A CULTURAL HISTORY OF TRAGEDY

VOLUME 5

A Cultural History of Tragedy
General Editor: Rebecca Bushnell

Volume 1
A Cultural History of Tragedy in Antiquity
Edited by Emily Wilson

Volume 2
A Cultural History of Tragedy in the Middle Ages
Edited by Jody Enders, Theresa Coletti, John T. Sebastian, and Carol Symes

Volume 3
A Cultural History of Tragedy in the Early Modern Age
Edited by Naomi Liebler

Volume 4
A Cultural History of Tragedy in the Age of Enlightenment
Edited by Mitchell Greenberg

Volume 5
A Cultural History of Tragedy in the Age of Empire
Edited by Michael Gamer and Diego Saglia

Volume 6
A Cultural History of Tragedy in the Modern Age
Edited by Jennifer Wallace

A CULTURAL HISTORY OF TRAGEDY

IN THE AGE OF EMPIRE

VOLUME 5

*Edited by Michael Gamer
and Diego Saglia*

BLOOMSBURY ACADEMIC
LONDON • NEW YORK • OXFORD • NEW DELHI • SYDNEY

BLOOMSBURY ACADEMIC
Bloomsbury Publishing Plc
50 Bedford Square, London, WC1B 3DP, UK
1385 Broadway, New York, NY 10018, USA

BLOOMSBURY, BLOOMSBURY ACADEMIC and the Diana logo are tracemarks of
Bloomsbury Publishing Plc

First published in Great Britain 2020

Copyright © Michael Gamer, Diego Saglia, and contributors, 2020

Michael Gamer, Diego Saglia, and contributors have asserted their right under the Copyright,
Designs and Patents Act, 1988, to be identified as the Authors of this work.

Series design by Raven Design

Cover image: *Taken by Surprise* by Edward Munch. Image sourced from
Darling Archive / Alamy Stock Photo

All rights reserved. No part of this publication may be reproduced or transmitted
in any form or by any means, electronic or mechanical, including photocopying,
recording, or any information storage or retrieval system, without prior permission
in writing from the publishers.

Bloomsbury Publishing Plc does not have any control over, or responsibility for, any
third-party websites referred to or in this book. All internet addresses given in this
book were correct at the time of going to press. The author and publisher regret
any inconvenience caused if addresses have changed or sites have ceased to
exist, but can accept no responsibility for any such changes.

A catalogue record for this book is available from the British Library.

Library of Congress Control Number: 2019949543

ISBN: HB: 978-1-4742-8807-1
       Set: 978-1-4742-8814-9

Series: The Cultural Histories Series

Typeset by RefineCatch Limited, Bungay, Suffolk
Printed and bound in Great Britain

To find out more about our authors and books visit www.bloomsbury.com
and sign up for our newsletters.

CONTENTS

List of Illustrations — vi
Notes on Contributors — viii
Series Preface — xi

Introduction: The Nineteenth Century: "Tragedy *in* the World" — 1
Michael Gamer and Diego Saglia

1 Forms and Media — 23
   Lissette Lopez Szwydky

2 Sites of Performance and Circulation — 45
   Katherine Newey

3 Communities of Production and Consumption — 61
   Sharon Aronofsky Weltman

4 Philosophy and Social Theory — 75
   Jonathan Sachs

5 Religion, Ritual and Myth — 91
   Jeffrey N. Cox

6 Politics of City and Nation — 105
   Michael Meeuwis

7 Society and Family — 121
   Dana Van Kooy

8 Gender and Sexuality — 139
   Cole Heinowitz

Notes — 155
Bibliography — 179
Index — 193

LIST OF ILLUSTRATIONS

INTRODUCTION

0.1	National Theater, Mannheim, 1782.	11
0.2	Drury Lane, London, 1795. Watercolor reproduction by Edward Dayes.	12
0.3	Covent Garden, London, 1804.	12
0.4	Drury Lane, London, 1812.	13
0.5	Théâtre de la Porte Saint-Martin, Paris, c. 1815–20.	13
0.6	Interior view of the Haymarket Theater, 1821.	14
0.7	The Grand Theater in Theater Square Moscow, c. 1850.	15
0.8	La Scala Theater, Milan, 1830.	15
0.9	San Carlo Theater, Naples, c. 1830.	16
0.10	Drury Lane Theater, c. 1840.	16
0.11	Berlin State Opera, Unter den Linden, c. 1850.	17
0.12	Mihály Zihy, *Auditorium of the Bolshoi Theatre*, Moscow, 1856.	17
0.13	Fire at Covent Garden, London, March 4, 1856.	18
0.14	Scene from *The Slave Market* by Dion Boucicault, New Adelphi Theater, London, 1861.	18
0.15	Theaters on the Boulevard du Temple, Paris, 1862.	19
0.16	Joseph Dantan, *An Interval with the Comédie Française*, 1886.	19
0.17	Savoy Theater, London, 1881.	20
0.18	Bomb Explosion in the Liceu Theatre, Barcelona, 1893.	20
0.19	Fire at the Théâtre Français (Comédie Française), March 8, 1900.	21
0.20	Henrik Ibsen on a sleigh in front of the National Theater, Oslo, 1900.	21

CHAPTER 1

1.1	Gustave Doré, *The Body of Elaine on Its Way to King Arthur's Palace*, 1867.	34
1.2	Julia Margaret Cameron, *The Corpse of Elaine Arriving in the Palace of King Arthur*, 1875.	35
1.3	Johann Heinrich Ramberg, *Ophelia Falling into the Water*, 1829.	35
1.4	John Everett Millais, *Ophelia*, 1852.	36
1.5	Alexandre Cabanel, *Ophelia*, 1883.	36
1.6	Frances MacDonald, *Ophelia*, 1898.	37
1.7	Anonymous, *To Henry Hunt, Esq. as chairman of the meeting assembled on St. Peter's Field, Manchester on the 16th of August, 1819*.	38
1.8	George Cruikshank, *Massacre at St. Peter's or 'Britons Strike Home'!!!*, 1819.	39
1.9	George Cruikshank, *Manchester Heroes*, 1819.	39

LIST OF ILLUSTRATIONS

1.10 Eugène Delacroix, *The Massacre at Chios*, 1824.   40
1.11 Joseph Mallord William Turner, *The Slave Ship (Slavers Throwing overboard the Dead and Dying, Typhon Coming On)*, 1840.   41
1.12 Francisco de Goya, *El Tres de Mayo, 1808*, 1814.   41
1.13 Pablo Picasso, *The Tragedy*, 1903.   42

NOTES ON CONTRIBUTORS

Jeffrey N. Cox is Vice Provost and Associate Vice Chancellor for Faculty Affairs at the University of Colorado Boulder where he is also an Arts and Sciences Professor of Distinction and Professor of English, of Comparative Literature, and of Humanities. He is the author or editor of ten books, including *In the Shadows of Romance: Romantic Tragic Drama in Germany, England, and France* (1987) and *Poetry and Politics in the Cockney School: Shelley, Keats, Hunt, and their Circle*, winner of the 2000 South Central Modern Language Association Best Book Award. His most recent book, *Romanticism in the Shadow of War: The Culture of the Napoleonic War Years*, was published in Fall 2014. He is the author of more than forty articles that have appeared in such journals as *Comparative Literature*, *ELH*, and *Studies in Romanticism*.

Michael Gamer is Professor of English and Comparative Literature at the University of Pennsylvania. His book publications are *Romanticism and the Gothic* (2000) and *Romanticism, Self-Canonization, and the Business of Poetry* (2017). He writes on collaboration and is fond of collaborative work, including (with Jeffrey Cox) *The Broadview Anthology of Romantic Drama* (2003), (with Dahlia Porter) *Lyrical Ballads 1798 and 1800* (2008), and (as part of the Multigraph Collective) *Interacting with Print: Modes of Reading in the Age of Print Saturation, 1700-1900* (2018). His writing on theater includes essays on hippodrama, the supernatural onstage, and theatricality offstage. He is currently at work on a book on melodrama and on a digital project asking what playbills can tell us.

Cole Heinowitz is a scholar, translator, poet, and Associate Professor of Literature at Bard College. She is the author of the critical study, *Spanish America and British Romanticism, 1777–1826: Rewriting Conquest* (2010). Her essays have appeared in journals such as *European Romantic Review*, the *Romantic Circles Praxis Series*, *The Boston Review*, *The Chicago Review*, *Nineteenth-Century Contexts*, and *The Journal of British Studies*, as well as in the edited collection *Romanticism and the Anglo-Hispanic Imaginary* and *The Oxford Encyclopedia of British Literature*. Heinowitz is the translator of Mario Santiago Papasquiaro's *Advice from 1 Disciple of Marx to 1 Heidegger Fanatic* (2013), *Beauty Is Our Spiritual Guernica* (2015), and *Bleeding from All 5 Senses* (2019), as well as *The Selected Late Letters of Antonin Artaud* (2014) and *A Tradition of Rupture: Selected Critical Writings of Alejandra Pizarnik* (2019). Heinowitz's books of poetry include *Stunning in Muscle Hospital* (2002) and *The Rubicon* (2008).

Michael Meeuwis is Assistant Professor at the University of Warwick. His first book, *Everyone's Theatre: Literature and Daily Life in England, 1860–1914*, is forthcoming. Michael works on English literature and performance culture from the eighteenth century to the present day. He is currently finishing a book-length project addressing home ownership in contemporary London drama, and beginning another revising the history of the novel around the idea of novels read out loud and in public. As an émigré to the

United Kingdom Michael continues to find the class system of Tesco pizza gradations fascinating, although he confesses the magic has begun to fade.

Katherine Newey is Professor of Theatre History at the University of Exeter. She is an historian specializing in nineteenth-century British popular theatre and women's writing. She has published widely on the nineteenth-century theatre and popular culture. Her books include *Women's Theatre Writing in Victorian Britain* (2005), *John Ruskin and the Victorian Theatre* co-authored with cultural historian, Jeffrey Richards (2010), and *Politics, Performance and Popular Culture* (2016), co-edited with Jeffrey Richards and Peter Yeandle. She is currently finishing a book on Victorian pantomime, *A Cultural History of English Pantomime, 1837–1901*. She has held major research grants from the Arts and Humanities Research Council (UK) on "Theatre and Visual Culture in the Long Nineteenth Century," "A Cultural History of English Pantomime, 1837–1901," "John Ruskin and the Victorian Theatre," and "Nineteenth Century Women Playwrights."

Jonathan Sachs is the author of *The Poetics of Decline in British Romanticism* (2018) and *Romantic Antiquity: Rome in the British Imagination, 1789-1832* (2010) and co-author, with the Multigraph Collective, of *Interacting with Print: Elements of Reading in the Era of Print Saturation* (2018). He is Professor of English at Concordia University, Montreal, where he also directs the inter-institutional Interacting with Print Research Group. In addition to grants from the Social Sciences and Humanities Research Council of Canada, his work has been supported by fellowship at the National Humanities Center (2014–15) and a membership at the Institute for Advanced Study, Princeton (2017–18).

Diego Saglia is Professor of English Literature at the University of Parma (Italy). His research centers on the Romantic period and in particular on such themes and areas as exoticism and orientalism, Gothic, national identity, and gender; as well as on several central figures of the period including Jane Austen, Lord Byron, Felicia Hemans, and Walter Scott. In the field of Romantic-period drama, he has published on Gothic theater, melodrama, tragedy, and women playwrights. He is the author of *Poetic Castles in Spain: British Romanticism and Figurations of Iberia* (2000) and *Reading Austen* (2016); and co-editor of *British Romanticism and Italian Literature: Translating, Reviewing, Rewriting* with Laura Bandiera (2005), of *Byron and Italy* with Alan Rawes (2017), and *Spain in British Romanticism 1800-1840* with Ian Haywood (2018). He is a member of the scientific committee of the Byron Museum in Ravenna, and his latest publication is the monograph *European Literatures in Britain, 1815-1832: Romantic Translations* (2019).

Lissette Lopez Szwydky is Assistant Professor of English at the University of Arkansas. Her research and teaching interests include Romantic and Victorian literature and culture, adaptation studies, gender studies, and professional issues in the Humanities. She has published articles on nineteenth-century stage adaptations of *Three-Fingered Jack*, Victor Hugo's *Notre-Dame de Paris*, Mary Shelley's *Frankenstein*, and others. Most recently, she has published essays in *Science Fiction in Film and Television* as well as in the following collections: *The Routledge Companion to Adaptation Studies* (2018; eds. Dennis Cutchins, Katja Krebs, and Eckhart Voight) and *Adapting Frankenstein: The Monsters Eternal Lives in Popular Culture* (2018; eds. Dennis Cutchins and Dennis Perry). Her forthcoming book *Transmedia Adaptation in the Nineteenth Century* traces the evolution of stories across page, stage, image, and other forms against the backdrop of industrialization and the rise of mass culture.

Dana Van Kooy is Associate Professor of Transnational Literature, Literary Theory and Culture and is Director of the English program in the Humanities Department at Michigan Technological University. Her research is grounded in romanticism and transatlantic and global perspectives of the literature and drama produced throughout the long eighteenth century. In her writing, she employs a range of theoretical approaches to explore formal and material intersections between literary, visual, and performance culture. Her publications include her book, *Shelley's Radical Stages: Performance and Cultural Memory in the Post-Napoleonic Era* (2016) and essays which have been published in *Studies in Romanticism, Modern Drama, Theatre Journal, The Keats-Shelley Review*, and *Literature Compass*. She has also edited and contributed to a collection of essays about teaching Romantic-period drama for *Romantic Textualities: Literature and Print Culture, 1780–1840*. Currently, she is working on a book project that examines the aesthetics of disappearance associated with the cultural configurations of colonialism, imperialism, and revolutionary resistance that inform Atlantic cultures and histories.

Sharon Aronofsky Weltman is the William E. "Bud" Davis Alumni Professor of English at Louisiana State University. Widely published on Victorian literature, theatre, and culture, her books include *Performing the Victorian: John Ruskin and Identity in Theater, Science, and Education* (2007) and *Ruskin's Mythic Queen: Gender Subversion in Victorian Culture* (Outstanding Academic Book, *Choice* magazine, 1999). She is North American Editor of *Nineteenth-Century Theatre and Film* and has recently completed a book manuscript entitled "Victorians on Broadway: Literature, Adaptation, and the Modern American Musical," which examines Broadway musicals from the second half of the twentieth century in conjunction with their Victorian sources. She is currently working on two projects: one considers Dickens, performance, and ethical embodiment; the other focuses on Victorian melodrama.

SERIES PREFACE

A cultural history of tragedy faces a daunting task: how to address tragedy's influence on Western culture while describing how complex and changing historical conditions have shaped it over two and a half millennia. This is the first study with such an extensive scope, investigating tragedy's long-lived cultural impact and accounting for its material, social, political, and philosophical dimensions.

Since antiquity, tragedy has appeared in a myriad of forms, reinvented in every age. It has been performed as opera, dance, film, and television as well as live theater. From the beginning, concepts of tragedy have also surfaced in other literary genres such as narrative poetry and novels, as well as in non-literary forms, including journalism, visual art, and photography. Tragedy never appears in a vacuum: the conditions of performance and production and its communal functions always affect its form and meaning. Tragedy has never belonged solely to elite culture, and who creates and consumes these forms of tragedy also makes a difference. Not only has the status of tragedy's producers—the writers, actors, artists, and performers—evolved over time, but so has the nature of the audiences, viewers, and readers as well, all significantly affecting tragedy's aesthetic and social impact.

Tragedy also does more than simply represent or perform human catastrophe or suffering; it is a mode of thought, a way of figuring the human condition as a whole. Philosophers and social and cultural theorists from Plato to Lacan have long pondered the idea of the tragic, while in turn literary models have influenced philosophy, social thought, and psychoanalysis. Tragedy has always had a complex relationship with religion and ritual practices, both complementing and conflicting with religious orthodoxies concerning fate, the power of the gods, and the meaning of suffering. At the same time, since its earliest staging in fifth-century Athens as a civic as well as religious event, tragedy has both echoed and challenged relationships of power and political events in societies experiencing conflict or change.

While tragedy in all its versions has thus profoundly tapped into broad social, intellectual, and political movements, it has often represented those themes through individual experiences, ranging from the titanic sufferings of princes to the sorrows of ordinary men and women. While tragedy's themes of ambition, authority, transgression, and rebellion are grounded in religion and politics, its plots often play out through family relationships that both mirror and conflict with social and political norms. When tragedy thus engages familial and personal themes, it often involves tensions of gender and sexuality. Sexuality is a powerful driver of tragic catastrophe, when desire is granted its own kind of fatal power.

As with other *Cultural History* series, here the story of tragedy writ large is divided into volumes covering six historical periods from antiquity to modernity. Although the boundaries between those time are necessarily fluid, the volumes are divided as follows: 1. Antiquity (500 BCE–1000 CE); 2. Middle Ages (1000–1400); 3. Early Modern Age (1400–1650); 4. Age of Enlightenment (1650–1800); 5. Age of Empire (1800–1920), and 6. Modern Age (1920–present). While such a history naturally focuses on Western culture and history, at the end it also touches on tragedy's later post-colonial adaptations, which put its fundamentally Western concerns in a global context. Each volume has its own introduction by an editor or co-editors presenting an original and provocative vision of tragedy's manifestations in one historical era. Each volume also covers the same eight topics as the others in the *Cultural History*: forms and media; sites of performance and circulation; communities of production and consumption; philosophy and social theory; religion, ritual, and myth; politics of city and nation; society and family; and gender and sexuality. Readers may thus follow one topic over a wide historical span, or they may focus on all dimensions of tragedy in one period. Either way they read, they will be able to appreciate the power of tragedy to shape our understanding of human experience, and in turn, how tragedy has changed over time, both reflecting and challenging historical conditions.

Rebecca Bushnell, University of Pennsylvania, General Editor

Introduction

The Nineteenth Century: *"Tragedy* in *the World"*

MICHAEL GAMER AND DIEGO SAGLIA

We open this volume on nineteenth-century tragedy in an unlikely year (1788), place (Edinburgh), and genre (the scholarly lecture). During that year in April, some fourteen months before the storming of the Bastille that started the French Revolution, Henry Mackenzie presented his "Account of the German Theatre" to the Royal Society of Edinburgh. The author of four plays and three novels and editor of *The Mirror* (1779–80) and *The Lounger* (1785–7), Mackenzie was arguably Edinburgh's most cosmopolitan man of letters, his *Man of Feeling* (1771) having made him famous throughout Europe, where he maintained a broad correspondence. The previous year he had effectively introduced Robert Burns to the city's literary circles by favorably reviewing *Poems, Written Chiefly in the Scottish Dialect* (1787). He was now doing the same, via his public lecture, for Gottfried Ephraim Lessing, Johann Wolfgang von Goethe, and Friedrich Schiller, whose tragedy *The Robbers* (1781) he singled out for sustained commentary and especial praise.

The fruit of months of labor acquainting himself with German literature, Mackenzie's address to the Royal Society was audacious, announcing the arrival of a new dramatic tradition. As in the case of Burns, literary gold had come from an unlikely place: a country of "small potentates" whose "limited revenues" made the establishment of good theaters nearly impossible. How, then, had such a revolution in taste occurred? Part of the answer, Mackenzie argued, lay in the nature of theatrical representation, which in "every country marks more strongly than any other of its productions, the features, both of its genius and of its manners."[1] The remainder, he surmised, lay in the national character of the German people, whose dominant bourgeoisie demanded plays about middle-class life in the tradition of George Lillo's *The London Merchant: or, The Tragedy of George Barnwell* (1731). In Germany, "the body of the people" had spoken, demanding "Dramas that rouse the passions and shake the soul."[2] The result was nothing less than a new tradition of tragedy.

Over the next decade, it is fair to say that British readers did more than take Mackenzie at his word. In a few short years German literature, especially tragedy, became one of the most acclaimed, popular, and controversial new literatures of the day. Inspired by Mackenzie's address, a translation of *The Robbers* appeared in 1792 in London; by 1800 dozens of German plays, most conspicuously those of August von Kotzebue, had been published or staged with great success in Europe, Britain, and North America. Readers also fueled a vogue for German poetry, particularly tragic ballads like Gottfried August Bürger's "Lenore," whose translators by 1797 included William Taylor of Norwich, the Poet Laureate Henry James Pye, Anna Seward, and a young barrister named Walter Scott, who at the time was penning several original tragedies in what he considered the "German" style. Though his *House of Aspen* (composed 1799, published 1830) was rejected for representation by Drury Lane, he had managed to sell his translation of Goethe's tragedy *Goetz von Berlichingen* (1798) for fifty pounds to J. Bell of London, thanks to the help of another popularizer of German drama, Matthew Gregory Lewis, who also published with Bell. During these same months, two other young writers, Samuel Taylor Coleridge and William Wordsworth, also composed tragedies for the London stage; like Scott, both received rejections, but this did not stop them from traveling to Germany in the autumn of 1798 in hopes of learning the language and meeting its greatest writers. Short on funds, Wordsworth spent a miserable winter in Goslar, learning little German but producing many of the poems that comprised the second volume of *Lyrical Ballads* (1800). Coleridge fared better, enjoying Göttingen's vibrant intellectual and artistic culture and, on his return, publishing his own translations of two of Schiller's historical tragedies, *The Death of Wallenstein* and *The Piccolomini*, in 1800. What had begun twelve years earlier as a single lecture delivered to a learned society had transformed itself, by the end of the century, into a burgeoning, truly international literature. Put another way, the years we customarily associate with the beginnings of Romanticism in Britain coincide with those that witnessed the discovery, dissemination, and appropriation of a new kind of tragic writing emanating from Germany—one that inspired an entire generation of young writers, from Joanna Baillie to Heinrich von Kleist, Lord Byron to Charles Nodier, Germaine de Staël to Victor Hugo.

The keywords of this volume, then, are transformation, proliferation, and hybridization. Our essays start from the recognition that tragedy did not die with Romanticism, as George Steiner famously argued, but rather transformed itself into multiple, vibrant forms with which it kept a constant dialogue.[3] With the notable exception of Shakespeare in Britain and a few other foundational figures in other national traditions, early modern tragedy might have lost its dominance in metropolitan theaters as the nineteenth century turned, but only because it was forced to share space with other mutating forms, both on the stage and off. For this reason, the contributors to this volume, far from limiting themselves to the stage, pointedly reach beyond it to tell this story of hybridization: across media, across genres, across demographics, across faiths both religious and secular, and across national boundaries. Some, like Jeffrey Cox and Jonathan Sachs, present tragedy as pan-European and emphasize its disciplinary crossings. Others, among them Cole Heinowitz, Michael Meeuwis, and Dana Van Kooy, focus more firmly on Britain to demonstrate the renewed energy with which nineteenth-century tragedy portrays the violence of gender and class relations. And still others, such as Katherine Newey, Lissette Lopez Szwydky, and Sharon Weltman, foreground tragedy's fondness for crossing boundaries of genre and of high and popular culture. Thanks to their different approaches, the eight essays contained in this volume capture tragedy's multiple trajectories and variations in the nineteenth century, providing a panorama rich in spatial, temporal, formal, and contextual concerns.

Far from announcing fragmentation or incoherence, this proliferation of tragedy in the nineteenth century heralded new questions that remain central to modern reflections on the tragic. In the years covered by this volume, the most pressing of these concerns is the relation between tragedy and politics—not just the question of tragedy's political valence, but also of what it means to bestow a tragic worldview on one's own present. Aptly, Hayden White in *Metahistory* reads the status of tragedy within the culture of nineteenth-century Europe as a crucial vehicle for "emplotment": a broad, almost archetypal, narrative structure used to interpret historical data.[4] As with romance, comedy, and satire, tragedy functions in White's account as an interpretive lens: a story we tell to understand our world and ourselves, both on and off the stage. Such stories, he argues, have the power to deepen and even transform everyday consciousness. Nineteenth-century theatergoers emerging late in the evening from a performance of *An Enemy of the People* (1882), for instance, might find themselves so moved by Ibsen's tragedy as to begin thinking differently along a number of lines: about the difficulty of acting on principle, about what it means to scapegoat a member of a community, and about the effects of moneyed interests in local politics. Reading a newspaper the following morning, they might find their evening reflections resonating anew with the stories in front of them, and might recast such events as "tragic."

This movement—between universal and ephemeral, abstract and material, transcendent and local—feeds not just nineteenth-century tragedy; it also has shaped critical writing on the subject since the 1960s. For George Steiner, these shifts in focus account for tragedy's so-called "death" in the nineteenth century, when a new interest in bourgeois experience transformed what was apparently universal into something seemingly more mundane. Steiner framed the problem as one of secularization: if tragedy for millennia had explored transcendent good and evil, then modern tragedy at best could question the possibility of meaning in a godless world.[5] Responding to Steiner, Raymond Williams recast these same terms to ask how tragedy captures human experience *in* the world:

> Tragedy, as such, teaches nothing about evil, because it teaches many things about many kinds of action. Yet it can at least be said, against the modern emphasis on transcendent evil, that most of the great tragedies of the world end not with evil absolute, but with evil both experienced and lived through. ... I believe that the meanings matter as such; in tragedy especially, because the experience is so central and we can hardly avoid thinking about it. If we find a particular idea of tragedy, in our own time, we find also a way of interpreting a very wide area of our experience: relevant certainly to literary criticism but relevant also to very much else.[6]

In moving from the possibility of Evil to the experience of it, Williams broadens his inquiry to include the "historical"—not to subsume earlier, "particular" meanings, but rather to place these contextual concerns in dialogue with metaphysical and transcendent ones. In this, he mirrors the movement of stage tragedy itself in the nineteenth century. As Jeffrey Cox's essay in this volume puts it succinctly, "history is the heartland of modern tragic drama."

If there is a politics of history emanating from nineteenth-century writers, it resides in what Williams calls "a tragedy of revolution." There, the potential for social change is undermined by a too dogged insistence on either individualism or idealism—or, as Jonathan Sachs frames it in his cogent survey of tragic philosophy and social theory, "freedom and necessity." In this formulation, modern tragedy at once emanates out of Romanticism while containing (as do many foundational texts of that literary and cultural phase) its own self-critique. For Jennifer Wallace, this same doubleness attends tragic performance, which by design involves audiences in the lives of characters even as it reserves painful ends for many of them. If tragedy is

> a matter of response, rather than purely aesthetic structure, then it immediately has implications for ethics. What is the purpose of stirring our emotions? We may feel sympathy for the hero's pain or shock at the cruelties inflicted on stage—Aristotle's pity or fear—but these feelings must have a function if the experience of tragedy is to offer anything other than a cheap thrill.[7]

Wallace's "must" nicely captures the uneasiness caused not just by stage tragedy but by any event, outcome, or life deemed "tragic." Given the presence of real, often unnecessary suffering, surely there must be some kind of reason for it. The alternatives—that there exists no providential meaning in the universe, that suffering and death are ultimately senseless, or that we might actually enjoy viewing or reading about the pain of others—are precisely what tragedy asks us to ask ourselves by interpolating us into action of at once harrowing and suspect status. Our point is not that people in the nineteenth century were the first to ask these questions. As Wallace's reference to Aristotle suggests, they are as old as tragedy. Rather, our volume suggests that part of the nineteenth-century's fascination with tragedy stems from the intensity with which readers and viewers had to confront the old question—is it human to garner pleasure from watching the suffering of another—in new ways. Indeed, Simon Goldhill, in *Sophocles and the Language of Tragedy* (2012), remarks that if there were a "nineteenth-century obsession with the tragic," this was because tragedy, for the nineteenth century, "became a structuring principle of the self-understanding of modernity, . . . history, and the suffering of humankind."[8]

Where might lie a convenient term to sum up what happens to tragedy in nineteenth-century Western culture, that bourgeois age of nations, revolutions, and empires, roughly delimited by the French Revolution and the First World War? And, more specifically, how to capture the ways in which tragedy met, was transformed by, and offered a lens to view what Georg Wilhelm Friedrich Hegel called "the prose of the world"? Taken from his lectures on aesthetics, Hegel's expression encapsulates the experience of the atomization—even pulverization—of the real that becomes increasingly pertinent as the nineteenth century progresses. For Hegel, "the prose of the world" referred to an increasingly fragmented perception of reality and history that made both seem comprised only of transient, even potentially insignificant, facts and events; and, as a result, the world in Hegel's vision had become almost mired in the material detritus of life.[9] This process bears essentially on what happens to tragedy and the tragic over the period covered by this volume, beginning with the bourgeois revolution in France that had rewritten the map of Europe by the time the nineteenth century turned.

Yet, as the essays of Katherine Newey and Lissette Lopez Szwydky remind us, this same material detritus can also chronicle tragedy's expansion into new media and sites of performance. In a Paris roiled by revolutionary turmoil, tragedy quickly began to mutate into a worldly, even everyday, mode for apprehending and representing drastic socio-political changes. This was most apparent in Paris's theaters, which in the 1790s saw a flourishing of the genre, especially that type of tragedy promoted by the Jacobins as a tool for educating the minds of the citizens. Firmly neoclassical and overtly intended as an instrument of propaganda, these plays were a staple of the early revolution. Yet, these same years also saw tragedy expand beyond the stage. No longer confined to the stage and to treatises on poetics, tragedy began to "walk the streets," in Matthew Buckley's evocative phrase.[10] And as the Terror spread death all around, tragedy became a crucial structure informing collective history and individual life experience. Writing on the politics of the city and nation, Michael Meeuwis finds these collective and individual histories speaking most poignantly in the stage sets of nineteenth-century tragedies, where objects frequently take on a durability that does not extend either to characters or societies. For Jonathan Sachs, it is precisely this willingness to consider the meaning of violence in history that makes tragedy so central to nineteenth-century philosophical discourses about social change.

INTRODUCTION

Increasingly, then, as ideas of tragedy and the tragic evolved and mutated, they did so according to a prevailing wind: away from the stage and into the world. Edward Bulwer Lytton, for example, tellingly included a symbolic, disoriented playwright in his survey of British culture and politics, *England and the English* (1833). Asked about the current state of theater, the playwright responds with his own question:

> In former times, then, there were reasons which do not exist at present, that rendered the Great the fitting heroes of the tragic stage. . . . Kings are no longer Destinies, and the interest they excited has departed with their power. Whither?—to the People! Among the people, then, must the tragic author invoke the genius of Modern Tragedy, and learn its springs.[11]

The passage is noteworthy not just for its critique of monarchy but also its association of tragedy with power. For Bulwer Lytton's fictional playwright, tragedy's class politics derive less from the innate dignity and nobility of tragic characters than from the power they possess. Once that power shifts away from a given class—in this case monarchs and aristocracy—so also does the tragic interest associated with that class. Especially significant, in this respect, is Bulwer Lytton's use of *among*, since it highlights his awareness that tragedy, having moved beyond the stages of elite theaters, has become a widespread, popular form for conveying individual and collective experience.

Writing in the early 1830s, Bulwer Lytton was able to mark a shift in tragic stage productions, particularly their practices of characterization, and even hypothesize its possible cause. What is clear from his pronouncements is that, far from dying, stage tragedy continued to function as a crucial genre across cultural traditions. As a defining yardstick of imaginative excellence, it still concentrated an enormous amount of cultural capital and prestige in the early nineteenth century, constituting one of the highest achievements in the *belles lettres*. It also, as Sharon Weltman convincingly argues, drew from new forms like melodrama, thus engaging in a sustained dialogue with the nineteenth-century's most popular dramatic form even as it sought to preserve its long-standing cultural primacy. Nearly half a century after citizens had stormed the Bastille, tragedy still could define the essence of a literary and dramatic tradition. And for emerging nations, it could shape debates over national character and cultural patriotism, as it did in the decades leading to Italian unification, when the Aristotelian unities became not just an aesthetic but also a cultural-political issue.

What *version* of tragedy, therefore, became a reigning question. Romanticism's revolt against the inherited system of genres may have meant that tragedy could no longer be exclusively associated with neoclassical taxonomies and templates, but what it was to become was far less certain. As early as 1819, William Hazlitt noted in a public lecture the existence of no fewer than "four sorts or schools of tragedy," each characterized by peculiar stylistic features. The "antique or classical," he surmised, followed the unities and nature, while "the Gothic or Romantic" was modeled on Shakespeare and eschewed "precise imitation of an actual event in place and time."[12] Eminently declamatory, "the French or common-place rhetorical style" found a marked contrast in the situational nature of German theater, whose violent events in turn inspired "certain extravagant speculative opinions, abstracted from all existing customs, prejudices and institutions" (325), its language "a mixture of metaphysical jargon and flaring prose" challenging conventions to the point of "immorality" (336).

Within this newly heterogeneous landscape, it is hardly surprising that tragedy's differing strands found their respective ways into a number of genres and cultural milieus, both on and off the stage. This sheer range is especially visible and emblematic in the works of Lord Byron, possibly the most international—even transnational—author in the nineteenth century. Across his career, Byron wrote tragedies in the style of both Alfieri and the Greek tragedians as well as in other modes of the tragic, including closet dramas (*Manfred* [1816]) and experimental "mystery" plays (*Cain* [1821] and *Heaven and Earth* [1823]). He also constantly reworked the tragic in his poetry, beginning with the first cantos of *Childe Harold's Pilgrimage* (1812) and *The Giaour* (1813) and continuing through to *Don Juan* (1819–24), most notably in the episode of the shipwreck in Canto II and the siege of Ismail in Cantos VII–VIII, with its graphic depiction of war as the backdrop for countless scenes of unmitigated horror. Aptly, in his landmark study of Romantic tragedy, *In the Shadows of Romance* (1987), Jeffrey Cox marks how the new dramatic traditions of Romanticism conjured up "chaotic world[s]" and "the collapse of traditional order," whose "protagonist[s] struggle to break through to a world remade."[13] The same might easily be said of tragedy crossing the genres during the nineteenth century.

Part of the attraction of the tragic to non-dramatic authors lay, as we have noted, in tragedy's long-standing cultural prestige. This is particularly true for writers of fiction, who in the previous century had been subject to critical attack in spite—or perhaps because—of their unflagging popularity with readers. Tragedy thus emerged repeatedly as a major element in this process of acquisition of authority and prestige through importation and admixture, as novelists experimented with form.[14] Within the English language tradition, in spite of its comic frame and prevailing aura of romance, Walter Scott's *Waverley; or 'Tis Sixty Years Since* (1814) wields a vision of history at once inevitable, irrevocable, and—for those taking up the Stuart cause other than Edward Waverley himself—unmistakably tragic. Mary Shelley's *Frankenstein* (1818), meanwhile, draws from Greek tragedy in its focused exploration of the psychology and the effects of *hubris*.[15] Looking later into the nineteenth century, Jeannette King has pronounced the works of George Eliot, Thomas Hardy, and Henry James not only to be infused by the tragic but also to offer a form of tragedy more fitting to contemporary cultural expectations. From this perspective, it is indisputable that "*Tess* must take its place among the great tragedies,"[16] and that similar claims could be extended to the productions of Emile Zola in France or Giovanni Verga in Italy.

Contra all this, however, Franco Moretti has contended that the prevalence in the nineteenth century of the *Bildungsroman*, or novel of education and personal growth, necessarily produces an outlook that is non-tragic. Nineteenth-century fiction may function through a constant negotiation of tragic events, he acknowledges, but it does so within a framework that tends to the narration of "normality" so that tragedy is always ultimately eluded or averted.[17] Though provocative in several respects, Moretti's interpretation depends, for its force, on reducing the rich tapestry of nineteenth-century fiction to a single sub-genre, flattening what was inclusive, varied, appropriative, and transformational. It also requires the more problematic conflation of form with mode, of "tragedy" with "tragic." As such, it diminishes the impact and scope of tragedy's infiltration into novel-writing while obfuscating their mutually constitutive dialogue with one another, not to mention tragedy's engagement with a host of other cultural forms. Among the essays in this volume, Dana Van Kooy's most explicitly addresses how tragedy "slips into and out of romance during this period," subjecting its idealisms to critique and unveiling its worlds as all too real.

As several essays in this volume also make clear, tragedy in the nineteenth century increasingly became a tool for describing, classifying, and responding to the real, whether in retrospect or in the face of contemporary events. To be sure, this was not a new idea. In 1818 Hazlitt had argued that the pleasures of tragedy ultimately resided in its connection to the world:

> The pleasure . . . derived from tragic poetry, is not any thing peculiar to it as poetry, as a fictitious and fanciful thing. It is not an anomaly of the imagination. It has its source and ground-work in the common love of strong excitement. As Mr. Burke observes, people flock to see a tragedy; but if there were a public execution in the next street, the theatre would very soon be empty. It is not then the difference between fiction and reality that solves the difficulty.[18]

Underlying Hazlitt's observation is the foundational question of the tension between tragedy on stage and tragedy in "reality." In this respect, Miriam Leonard notes, tragedy in modernity "becomes connected to life," so that reality, we might add, comes to be perceived as a narrative punctuated by tragic events: the Terror and beheading of Louis XVI, Napoleon's rise and fall, the Crimean and Franco-Prussian wars, the 1908 earthquake of Messina and Barcelona's 1909 "Tragic Week," the sinking of *Titanic* in 1912, the Battle of the Somme in 1916 and the Italian rout at Caporetto in 1917.[19] The list could continue indefinitely.

Placed at the meeting point of all these fields of experience and representation, tragedy in the nineteenth century inevitably becomes a major philosophical concern. As Jonathan Sachs notes in his contribution to his volume, this is especially so in the German tradition, with tragedy functioning as a key problematic in the works of Friedrich Hölderlin, Friedrich Wilhelm Joseph Schelling, Hegel, Friedrich Wilhelm Nietzsche, Karl Marx, Sigmund Freud, and Walter Benjamin, to name but some among the most representative figures. As the century unfolds, the philosophy of the tragic evolves into more and more neatly delineated arenas of thinking. Most, as we have noted, have their roots in the upheaval of the French Revolution and questions of unnecessary suffering. As our contributors demonstrate, nearly all accumulate new meanings as they traverse boundaries, whether those of nation or medium, gender or genre. Their work amply testifies to the richness of tragedy's engagement with the full breadth of nineteenth-century life.

Lissette Lopez Szwydky provides a powerful survey of this rich tapestry in this volume's opening essay on "Forms and Media," which she approaches through the lens of adaptation. Tragedy's malleability in the nineteenth century, she argues, enabled its deployment as a mode across a range of sites, both formal and ideological. Her opening case study—a toy theater for a play called *The Guillotine*, which young children at the turn of the twentieth century used to stage the "very exciting and terribly tragic" stories of Louis XVI and Marie Antoinette—beautifully concretizes her topic's overarching concerns. Here are multiple crossings of medium: a historical event frequently dramatized across Europe now acquiring new form as a toy theater for American children. Coming at the end of a century that most often dramatized the French Revolution as a calamity, what are we to make of this subsequent transformation from the stage to the nursery? What can it tell us about tragedy's status and reach as the nineteenth century closed? Part of her answer, Szwydky acknowledges, can be found in Romantic challenges to generic norms and the censorship regimes that required new hybrid forms if artists were to evade them. Still more, however, lies in the nineteenth century's multiplication of media. Tragedy thus becomes a vehicle in this chapter for "transmedia storytelling" and "convergence culture," terms by which contemporary media theorist Henry Jenkins has described the existence of multiple, coordinated narratives owned by a single source but licensed and disseminated via a range of media platforms and providers. Understanding tragedy's development in the nineteenth century requires comprehending the media economies that proliferate it.

Following Szwydky, Katherine Newey's contribution on "Sites of Performance and Circulation" also considers tragedy's mobility, but here the crossings are national and generic. Magisterial in its scope, her essay canvases French, German, and British dramaturgies as well as considering the role of actor-managers and dramatic historians, including Dion Boucicault, Christian Dietrich Grabbe, and William Charles Macready. Surveying tragedy's many homes in the nineteenth century, she reminds us that theatrical practices are necessarily site-specific, shaped by the venues that house them and the performers who bring them to life. What keeps tragedy vibrant, in fact, is this local currency: "However much an intellectual (or metaphysical) concept, . . . tragedy survived in mainstream nineteenth century theater because of its contact with the very demotic and popular forms thought to be causing its decline." Traditional manifestations of tragedy might survive in national repertories, but its ongoing renewal depends on its ability to act as a site for radical generic and technological innovations, which are most visible in melodrama. Indeed, against long-standing accounts of the "decline of the drama" in the nineteenth century, Newey presents a palpably robust tragic stage: a place of modernization and experimentation fueled by the energies of so-called "illegitimate" genres and "audience desires," as she adroitly puts it, for "new imagined worlds on stage."

Where proliferation and innovation govern the forms of tragedy and its sites of production, it is hardly surprising to find these same phenomena attending artists, authors, and audiences as well. In her cogent treatment of nineteenth-century "Communities of Production and Consumption," Sharon Weltman takes up this recurrent theme—that tragedy disperses and mutates—to track its forays into untraditional venues and publics. Melodrama plays a central role in her essay, too, particularly through its ability to turn specific conventions of tragedy to new account. And conversely, understanding tragedy's various transformations during the nineteenth century means recognizing how it consumed other genres even as it was consumed by them. Melodrama's meteoric rise, in other words, enables its co-evolving and mutually constitutive relation with tragedy, one that in turn dictated how a range of communities produced and consumed both forms, often in the same evening. Her essay thus looks beyond tragedy's usual haunts to examine transnational exchanges of texts and performers, class-related contexts, and the impact of women authors and performers. Considering plays by Victor Hugo, Caroline Boaden, Elizabeth Polack, Dibdin Pitt, Henri Meilhac, and Ludovic Halévy, she reveals an animating scene, one that captures the overwhelming diversity of tragic productions in Europe in these years.

If nineteenth-century drama lacks, as Jeffrey Cox's fine essay on religion puts it, "that necessary providential grounding," it is because its concerns are "located elsewhere, in a struggle with history or with society or, perhaps most interestingly, with a post-providential world that might appear meaningless or absurd." For Cox, this vexed relation between tragedy and religion commences in the Romantic period and spans the nineteenth century. It manifests itself, moreover, across a range of sites: from state censorship and the non-representation of religious rituals on stage, to problems over staging the supernatural, to religious eclecticism and comparative mythology, to historicizing religion. Far from rendering religion invisible, he finds, this "post-providential world" produces some of the most powerful religious tragedies we have, including Goethe's *Iphigenia* (1779), Charles Robert Maturin's *Bertram* (1816), Percy Shelley's *The Cenci* (1819), Byron's *Cain* (1821) and *Heaven and Earth* (1823), Charles Algernon Swinburne's *Atalanta in Calydon* (1865), Henrik Ibsen's *Brand* (1867), and August Strindberg's *Easter* (1901) and *To Damascus*

(1898–1904). Each presents its audience with a world no longer organized by traditional ideas, whose characters must "come to understand that they must define themselves in a world no longer governed by the divine." In Cox's account, this struggle between new and old, between flux and fixity, produces "a new kind of tragic drama."

Similar questions govern Jonathan Sachs' essay on philosophy and social theory, which addresses the crossing of philosophy and tragedy so strongly present in the nineteenth century. If a "philosophy of the tragic" resides anywhere in these years, he contends, it dwells in "German idealist thinking." His essay provides a highly readable and dexterously synthesized account of tragedy's entree into Western philosophical discourse, one that also traces its impact on nineteenth-century social theory. Especially important is what might be called tragedy's double life: its increasing relevance both as a specialist term for literary and philosophical analysis, and as a popular term to describe sudden reversals in private life and in the news of the day. Sachs' essay thus examines "tragedy as an experience, tragedy as a literary genre, and tragedy as an idea," tapping sources both expected (the work of Raymond Williams and Terry Eagleton) and unexpected (Tom McCarthy's novel *Satin Island* [2015]). Here again the French Revolution plays a foundational role, but in ways not restricted to materialist thought. In Sachs' formulation, the event also generates a line of "thinking that turned away from an explicit sense of politics and towards the abstraction of politics into metaphysical and aesthetic terms." Accordingly, he traces this development through the works of Schelling, Hegel, Arthur Schopenhauer, and Nietzsche before transitioning to Marxian social theory by way of Shelley. The resulting essay not only elucidates two philosophical traditions of the tragic, the immaterial and material, but also usefully illuminates their relation.

Michael Meeuwis also takes up these twin poles in order to offer an original angle on tragedy and the politics of the "polis" and the nation. His essay opens by examining the changing conditions that attended nineteenth-century tragic performances, which in turn generated new ideas in new communities. "Politics of City and Nation" begins not on the largest of scales, but rather its opposite: the intimate, even cramped, spaces where tragedy thrived in the decades after Waterloo. In a century dominated by Hugo and Scott, one might expect massive canvases chronicling social change. Instead, Meeuwis looks to the domestic scenes and intimate tableaux that dominate nineteenth-century tragedy. These "enameled veins," he argues, repeatedly take on a universal quality on the stage, allowing playwrights to reach across the divides of nation, class, and gender. The essay is particularly astute in its analyses of key stage props, which come to stand in for other kinds of permanence lost to modernity. Surveying James Sheridan Knowles' *Virginius* (1820), Georg Büchner's *Woyzeck* (1836–7), Leopold Lewis's 1871 translation of Erckmann-Chatrian's *Le Juif Polonais* (1867), and Henrik Ibsen's *Ghosts* (1882), he shows how objects transcend their usual, mundane functions to become in these tragedies stage devices in and of themselves. Asking why nineteenth-century stage tragedies are so "cluttered with domestic objects," he demonstrates how objects come to stand in for relations between individual, metropole, and nation—whether acting as silent witnesses to the action or simply enduring beyond the fall of the final curtain, "fated to outlast the action of the tragedy itself."

Meeuwis's focus on domesticity and intimacy nicely sets up the final two essays of this volume: Dana Van Kooy's treatment of "Society and Family" and Cole Heinowitz's "Gender and Sexuality." The former essay considers tragedy in the unstable context of changing ideas of power and authority. As Van Kooy astutely notes, these two concepts depend on a host of other political discourses: on social norms, on the ethics of violence and warfare, and on the often contradictory loyalties demanded by family, community, and nation. She confronts these tectonic shifts through analyses of Schiller's *The Robbers*, Byron's *Sardanapalus* (1821) and *Cain*, Goethe's *Iphigenia*, Boucicault's *Octoroon* (1859), and Ibsen's *The Master Builder* (1892). Surveying the century's output, she notes its mixings with romance and melodrama. At the same time, she also notes a key difference running through these plays, which repeatedly present "isolated and alienated men" who are matched by "strong-willed, intelligent, and capable women [who] attempt to restore some sense of home and family in war-torn societies," but whose "efforts are thwarted." The resulting domestic portrait is one fractured by clashing codes of vengeance, violence, and displacement affecting relations between husband and wife, parent and child, and the individual and social institutions.

Closing the volume, Heinowitz focuses on the social relation that most often underwrote the new bourgeois tragedy: that of fathers and daughters. Given the continued presence of primogeniture laws that institutionalized material bonds between fathers and their eldest sons, she reasons, why do tragedians look to daughters when writing about middle-class life? In answer, she argues that nineteenth-century tragedies reimagine the nature of paternal inheritance as focused not on property but on genetic material—or "blood" to use the dominant term of the times. Across a broad range of plays—including Baillie's *Orra* (1812), Shelley's *The Cenci* (1819), Ibsen's *A Doll's House* (1879) and *Ghosts* (1882), Strindberg's *The Father* (1887), George Bernard Shaw's *Mrs. Warren's Profession* (1893), and Oscar Wilde's *Salome* (1893)—Heinowitz shows how nineteenth-century tragedies repeatedly present the *pater familias* occupying his customary "seat of command over the bourgeois household" only to be exposed, diminished, and ultimately emasculated by the play's conclusion. Stripped of "his affective mantle of tenderness and decency" that served to justify his political prerogative from the eighteenth century onward, she notes, the foundational paternal figure "could be seen for what he truly was" by century's end.

Our own introductory chapter ends with an appendix entitled, "The Venues": twenty illustrations of sites associated with tragedy during the nineteenth century. Here, we provide images of some of the most significant theatrical venues across—in view of the volume's focus on Western cultural traditions—major cities and capitals in Europe. In this sense, they reflect the centrality of urban environments in the development of cultural phenomena in this century, as Walter Benjamin argued in his *exposés* on Paris in "Paris Capital of the Nineteenth Century" (1935, 1939). Ordered chronologically, the images render starkly visible the issues of size and space that at once shaped tragedy in the nineteenth century and also prompted its practitioners to look outside of the theater as well. We thus begin with a 1782 image of the Mannheim Theatre where *The Robbers* was first performed (Figure 0.1). From here, theaters at once grow larger (Figures 0.2, 0.3, 0.5, 0.7, 0.8, 0.9, 0.11, 0.12, 0.15) and smaller (Figure 0.6); even as major theaters swell with the urban populations they serve, so also do "minor" theaters flourish, performing melodramas and other competing forms of tragedy to full houses (Figures 0.14, 0.16, 0.17). Our images also include several of the grand opera houses that during the century became crucial hubs for the performance and consumption of the tragic. Appealing to a broad spectrum of social classes, from the aristocracy to the lower orders, tragic operas not only enjoyed great popularity but also functioned as objects of national pride. In their highly ornate interiors and monumental exteriors, nineteenth-century opera houses become symbols of civilization, refinement, and collective identity. In this case, our closing photo, of Ibsen in front of Norway's National Theater (Figure 0.20), is deeply significant. Here a country's eminent playwright, the founder of its national dramaturgy, poses in front of the nation's theater in a two-way exchange of personal and communal lines of definition. Yet, our images also bear witness to the tragedies that might happen to theaters (particularly fire—Figures 0.4, 0.10, 0.13, 0.19) or inside them, as with the arresting image of the bomb exploded on November 7, 1893 by anarchists at the Liceu Theatre in Barcelona (Figure 0.18), killing twenty people and injuring several more.

What Henry Mackenzie, speaking a century earlier to a largely male and genteel Edinburgh audience, would have made of such events—or of the tragedies of Strindberg and Wilde, or even of Ibsen and Shaw—is an open question. Still, he likely would have recognized in Shelley's Beatrice, Ibsen's Nora, and Shaw's Vivie the true heirs of Schiller's Karl Moor. At the very least, the aesthetic bloodlines would have been clear to him. Like Beatrice, Moor finds himself a victim of sadistic malice and without legal redress; like Nora, he finds himself banished by a patriarch fed on slander and acting on whim; like Vivie, he rejects the conventions of romance—and the social institutions associated with them—to choose a purer, more solitary fate. Each heroine must act, and each does so decisively in ways Mackenzie would have recognized and possibly approved. What would have surprised Mackenzie more, we believe, would have been tragedy's thriving life *off* the national stage: its secret and not so secret lives in fiction and cabarets, in playrooms and pamphlets, in tabloid dailies and philosophical treatises. Whether this popular dispersal of the tragic would have distressed or pleased him is uncertain; given Mackenzie's mix of classical learning and literary populism, we expect both. One thing is certain: instead of uncovering a genre neglected and dying, he would have encountered an aesthetic mode so dispersed as to be almost omnipresent—proliferating across media, classes, and cultures, and irreversibly altered by the transformative effects of time and travel.

APPENDIX: THE VENUES

FIGURE 0.1: National Theater, Mannheim, 1782, the year *The Robbers* premiered. Etching by Johann Sebastian and Johann Baptist Klauber, after Franz von der Schlichten (by permission of Getty Images).

FIGURE 0.2: The redesigned Drury Lane Theater, London, 1795. Watercolor reproduction by Edward Dayes (by permission of Getty Images).

FIGURE 0.3: Interior of Covent Garden Theater, London, 1804 (published 1900; by permission of Getty Images).

FIGURE 0.4: Drury Lane Theater, London, 1812, rebuilt after being destroyed by fire in 1809 (by permission of Getty Images).

FIGURE 0.5: Théâtre de la Porte Saint-Martin, Paris, *c.* 1815–20 (by permission of Getty Images).

FIGURE 0.6: Interior view of the Haymarket Theater, 1821 (from *The British Stage*, August 1821; by permission of Getty Images).

FIGURE 0.7: The Grand Theater in Theater Square Moscow, *c.* 1850 (built in 1824, it burnt down in 1853 and was later rebuilt as the modern Bolshoi Theatre; by permission of Getty Images).

FIGURE 0.8: La Scala Theater, Milan, 1830 (by permission of Getty Images).

FIGURE 0.9: San Carlo Theater, Naples, *c.* 1830 (by permission of Getty Images).

FIGURE 0.10: Drury Lane Theater, *c.* 1840. An engraving of Drury Lane Theater from the stage during the performance (by permission of Rischgitz/Getty Images).

FIGURE 0.11: Berlin State Opera, Unter den Linden, *c*. 1850. Engraving by A.H. Payne after A. Carse (by permission of Getty Images).

FIGURE 0.12: Mihály Zihy, *Auditorium of the Bolshoi Theatre*, Moscow, 1856 (by permission of Getty Images).

FIGURE 0.13: Fire at Covent Garden, London, March 4, 1856 (from *L'Illustration*, March 15, 1856; by permission of Getty Images).

FIGURE 0.14: Scene from *The Slave Market* by Dion Boucicault, New Adelphi Theater, London, 1861 (from *The Illustrated London News*, November 30, 1861; by permission of Getty Images).

FIGURE 0.15: Theaters on the Boulevard du Temple, Paris, 1862 (by permission of Getty Images).

FIGURE 0.16: Joseph Dantan, *An Interval with the Comédie Française*, 1886. Private Collection (by permission of Getty Images).

FIGURE 0.17: Savoy Theatre, London, 1881 (by permission of Getty Images).

FIGURE 0.18: Bomb explosion in the Liceu Theatre, Barcelona, 1893 (from *Le Petit journal*, November 25, 1893; by permission of Getty Images).

INTRODUCTION 21

FIGURE 0.19: Fire at the Théâtre Français (Comédie Française), March 8, 1900 (by permission of Getty Images).

FIGURE 0.20: Henrik Ibsen on a sleigh in front of the National Theater, Oslo, 1900 (by permission of Getty Images).

CHAPTER ONE

Forms and Media

LISSETTE LOPEZ SZWYDKY

What can a child's toy teach us about tragedy? The diary of twelve-year-old Benjamin Musser, written in 1902, provides an opportunity to answer this question, as the adolescent describes a play he has written to produce on his toy theater:

> Saturday [November] 21. Our first play will be next Saturday and will be called *The Guillotine*, dealing with Marie Antoinette, Louis XVI, etc. It is very exciting and terribly tragic, I made it just as tragic as I could so the audience (Julia) would be fearfully moved and cry maybe. The prison scene is horrible, where they stick Princess Lamable's head through the bars and tear the dauphin from his mothers arm. . . . Fred says I'm a royalist, and I said he bets his life I am at least regarding France, and Fred said then I ought not to let my own feelings show in things I write. Well but whose feelings out to show, that's what writers are for.[1]

Ben and Fred made sense of the world, of history, and of writing through this toy that put storytelling, performance, and interpretation in the hands of children. Their understanding of the French Revolution was informed by the century and ocean separating imaginative children from the violence, suffering, and contexts (philosophical, domestic, national, and continental) of war.

Musser's musings raise questions about history, form, and the purpose of modern authorship, while providing an entry point to examine the trajectory of nineteenth-century tragedy. The twelve-year-old defines tragedy in broad terms, invoking its political, domestic, and artistic dimensions. He portrays a grand historical event through the deaths of its most iconic and pathetic figures. He intends to create strong emotional responses in the audience (to make his sister Julia "be fearfully moved and cry maybe"). He conflates emotions, politics, and aesthetics, his emotions and emerging political allegiances. All of these elements are central tenets of European Romanticism, from its eighteenth-century roots in England, France, and Germany, to its long-term effects on modern art and culture. Musser's miniature toy theater from the turn of the twentieth century thus functions as a site of remediation between the past and the present, providing a small-scale venue to explore large-scale suffering.

Traditionally defined through genre (tragedy), form (drama), and medium (the stage), "tragedy" might refer to a specific type of art or an unfortunate incident. Terry Eagleton calls attention to this disconnect between academic and public discourses (already in place during the nineteenth century) where, "For most people today, tragedy means an actual occurrence, not a work of art. Indeed, some of those who nowadays use the word for actual events are probably unaware that it has an artistic sense at all . . . [and] might be puzzled to hear it used of a film or novel."[2] Modern tragedy's diffusion from high art to the description of everyday occurrences is an opportunity to reframe conversations and rethink the cultural function of tragedy both now and in the past. Adrian Poole, for example, sees modern tragedy "liberated from the realm of art" (while not abandoning it entirely), partly an effect of "the development of the modern media that disseminate what we call 'the news' . . ." over the last two hundred years.[3] Today's colloquial use comes from eighteenth- and nineteenth-century illustrated newspapers that regularly invoked "tragedy" to describe a range of unfortunate events because "'Real life' . . . has to be turned into words, stories, and plots" in order to "hold our protracted attention."[4] Rebecca Bushnell identifies a similar process that positions literature and art as meaning-making devices: "Tragedy can shape experience and history into meaning" so that "knowledge might emerge out of the chaos of human suffering."[5] Bushnell focuses on drama and Poole surveys many forms, yet both scholars agree that the cultural function of tragedy primarily demonstrates how art creates and mediates understanding.

The following chapter approaches tragedy not as a genre but as a malleable mode crossing genres. As Rita Felski has noted, mode's elasticity as a term "lends itself especially well to the complicated history and vicissitudes of tragic art."[6] Tragedy thrives across artistic forms and media, as well as across social and political contexts. Tragic modes help us to negotiate between scholarly and vernacular uses, moving beyond limited formalist and disciplinary approaches to reconsider the multiple contexts that inform cultural production in the past as well as the present. To this effect, Stephen Dowden argues for interdisciplinary approaches to tragedy because "literature, philosophy, history, politics, and the arts intermingle productively when seeking to understand tragedy and the tragic. They are so blended that to separate them out into discrete units would mask something crucial: namely, that tragic experience precedes our disciplinary structures."[7] The disciplinary silos of the modern university have tended to promote a limited understanding of tragedy by focusing too narrowly on singular genres, forms, and media instead of emphasizing comparative approaches. Even George Steiner (whose definition of tragedy is remarkably narrow) admits that medieval writers including Geoffrey Chaucer and Dante Alighieri used "tragedy" to describe any "narrative recounting the life of some ancient or eminent personage who suffered a decline of fortune toward a disastrous end" regardless of the form in which the story was told.[8]

Writers and artists rarely limit themselves to single forms, and in the nineteenth century regularly mixed genres and media. Johann Wolfgang von Goethe, Elizabeth Inchbald, Charlotte Smith, William Godwin, Samuel Taylor Coleridge, Victor Hugo, Alexandre Dumas, Thomas Hardy, Fyodor Dostoyevsky, and Mikhail Lermontov all distinguished themselves across a range of forms and genres while employing tragic elements in their works. Far from confining itself to the stage, nineteenth-century tragedy stayed culturally relevant through visual art and other forms. The following essay thus surveys a range of nineteenth-century tragic forms and media in three representative mediums through which tragedy circulated: theater, textual forms, and visual culture.

THE DEMOCRATIZATION OF CULTURE AND THE EVOLUTION OF GENRES

Raymond Williams' *Modern Tragedy* (1965) challenged Steiner's claim that post-Enlightenment secularism and the French Revolution caused the "death of tragedy." Both scholars tie tragedy's transformation to the period's larger democratic project as it played out politically, socially, and aesthetically, requiring a fundamental restructuring of the mystical and hierarchal paradigms that dominated classical tragedy. Yet, where Steiner scorned the aesthetic revolution that elevated common experience as a worthy subject for poetry, Williams welcomed this radical turn, applauding "the movement of civilization" toward progressive social changes.[9]

Though it was not the only political revolution of its time, the French Revolution marked a major shift in how tragedy and the tragic mode have been conceptualized for more than two centuries across Europe. According to Matthew Buckley:

> [T]he transition from traditional to modern drama is best understood not as an aggregate of disconnected ruptures—of isolated and irreconcilable formal experiments gathered about the French Revolution's epistemological void—but as a continuous and extended crises, worked out not only in literature and the theater but also in political and social performance, of the drama's authority as a narrative form.[10]

Tragedy reflects how we process, speak about, understand, and perform social and political ruptures. The French Revolution was a highly dramatic event that changed European political structures as well as artistic and social expression. While certainly informing the stage, its violence and tragic narratives also permeated culture throughout the continent.

Political rhetoric regularly employed the tragic mode. In the famous pamphlet debate between Edmund Burke and Thomas Paine, both authors invoke tragedy and use theatrical metaphors. For Burke in *Reflections on the Revolution in France* (1790), the French Revolution presented a "monstrous tragicomic scene"; responding to Burke in *The Rights of Man*, Paine had mocked Burke's histrionic rhetoric:

> As to the tragic paintings by which Mr. Burke has outraged his own imagination . . . they are very well calculated for theatrical representation, where facts are manufactured for the sake of show, and accommodated to produce, through the weakness of sympathy, a weeping effect. But Mr. Burke should recollect that he is writing history, and not plays, and that his readers will expect truth, and not the spouting rant of high-toned exclamation.[11]

Their exchange exemplifies "the emphatic, contested theatricality of politics in both France *and* England during this period" that Paine hoped to eliminate from public discourse.[12] Readers today might also notice how Steiner and Williams echo the tension between Burke and Paine. The Revolution in France—especially in the context of the transformational revolutions in the American colonies and in Saint Domingue—marked a major turning point in the cultural function of tragedy in the popular imagination, including the socially conscious art that followed in the Romantic period across forms and media.

Even in its emphasis on originality, European Romanticism was defined by hybrid genres that recreated old forms in a complex network of forms and media. As David Duff explains, "genres cannot be studied in isolation" because all "genres grow out of one another, a new genre being always a reworking of old ones, and complex genres being built up out of simple ones."[13] Duff's focus is the British Romantic tradition, but similar points have been made about French Romanticism too, as when Victor Brombert argues for "[Victor] Hugo's unwillingness to establish fixed boundaries between genres."[14]

To what extent, then, are any of the characteristics of the tragic mode unique to dramatic form or high culture? Tragedy shares much in common with other nineteenth-century artistic modes such as melodrama and the gothic, whose convergence in both print and performance can be found in the careers of several Romantic-period writers. Horace Walpole not only penned the first English gothic novel *The Castle of Otranto* (1764), but also wrote the gothic-infused drama *The Mysterious Mother: A Tragedy* (1768). Irish writer Charles Robert Maturin is best remembered for his Faustian-inspired gothic novel *Melmoth The Wanderer* (1820), but his repertoire included several five-act tragedies, including *Bertram; or, The Castle of St Aldobrand* (1816), *Manuel* (1817), and *Fredolpho* (1819). Percy Bysshe Shelley published two gothic novels before penning *The Cenci: A Tragedy in Five Acts* (1819), itself the product of an earlier generic hybrid, gothic drama, as Diego Saglia explains:

> The Gothic stage ... both endorsed canonical forms such as tragedy and subverted hierarchies by dissolving and reconfiguring existing models, usually by mixing high and low forms or adapting from other genres. Instigating hybridity through its characteristic cross-fertilisation of modes and types, stage Gothic undermined conventions—both literary and theatrical—and forced their redefinition, as well as ... the epistemological principles and ideological frameworks they encapsuled.[15]

Gothic drama was not alone in this formal experimentation for both artistic and political purposes. Melodrama was also a sophisticated discursive mode that emerged, according to Elaine Hadley, "as a polemical response to the social, economic, and epistemological changes that characterized the consolidation of market society in the nineteenth century" whose reach extended well beyond the stage to include speeches, physical gestures, clothing, and political actions.[16] Gothic and melodrama both borrowed from the tragic mode through their focus on human suffering, while redeploying its tropes for new readers and audiences. Tragic art, in turn, adapted the techniques of popular forms like gothic and melodrama, both textual and dramatic. The picture that emerges is what Duff calls a "genre-system," where competing genres and media adapt and transform one another.[17]

Contemporary theories of adaptation and transmedia storytelling show us how the nineteenth century transformed tragedy from one of the most revered genres of "high" art into an accessible and popular mode. Instead of seeing the decline of an older form, we should celebrate how tragedy adapted to new political and social environments. Gary Bortolotti and Linda Hutcheon's biological model of cultural adaptation is particularly helpful here because it challenges our tendency to fixate on differences when evaluating the cultural evolution of narratives. "If a narrative is adapted into many media," they write, "we might use this proliferation of forms as a measure of success. The new versions would in turn allow other opportunities for future adaptations and thus insure longevity because of the medium change...."[18] In this approach, difference and diversity become primary markers of success. Bortolotti and Hutcheon are interested in adaptation as both a product and a process, and their observations apply to single narratives as well as genres more broadly. Tracing the cultural history of tragedy means celebrating how tragedy has evolved over time instead of focusing too intensely how it has changed. The political, social, technological, and aesthetic revolutions of the day required tragedy to evolve. To borrow an analogy from evolutionary biology: myriad environmental changes altered tragedy's main habitat—the stage. Censorship, regulation, and the growing commercialization of the theater created an increasingly inhospitable environment for tragedy to thrive in a single site. Some of the older form survived, but there was not enough freedom or resources for tragedy to maintain its classic form. And so, tragedy migrated. Tragedy could not have survived without being adapted, appropriated, and dispersed into the various forms and media of the day.

CENSORSHIP OF THE STAGE AND THE RISE OF HYBRID FORMS

As Saglia explains, "If there is no death of tragedy in the Romantic period, then what we have to confront is an array of multiple and simultaneous reinventions of it."[19] Tragedy remained a culturally relevant form even if it was no longer the most prevalent dramatic genre. In competing with an array of new forms, tragedy was transformed and reworked, becoming "visible as an aesthetically, historically, and ideologically conditioned set of rules or frames . . . to conform and express the evil of suffering."[20] Victor Hugo exemplified this hybrid vision, breaking with classical tragedy to appeal to modern audiences. His dramas blended old forms and new, collapsing the distinctions between noble and popular, tragic and comic, sublime and grotesque, to represent a fuller range of lived experience.[21] Another innovator, Alexandre Dumas "helped to transform serious drama in France by combining the dynamism and spectacle of melodrama with the gravity of tragedy" in plays such as *Henri III et sa cour* (1829) and *Antony* (1831).[22] Both writers exemplified the new tragic stage theorized by Stendhal in France and Schlegel in Germany.

Tragedy's shifting political and social sensibilities began several decades before the French Revolution. As Williams writes, "a determined attempt was made in England to adapt tragedy to the habits of thinking of middle-class life . . . [with] little immediate success, though the imitation of its example in France and Germany provided one of the elements for the emergence of serious modern tragedy."[23] Jeffrey Cox corroborates this view, noting that for "the Romantics, the tragic was no longer identified with a particular aesthetic form, but rather with a vision or philosophy of life."[24] Cox sees the beginnings of a more democratic tragic sensibility in George Lillo's *The London Merchant; or, The History of George Barnwell* (1731), which explicitly calls for tragedy to convey the misfortunes and errors of characters from all walks of life.[25] As the stage embraced new theatrical genres including pantomime, burlesque, farce, and especially melodrama, tragedy spread to these more visible forms.

Not just part of a new ideologically infused aesthetic, these changes were largely informed by strict censorship. Beginning with the restrictive Theatre Licensing Act of 1737, the British stage found itself increasingly regulated in ways that permanently shifted the trajectory of all dramatic forms. Only two theaters in London—Drury Lane and Covent Garden—were "licensed" to stage spoken-word drama in the "legitimate" genres of tragedy and comedy. (The smaller Haymarket Theatre acquired a third license in 1766 to operate during the summers.) Competing theaters—the "minor" houses—could only stage pantomime, opera, burlesque, farce, and other "illegitimate" forms. The Licensing Act created a class structure around theatrical genres, but these divisions between "legitimate" and "illegitimate" forms did not apply both ways. The minor theaters were not allowed to stage "legitimate" drama, but the patent theaters included many "illegitimate" pieces in their repertoires. Thus, "illegitimate" forms had a much wider reach than the "legitimate" drama, and they borrowed as much as they could from the traditional genres to satisfy both regulatory structures and popular tastes.

The second aspect of the law in England required all dramas (both "legitimate" and "illegitimate") to receive licenses from the Examiner of Plays, under the direction of the

Lord Chamberlain. The practice is often a source of confusion leading to the assumption that "illegitimate" forms were not subject to the same censorship as "legitimate" dramas. Minor theaters, music halls, and saloons often staged pieces that fell under the radar of the Examiner of Plays (or were intentionally ignored), but not always. Some non-patent theaters relied on the perceived respectability afforded by the Lord Chamberlain's office, especially when staging potentially controversial pieces.[26] Back at the patent theaters, licenses were acquired for "legitimate" and "illegitimate" pieces alike.

The Theatre Regulation Act of 1843 removed this two-tiered system of legitimacy.[27] Deregulation of the patent system made all dramatic entertainment equal. Yet, because the censorship rules did not change, this new system brought all dramatic forms equally under the purview of the Lord Chamberlain. Continued government oversight meant that what could have galvanized the stage, hampered by more than a hundred years of regulations, effected little change. As London's population steadily increased, the most important goal for theater entrepreneurs was a steady number of customers. The biggest draw for patrons was the prospect of seeing something innovative, and the theater prospered by focusing on spectacle. The relationship between literary and theatrical production strengthened. Adaptation was steadily on the rise.[28]

Outside of England and France, comparative studies of nineteenth-century European theatrical censorship are hard to come by. Still, existing evidence shows regulation of the stage to be widespread across the continent, shaping not only the politics of the stage but also its aesthetics. Though varying from country to country and growing out of nuanced cultural contexts, these censorship regimes shared a number of traits. Where class divisions engendered anxiety among the ruling and upper classes, the stage was considered threatening because of its ability to reach literate and illiterate audiences alike. Any medium possessing the power to stir the emotions of a large group could enable mob violence. By contrast, print was more easily controlled, confiscated, and regulated. Censored topics varied by country, year, and the idiosyncrasies of individual censors. Explicit references to ruling heads of state and religious topics received the most immediate attention, but historical dramas too were affected, especially political ones. In the German state of Bavaria all plays that invoked German history were banned in the 1790s.[29] In its most extreme manifestations, theatrical censorship included gestures and costuming.

Censorship was commonplace and practiced by government officials, theater managers, and actors making changes or refusing to speak parts. As L.W. Conolly explains regarding the 1737 Licensing Act in England: "Before the manuscript of a new play ever reached the Examiner, several people might have meddled with it. Managers ... altered texts a good deal and in doing so saved the censor a considerable amount of work."[30] Preemptive changes could be prompted by political, economic, or practical reasons ranging from projected production expenses to a play's potential for inciting riots in a crowded building (combining political, safety, and economic risk for theater managers). Censorship resulted in the rise of non-verbal—hence harder to censor—spectacle that included new technologies and theatrical effects and investment in costuming, scenery, and other visual elements over writing.

Dramatic genres were profoundly shaped by these new practices. Traditionally one of the most political of theatrical genres and second only to political satire, tragedy was particularly affected. As Rebecca Bushnell explains, "Tragedy's original form was shaped as much by Athenian democracy as it was by ancient religion, and its survival in European and American culture has been intertwined with the fate of dynasties, revolutions, and crises of social change."[31] As it found its way into new media and theatrical forms, the tragic mode provided an aesthetic framework for stories told on the stage as well as a system for synthesizing both real events and fictional narratives. It infused history and historiography by providing

> a familiar way of reading history ... certain exemplary stories within it, such as those which tell the rise and fall of political leaders from Napoleon onwards, or the fate of ambitious political movements, especially those aimed at radical or revolutionary change. Where these involve signal loss of life, tragedy and history seemed fused together.[32]

Tragedy and history productively coalesce when tragedy sheds light on revolutionary failures and feeds anxieties of radical change.

The Age of Revolutions impacted Europe at large, and its accompanying tragic vision traversed national boundaries while simultaneously reinforcing them. For example, Ilya Kliger underscores the interdependence of tragedy, history, and nationalism in Dostoevsky's oeuvre, highlighting the importance of a tragic vision for both the Russian writer and the trajectory of the nineteenth-century European novel's engagement with continental philosophy. For Kliger, tragedy and the novel revolve in a "tragic Mobius strip" with a new understanding of history and the individual's place in the world, connecting Europe around a tragic vision situated in a historical crisis: "For both Dostoevsky and Nietzsche—or rather for the 'tragic nationalist' vision constructed somewhere at midpoint between them—the problem is historical in nature."[33]

Beyond history, politics, and aesthetics, tragedy and other traditional forms were refashioned in the nineteenth century by technological advances ushered in by the Industrial Revolution. Printing innovations steadily decreased the price of texts and introduced new ways of producing and consuming art, which in turn brought a new array of challenges and opportunities. For example, though many of the century's important tragedies were not performed during their authors' lifetimes, they still existed in print form (a more permanent form than the ephemeral stage). Joanna Baillie may have seen only a third of her *Plays on the Passions* performed before her death in 1850, yet her works circulated well thanks to the period's vibrant print culture.[34] The printed page thus became a key way that the tragic mode dispersed from the stage into other areas of nineteenth-century European cultural production.

TRAGEDY'S TEXTUAL FORMS

The most straightforward transition between the tragic stage and the tragic page is in nineteenth-century dramatic poetry, especially closet drama and dramatic monologue. Closet dramas of the early part of the century illustrate the censorship of the stage and the comparative freedom of the page, although printed texts could still be banned or prosecuted for libel or obscenity.[35] Lord Byron and Shelley, whose radical politics and personal scandals drove them from England to Italy, exemplify this shift. While living in Italy, Shelley wrote three dramas with strong connections to tragedy—*The Cenci* (1819), *Prometheus Unbound* (1820), and *Hellas* (1822)—the last two signaling their direct connection to classical Greek tragedy vis-à-vis Aeschylus. Also living in Italy during these years, Byron penned *Manfred* (1817), *Sardanapalus* (1821), *Marino Faliero* (1821), and *The Two Foscari* (1821). And while Byron famously refused to try his hand at stage drama despite being a lifelong patron of the theater, his plays were nonetheless performed and adapted, sometimes in the tragic mode they were written in, but often reworked into comic or illegitimate forms.[36]

Similarly, the rise of the novel during the eighteenth and nineteenth centuries provided opportunity to test the conventions of tragedy in a new literary form. As they gained popularity and critical recognition, novelists adapted the aesthetics of tragedy into a variety of fictional modes, from epistolary fiction to the gothic. Both Samuel Richardson's *Clarissa; or, The History of a Lady* (1748) and Goethe's *The Sorrows of Young Werther* (1774), for example, chart the tragic deaths of young protagonists who succumb to rigid and pitiless social structures that leave youth vulnerable to their passions. Similarly, gothic novels were steeped in the tragic mode, especially in their portrayal of women made victims by an array of social circumstances wrongly framed as defective character or gendered weaknesses. Both Ann Radcliffe's *The Mysteries of Udolpho* (1794) and Mary Wollstonecraft's unfinished novella *Maria; or, The Wrongs of Woman* (1798) blend sentimental, gothic, and tragic modes to advance a social critique of patriarchal oppression that would shape women's fiction for the next two centuries. Drawing on these traditions, Mary Shelley's *Frankenstein; or, The Modern Prometheus* (1818) provided the century with a tragic hero, Victor Frankenstein, still recognizable today. Whether Victor's downfall is the cause of narcissistic and obsessive self-destruction (as we see in the 1818 edition) or an unavoidable destiny set in motion by accident (as many of the revisions in the 1831 edition suggest), it still comes directly from tragic tradition. In both versions, the main source of conflict is internal rather than external, produced by Victor's character and actions rather than from outside events impacting him. The ethical slippages between creator and monster—not to mention their similarity to one another—also closely follow the conventions of tragedy by resisting the more clearly defined character types of melodrama.[37] All of Shelley's novels include at least some aspects of tragedy whether embodied in protagonists that closely follow the conventions of the classic tragic hero as we see in *Frankenstein*, or in the apocalyptic vision of *The Last Man* (1826), a novel of personal mourning and a tragic, pessimistic outlook on the fate of humanity.

In the second half of the nineteenth century, realism also embraced the tragic mode. "One of the greatest achievements of the 19th-century realist novel," Adrian Poole notes, "was to find ways of representing apparently ordinary, inevitable forms of suffering and give them the special attention by virtue of which they would strike the reader as extraordinary, un-inevitable, and therefore tragic."[38] Jeannette King sees a direct engagement with classical tragedy in the novels of George Eliot, Thomas Hardy, and Henry James: "In turning to the novel and new versions of tragedy, writers did not . . . completely reject traditional tragic theory and practice. At a time when knowledge of the classics was far more widespread among the educated and the literary than it is now, it is unlikely that any writer could form his ideas of tragedy in a void."[39] King connects the Victorian realist novel to earlier forms, arguing that the novel replaced drama as the primary form of the tragic vision.

Similar developments characterize fiction in France, especially those by Hugo and Gustave Flaubert (representing the Romantic and realist novel respectively). Hugo's historical novels *Notre-Dame de Paris* (1830) and *Les Misérables* (1862) blend dominant tropes of European Romanticism (historical consciousness, commentary on political and cultural revolutions, emotional intensity, and social empathy) packaged in a reflective, tragic vision. Brombert notes that *Notre-Dame de Paris*, a historical romance, is ultimately a novel about death—and fate. Characters and ideologies die, and all of this is predestined and foreshadowed by the engraving of a single word on a wall of the cathedral: *anankē*, the Greek word for "fate," linking the novel's tragic sensibility in the classical tradition while giving it a modern facade.[40] In *Les Misérables*, the sentimental and the grotesque are grounded in the brutal realism of poverty. Both novels use the disabled, the poor, orphans, and criminals to portray the tragic outcomes of disenfranchisement and other forms of systemic exclusion.

The class context changes in Flaubert's fiction, which approaches the tragic isolation of modernity on the individual grounded through realistic portrayals of everyday solitude in bourgeoisie society. According to Brombert, *Madame Bovary* (1856) is a "tragedy of dreams" that seeks to redefine "a new form of tragedy: [in] a period which discovers the pathos of the unheroic hero [and] also discovers the tragedy of the very absence of Tragedy."[41] Similarly, In *L'Éducation sentimentale* (*Sentimental Education* 1869), the protagonist "suffers most from the tragedy of cognition because . . . he is torn between egotism and selflessness. The simultaneous presence of the two urges gives him the sense that he is not in control of his fate."[42] The novel is set during the French Revolution of 1848 and the establishment of the Second French Empire, extending the crisis of modernity sparked by the French Revolution of the 1790s.

Russian fiction also confronted the tragic conditions of nineteenth-century modernity. Alexander Pushkin's hybrid texts are steeped in tragic aesthetics, such as the verse novel *Evgenii Onegin* (1833), where the protagonist's "vision approaches the tragic."[43] Similar observations have been made of his dramas *Boris Godunov* (1825) and the four plays that comprise the *Little Tragedies* (1830). According to Caryl Emerson, Pushkin's theatrical ideals included "tough-minded hopes for a hybrid drama combining the best of classical (and neo-classical) restraint with the flexibility of Shakespeare as revived by French and German Romanticism."[44] Dostoevsky's works are also characterized by a tragic sensibility. Calling Dostoevsky "the new Aeschylus," Kliger sees the writer as a "tragic poet" who "takes up the key motifs of the tragic tradition." However, she argues that Dostoevsky's novels "are only privately tragic, representing the last throes of a great form, the collapse of tragic consciousness in modernity."[45] Kliger connects Dostoevsky's works to a larger-scale modern reconceptualization of the possibilities of the tragic vision and the novel, where readers find themselves "at the threshold between two genres. Two epochs, two conceptions of the individual traverse in a single narrative, turning it into a transmodern hybrid form, a 'novel-tragedy.'"[46] If Enlightenment philosophy ushered in an age of skepticism, then the novel discovered potential ways that doubt might play out individually—as mechanisms of both survival and destruction. Werther, Frankenstein, Jean Valjean, Emma Bovary, and Rodion Raskolnikov each portray the individual's isolation from a ruthless society. Whether that isolation is self-imposed or the result of social ostracizing, it is always expressed as tragedy.

Beyond the novel, the tragic mode dominated discourses of social action across an array of textual forms and genres, including memoir, poetry, popular ballads, and political pamphleteering. The major societal questions of the day, from the abolition of slavery to workers' rights to the status (and fate) of women in society, found voice in the tragic mode, especially in Britain.[47] Between the 1780s and the Slave Trade Act of 1807 that ended the British slave trade, England saw a significant output of poetry and ballads supporting the abolitionist cause.[48] Later in the century, as attention turned to ending slavery in the United States, writers continued to employ tragic elements in poetry supporting this global crisis. Elizabeth Barrett Browning's dramatic monologue *The Runaway Slave at Pilgrim's Point* (1848) stands out for acknowledging how several tragic tropes—slavery, rape, murder, infanticide, suicide—informed the lived experience of millions of enslaved people. The speaker insists in Stanza IV that God must have cast her away in favor of his white creations, adding a religious determinism or predestination to the poem that echoes the mysticism and role of fate of classic tragedy.

The tragic visions of abolitionist poetry are also characteristic of nineteenth-century poetry written by women, which regularly relied on tragic tropes and language. Felicia Hemans' *Records of Woman* (1828) shows how the tragic mode could bring together the idea of disparate voices in a cohesive poetic whole. Drawing from a combination of historical persons and fictional subjects, Hemans crafts a collection that asks the reader to read women's history through a tragic lens. From the imagined historical voices of Arabella Stuart, Properzia Rossi, and Joan of Arc to the fictional ones interspersed throughout the collection, most of the poems in *Records of Woman* end with the speakers dead or in various stages of despair. Hemans dedicates the volume to Joanna Baillie, suggesting a multi-genre connection in the tragic mode. Several epigraphs are included throughout the volume, quoting tragic works by Goethe, Byron, Schiller, and Baillie. For Hemans and other nineteenth-century women writers, art (regardless of form, genre, or medium) provided an opportunity to aestheticize political and social action.

Tragic works were often infused with social commentary that led to anachronistic adaptations notable for their historical displacement. Such fusions of past and present via the tragic mode characterized much of the art and literature of the period, particularly in medieval revivals such as those of Alfred Lord Tennyson. Tennyson's adaptations often recast morally ambiguous characters in a new light, so that Guinevere, in Maureen Fries' estimation, "emerges not as one participant in a complex tale of sin and betrayal, as in Malory, but as almost sole cause of what has instead become a simple (not to say simplistic) tragedy."[49] Tennyson's rewriting of Arthurian tradition employs several conventions of tragedy, specifically through the downfalls of aristocratic heroes. Nobility is constructed through bravery, the willingness to fight unwinnable wars. The heroes of Tennyson's poems are fated to die, either by their own hand or that of others, a fatalistic view characteristic of nineteenth-century tragic texts. It also served as the inspiration for much of the period's visual art, which also embedded the tragic mode in other forms of adaptation and appropriation.

PAINTING, ILLUSTRATION, AND TRANSMEDIA STORYTELLING

The Industrial Revolution also brought increased demand for spectacle on stage and other visual forms including sculpture, painting, and engraving. Illustrated texts became popular as technology made the reproduction of images financially feasible for printers and publishers. Pictorial texts—whether novels, gift books, or illustrated newspapers—dispersed and increased the consumption of visually supported, dynamic storytelling across a range of forms and media. Tragedy's adaptability to non-performative visual media dates back to its root in antiquity where, as Edith Hall explains, "Ancient historians described events as if they were episodes in tragic drama . . . poets composed ekphrasis of scenes derived from tragic theatre; sculptors and potters carved and painted figures from individual tragedies."[50] What we see in the nineteenth century is an intensification of visual appropriations of the tragic mode made possible as new printing technologies lowered the costs of producing and consuming these visual texts.

Throughout the nineteenth century we find early sites of "transmedia storytelling" and "convergence culture," terms coined by contemporary media theorist Henry Jenkins to describe coordinated narratives owned by a single source but licensed and disseminated via a range of media platforms and providers as we see in today's mega-franchises like *The Matrix* or *Star Wars*. In "true" transmedia storytelling, all of the narrative-based tie-ins produce unique yet "authoritative" additions to the storyline—each piece is embedded in the process of world building. Nineteenth-century forms of entertainment and storytelling wouldn't (or couldn't) qualify as a "pure" form of transmedia storytelling because of the lack of strict copyright laws; yet, they still represent early examples of convergence culture, an umbrella term that theorizes "the flow of content across multiple media platforms, the cooperation between multiple media industries, and the migratory behavior of media audiences who will go almost anywhere in search of the kinds of entertainment experiences they want."[51] The lack of copyright on adaptations until the late nineteenth century created an artistic, cultural, and commercial climate that allowed transmedia storytelling to become a central process of cultural production.[52] Each version of a story worked individually, yet collectively they created shared narratives many of which were conceptualized through the tragic mode. Relatedly, although many versions of a story drew their inspiration from a range of earlier sources, there was no single "authoritative" version of the story—just a range of forms and media converging to popularize a story.

Tragedies from ancient Greece through the Early Modern period inspired Romantic and Victorian poets from Blake to Tennyson, not to mention the visual artists who adapted their works into paintings, sculptures, and other forms of illustration. Historical and fictional persons were reimagined or reinterpreted as tragic subjects, with different forms and media converging and turning fashionable figures into cross-cultural icons across Europe. For example, Byron's blank-verse drama *Sardanapalus: A Tragedy* (1821), inspired by quasi-historical sources, was first given visual form in Eugène Delacroix's oil painting *The Death of Sardanapalus* (*La Mort de Sardanapale*) in 1827. Byron's tragedy spurred additional renderings in multiple forms and media in the following decades including a song in the genre of a cantata by French composer Hector Berlioz (1830), an unfinished opera by Hungarian composer Franz Liszt (which he worked on throughout the 1840s), as well as several other completed operas in Italy by Giulio Alary (1852) and in France by Victorin de Joncières (1867) and Alphonse Duvernoy (1882).

Nineteenth-century visual artists refashioned characters according to Romantic aesthetics or Victorian social mores. The Pre-Raphaelite Brotherhood was particularly fond of tragic subjects from drama, literature, and myth—bringing them to life in intricate paintings and book illustrations. We see one of the most visible convergences of genres, forms, and media in the tragic mode around Arthurian legend—including some of its minor characters—as poets and painters reimagined medieval subjects for Victorian audiences. Dozens of paintings and book illustrations of Elaine of Astolat and/or the Lady of Shalott, were inspired by Tennyson's 1833 poem, with increased interest after the publication of *Idylls of the King*.[53] Multiple editions were published, and artists took turns visualizing Tennyson's poems, including the three original members of the Pre-Raphaelite Brotherhood, all featured in the 1857 edition of Tennyson's *Poems* published by Edward Moxon. Gustave Doré illustrated Tennyson's poems (Figure 1.1), whose gift books were especially popular and profitable. Moxon brought volumes dedicated to Elaine, Guinevere, Vivien, and Enid before collecting them together as *Idylls*; all were translated and published in France, the Netherlands, and the United States between 1860 and 1900.[54] Tennyson also commissioned the celebrated Victorian photographer Julia Margaret Cameron to illustrate an 1874 edition of *Idylls* in this new, popular medium. She produced

FIGURE 1.1: Gustave Doré, *The Body of Elaine on Its Way to King Arthur's Palace*, 1867 (by permission of SuperStock/Alamy Stock Photo).

more than 200 images for the project, which failed commercially because of the expense of the project, and which only exists in a relatively limited format (Figure 1.2).

Although details differ between the stories of Elaine of Astolat and the Lady of Shalott, all Victorian versions align in their depiction of the heroine's tragic death. Whether they imagined her at the window, at her loom, on her final boat ride, or arriving dead in Camelot, artists found in her an endless source of inspiration for visualizing unrequited love and woman's social entrapment. Painters, illustrators, and sculptors made the tragic vision central to nineteenth-century British art by drawing heavily from Greek mythology, Biblical stories, Shakespearean tragedies, and other literary sources.

Transnational in scope, this practice of adapting existing texts to visual media popularized the tragic as a mode in high and mass culture alike. Visualization transcended language barriers. It created iconography, making narrative associations across media. Such was the case with Ophelia, a popular subject repeatedly depicted by nineteenth-century European painters including Delacroix (1838 and 1858), Arthur Hughes (1852 and 1865), and John William Waterhouse (1889, 1894, and 1910), whose depictions added dimensions not found in Shakespeare's tragic play. For instance, Hughes and Waterhouse portray Ophelia as an object of desire undone by idealized innocence, while Delacroix fixates on the young woman's tragic death. Many nineteenth-century paintings and sculpture follow Delacroix's interest in depicting the death of Ophelia and demonstrate how imagery established in visual form inspired new iterations of the same story or scene (see Figures 1.3 to 1.6).

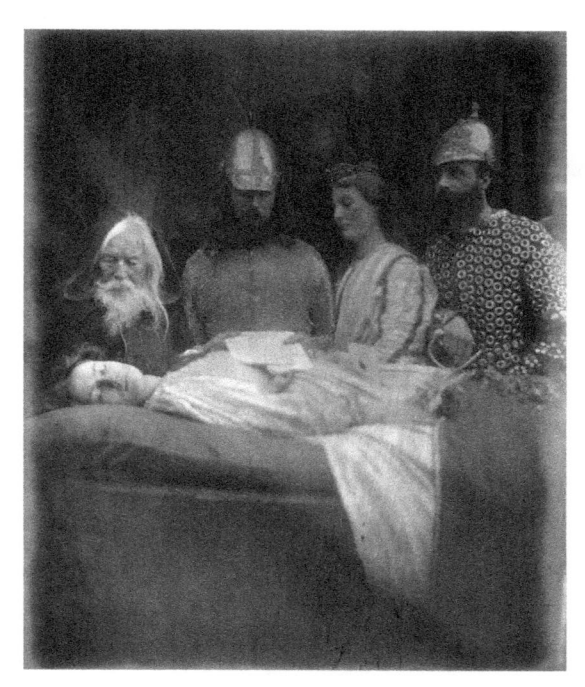

FIGURE 1.2: Julia Margaret Cameron, *The Corpse of Elaine Arriving in the Palace of King Arthur*, 1875 (courtesy of the Getty's Open Content Program).

FIGURE 1.3: Johann Heinrich Ramberg, *Ophelia Falling into the Water*, 1829 (by permission of the Folger Shakespeare Library).

FIGURE 1.4: John Everett Millais, *Ophelia*, 1852. Tate Gallery, London (by permission of Erich Lessing/Art Resource, NY).

FIGURE 1.5: Alexandre Cabanel, *Ophelia*, 1883. Private Collection (by permission of Alamy Stock Photo).

FORMS AND MEDIA 37

FIGURE 1.6: Frances MacDonald, *Ophelia*, 1898. Private Collection (by permission of Alamy Stock Photo).

Produced in four countries across eight decades, all of these works illustrate Ophelia's death scene, a moment from *Hamlet* that is described in detail by Queen Gertrude, but does not take place onstage in Shakespeare's play.[55] The artistic interest in rendering this tragic scene visible follows Martin Meisel's understanding of how illustration was understood by visual artists in the nineteenth century as carrying "a sense of enrichment and embellishment beyond mere specification; it implied the extensions of one medium or mode of discourse by another, rather than a materialization with a minimum of imaginative intervention."[56] Later nineteenth-century art would continue the trend of visualizing Ophelia's death including Antoine-Augustin Préault's bronze bas-relief sculpture completed in 1876, as well as actress and visual artist Sarah Bernhardt's marble sculpture completed in 1880 followed by a performance in 1886, where she became the first person to appear onstage as Ophelia's corpse (as opposed to in a coffin).[57] Together, all of these forms show us how the "shared structures in the representational arts helped constitute not just a common style, but a popular style" in the nineteenth century that Meisel terms the process of *realization*, connecting the representational arts of literature, drama, and picture where "each form and each work becomes the site of a complex interplay of narrative and picture" and storytelling.[58]

Nineteenth-century history painting portrayed subjects both fictional and real, all of which could be rendered in the tragic mode. As art historians Robert Rosenblum and H.W. Janson note, "many [nineteenth-century] artists from West and Copley to David and Goya . . . painted newsworthy events in the language of heroic tragedy."[59] These events ranged from battles with international reach and major historical impact to local occurrences that captured the suffering of everyday life among the poor. The French Revolution, the Napoleonic Wars, and subsequent revolutions inspired European visual art for decades which was both celebratory and critical, participating in national mythmaking and the aestheticization of revolutionary ideals.

Transmediations across art forms functioned both globally and locally, as seen through the artistic attention given to the tragic events at St. Peter's Field in Manchester on August 16, 1819. On that day, 60,000–80,000 people gathered to protest parliament and demand better representation; cavalry forces charged the peaceful demonstration, killing

FIGURE 1.7: Anonymous, *To Henry Hunt, Esq. as chairman of the meeting assembled on St. Peter's Field, Manchester on the 16th of August, 1819*. British Museum, London (by permission of The Trustees of the British Museum).

several protesters. Although literary scholars know the "Peterloo" Massacre best through poems written in response to this violent event such as Shelley's "England in 1819" and "The Mask of Anarchy," the attack also inspired other poems, paintings, sketches, and caricatures that circulated in illustrated periodicals, broadsides, and a host of commemorative items. An anonymous print dedicated to Henry Hunt (the featured speaker arrested at the rally, Figure 1.7) and two cartoons by George Cruikshank (Figures 1.8 and 1.9) depict the massacre through the tragic mode to critique excessive use of military force. All three images foreground women and youths, specifically mothers embracing their children in pathetic appeals: a common trope from tragedy and melodrama. Such representations were deployed by radicals and conservatives either to celebrate or criticize women's increasing participation in the public sphere.[60]

Cruikshank's depictions exemplify the mixture of horror, dismay, and suffering by choosing to zoom in on the violence (as opposed to other contemporaneous illustrations that emphasize the magnitude of the crowd). His cartoons demonstrate how even a strictly popular visual form such as caricature could function as a democratic tool that communicated urgency, outrage, and sympathy through a tragic lens.

A common element among the period's visual art includes the notable infusion of tragic sensibility as it was being renegotiated across class. As the revolutions of the eighteenth and nineteenth centuries permanently shifted the tragic vision away from the aristocratic world to the common people, visual art increasingly portrayed grand events alongside everyday concerns and the suffering of the masses, as in *The Massacre at Chios* (1824), a massive oil on canvas by Delacroix (Figure 1.10), inspired by the 1822

FORMS AND MEDIA 39

FIGURE 1.8: George Cruikshank, *Massacre at St. Peter's or "Britons Strike Home"!!!*, 1819. British Museum, London (by permission of The Trustees of the British Museum/Art Resource NY).

FIGURE 1.9: George Cruikshank, *Manchester Heroes*, 1819. British Museum, London (by permission of The Trustees of the British Museum).

FIGURE 1.10: Eugène Delacroix, *The Massacre at Chios*, 1824. Musée du Louvre, Paris (by permission of Stéphane Maréchalle/Adrien Didierjean, RMN-Grand Palais/Art Resource, NY).

attack that left thousands dead and spurred international support for the Greek War of Independence. In its lower right-hand corner, the painting extends the iconography of the suffering or dying mother with child seen in other examples of political painting, illustration, and cartoons. No longer limited to the suffering of aristocrats, violent massacres and crimes against humanity form the subjects of a diverse range of nineteenth-century art. In *The Slave Ship* (1840), J.M.W. Turner paints a haunting vision of the mass murder of 133 Africans tossed from the British slave ship *Zong* in 1781 (Figure 1.11), fusing the horrors of slavery and the natural sublime, the sea is a site of tragic loss and a reflection of human cruelty.

Repeated returns to the plight of the enslaved, oppressed, and poor permeate nineteenth-century European visual culture. Various styles including Romanticism, Symbolism, and Realism adapted the tragic mode to gain support for political and social reforms. Tragic sensibility crosses class and national boundaries across the century, whether the topic is a national calamity with international reach as depicted in George Frederic Watts' *The Irish Famine* (1850), the horrors of war and abuses of government power and military force as shown in Francisco Goya's *The Third of May 1808* (1814; Figure 1.12) or intimate, familial grief as portrayed in Pablo Picasso's *The Tragedy* (1903;

FIGURE 1.11: Joseph Mallord William Turner, *The Slave Ship (Slavers Throwing overboard the Dead and Dying, Typhon Coming On)*, 1840. Museum of Fine Arts, Boston (by permission of Museum of Fine Arts, Boston, Massachusetts. Photo credit: HIP/Art Resource, NY).

FIGURE 1.12: Francisco de Goya, *El Tres de Mayo, 1808*, 1814. Museo del Prado, Madrid (by permission of Museo Nacional del Prado/Art Resource, NY).

FIGURE 1.13: Pablo Picasso, *The Tragedy*, 1903. National Gallery of Art, Washington, D.C. (by permission of Estate of Pablo Picasso/Artists Rights Society).

Figure 1.13). Spanish painters Goya and Picasso conveniently bookend the range of the tragic mode in nineteenth-century European art. Goya was a prolific producer of tragic art aimed at capturing the violence and suffering of imperialism. His posthumously published *The Disasters of War* project, a series of eighty-two engravings produced between 1810 and 1820, are driven by a tragic view of the Napoleonic Wars (specifically the Peninsular War) as experienced by ordinary people. We see a similar focus on everyday suffering and poverty in Picasso's early career, especially the paintings produced during what is known as Picasso's "Blue Period" (1901–4) before the painter created his signature cubist style. Witnessing the tragic elements of violence, political abuses, natural disasters, and personal suffering, the paintings connect in their critique of poverty—the most widespread social and political disease of all.

According to Kraus, Goldhill, Foley, and Elsner, visualization is key to understanding "the diffuse formation of the genre of tragedy," from the importance of the vivid descriptions of battle scenes in epic poetry to the allegorical images painted on Athenian pottery in the fourth century BCE.[61] Seeing tragedy as an inherently affective mode permeating the literary, visual, and performing arts illuminates how representational acts engage us through allusion, parody, and other mimetic processes. Tragedy's dramatic, textual, and visual forms provide insight into how practices of adaptation and appropriation permeated high art and mass culture alike, while also influencing how printed texts were produced and read. Unhindered by language barriers, visual forms were also able to cross national and cultural boundaries more easily through a fusion of historical, dramatic, textual, and visual forms, we are able to better appreciate the tragic mode's ability to cross class, culture, and even generations.

Young Musser's toy theater can be seen in new light after surveying nineteenth-century tragedy's dispersal among various forms and media. The twelve-year-old's playful reenactment of a transformative historical event on a miniature stage shows us the transhistorical, transcultural, transatlantic, and transmedial reach of the tragic mode once it is unbound by generic definitions and conventions. A century and an ocean may have stood between Benjamin Musser and Marie Antoinette, yet this young American reenacts the fall of a French monarch in the comfort of his home and records the experience in the privacy of his diary, comfortably removed from the violent revolutions that birthed modern democracy. His Royalist sympathies—to the extent that they apply to American and French Revolutions but do not translate to his own place and time—are mediated by the tragic mode. Twenty-first-century readers might draw parallels between those two periods of history and tragedy's function across various forms and media in our own day. Without a doubt, tragedy has changed over time—and while a traditionalist might lament these changes, interpretation depends largely on one's commitment to the preservation of genres, forms, and media. Instead, as I have shown in this essay, we should recognize new iterations as evidence of growth, evolution, and continued social relevance. In this spirit, we should celebrate the transformations tragic art underwent throughout the nineteenth century, making it possible for us to continue remaking tragedy in the forms and media that speak to current and future generations.

CHAPTER TWO

Sites of Performance and Circulation

KATHERINE NEWEY

This chapter explores the mutability of tragedy, both as a mode and as a coalescence of theatrical practices. I explore how tragedy in the nineteenth century circulated spatially, temporally, and generically. The troubled relationship of tragedy to melodrama is central to any understanding of the mobility and circulation of tragedy in Europe after the French Revolution. This relationship is at the center of many of the debates and conflicts over the position of tragedy in European theaters in the first half of the nineteenth century, and markedly present in public discussions and histories of the theater in this period. While it may at first seem secondary to the material practices of performance, a study of the sites and circulation of tragedy in performance must necessarily include a discussion of this kind of critical history and historiography of tragedy. To a greater or lesser extent, theater practices in this period were produced discursively; what could or could not be imagined for the stage was framed by the legislative language of regulation, censorship, and ownership (of writing, of productions, of places of performance). Melodrama and the melodramatic mode challenged existing discourses of theater theory, theater legislation, and theater criticism, and had an embodied material effect on the ways in which tragedy and serious drama circulated and were performed and understood.

I start from the assumption that tragedy did not die in the nineteenth century. This is in contrast to powerful critical opinion in the nineteenth century and since, which has placed tragedy at the pinnacle of human expression—claiming this status as well for Western civilization, of course. George Steiner writes "that representation of personal suffering and heroism which we call tragic drama is distinctive of the western tradition."[1] Robert Heilman defends tragedy as "a specific form of experience that needs to be differentiated from all other catastrophic disturbances of life."[2] This reification of tragedy and the tragic was embedded in class-based and sex-segregated education for men across Europe, through training in Greek and Latin language and literature, becoming self-sustaining through the role of this education in the reproduction of elite and clerical cultures. In his study of the "sweet violence" of the tragic, Terry Eagleton argues that for a "lineage of modern thinkers, . . . tragedy represents a privileged mode of cognition, a spiritual experience reserved for the metaphysically minded few."[3] It was this rarefied and reified notion of tragedy that was felt to be under attack in post-Revolutionary literary and theatrical cultures. Even theater practitioners working within the popular theater of the time internalized the intellectual focus of tragedy and its variants. In Britain in 1832, we have a rich cache of evidence of the complex (and often confused) thinking around the idea of tragedy, and its performance, in the Report from the Select Committee on Dramatic Literature. In this enquiry into the standards and regulation of the London theater, much of the focus was on the groundwork of defining the "legitimate" drama—the plays of Shakespeare and his contemporaries, high comedy, and the traditional repertoire of the English stage. Douglas Jerrold's evidence encapsulates the thinking of the period:

> I describe the legitimate drama to be where the interest of the piece is mental; where the situation of the piece is rather mental than physical. . . . Q. 2844. A piece rather addressed to the ear than to the eye?—Certainly.[4]

Jerrold's own situation here is ironic and conflicted, and demonstrates some of the complexity of the material practices in the London theater industry at the time. Jerrold's work addressed the eye rather than the ear. Indeed, as the author of *Black-Ey'd Susan* (Surrey, 1829), Jerrold's deft use of melodrama and its telling situations naturalized melodrama as the "domestic drama" for English audiences. His play *The Rent Day*, which realized well-known domestic genre paintings by David Wilkie, was produced at Drury Lane, drawing on the superior scenographic capacities of that theater, but also continuing the performance of melodrama—the very form which was felt to threaten the legitimate drama—at a Patent theater, the supposed guardian of the national canonical repertoire. However much an intellectual (or metaphysical) concept of tragedy attempted to situate tragedy away from the demotic, the popular, and the commercial, tragedy survived in mainstream nineteenth-century theater because of its contact with those very demotic and popular forms thought to be causing its decline.

Tragedy survived in the nineteenth-century theaters of Europe in two ways. Firstly, through the preservation of national repertoires, continually renewed by spectacular performances and innovative scenography, fueled by the burgeoning visual culture of nineteenth-century modernity, and circulating nationally and internationally. I discuss this phenomenon in London below, with the work of actor-managers such as William Charles Macready, Charles Kean, and Henry Irving. Secondly, tragedy circulated and was renewed through radical generic and aesthetic change, so that what might be considered theatrical tragedy at the end of the nineteenth century would have been unrecognizable (and probably undesired) at the beginning of the period. Melodrama is key here. Rather than being the blight of tragedy, it was the means by which a renewed and revivified tragic form circulated in the nineteenth century.

The historiography of the performance and circulation of tragedy in the nineteenth century is marked by a central contradiction, and one which has persisted in historical, anecdotal, professional, and personal narratives of European theater until very recently. Discussions about tragedy in the public sphere across Europe follow remarkably similar narratives: largely, a narrative of decline or disappearance of traditional theatrical forms such as tragedy and high comedy. This perception of what was labeled in Britain as "the decline of the drama" was linked to unease about new audiences, new theaters, and new approaches to performance. Yet, the overwhelming evidence of a century of theater programmes, advertisements, playbills, reviews, and practitioners' careers, is that theater—and tragedy within it—survived very well in performance. Indeed, the performance of national tragic repertoires was at the forefront of the national and international mobility of theater and theatrical cultures. There is a fairly general agreement in recent revisionist histories of European national theaters that the "decline of the drama" was not actually a decline, but rather a specific ideological approach to changes to the material and aesthetic practices in national theater industries. The theater industry itself was not in decline. It was a place of innovation and experimentation, with the new energies of the mass cultural "illegitimate" genres developing and fueling new audiences' desires for excitement, entertainment, and new imagined worlds onstage. Most notable was the flourishing of the Shakespearean repertoire, which attained a unique position as an international and transhistorical phenomenon. Other "national poets" such as Jean Racine and Friedrich Schiller had a similarly consistent and successful existence in the French and German national repertoires at the highest level.

In whatever ways twenty-first-century histories are helping to redirect our theoretical gaze, understanding this normative discourse about the presence of tragedy in the theatrical repertoire remains essential. It represented both what were felt to be the limits of theater practice, and the boundaries against which waves of *avant-garde* practitioners could protest. Time and again, critics, actors, playwrights, and legislators wielded stories of the theater in decline as disciplinary tools—the most obvious example being the establishment in Britain in 1832 of the House of Commons Select Committee into Dramatic Literature. In separate national theatrical cultures, there were repeated attempts to ensure the preservation of the canonical repertoire of dramatic tragedy, matched only by an unease about the production of new tragedies, and outright anxiety about the new form most threatening to tragedy: melodrama. This desire to protect national dramatic repertoires from a perceived decline in the drama in post-Revolutionary Europe fed into the regulation of the theater in France and Britain, justified state censorship and regulation across Europe, and generated countless editorials, critical articles, essays, and books on the state of the drama. Most writers started from the assumption that the theaters were in decline, and that national dramatic repertoires performed in stable organizations to knowledgeable audiences were being replaced by poor quality novelties, performed to mass audiences with little discrimination except the desire for novelty, pleasure, and sensation.

Conventional national histories of theater in France and Germany continue to reinforce this orthodoxy. In standard narratives of national theater histories, both Marvin Carlson and Erika Fischer-Lichte seek the new and the inventive through writing which aspired to the status of classical or canonical drama, but overlook the innovations in stagecraft and performance styles in melodrama, as well as its carriage of much of the aesthetic and intellectual force of Romantic revolutionism.[5] Counter-narratives, however, can be found. They offer examples of local and national material practices of management, production, and performance which suggest that new repertoire, understood intertheatrically, offered a continuation of the serious concerns of tragedy, staged together with the newer forms of bourgeois drama and melodrama which addressed contemporary life. Immerman's theater in Düsseldorf in the 1830s, for example, staged new writing and older classic repertoire together:

> Our repertoire would be admirable for its richness and splendour even if it were badly acted. . . . When he [Karl Immerman] took over direction, there were newly produced and performed between 28 October [1834] and 1 April [1835] *among other things*, [the following] tragedies, historical and romantic dramas: *Prinz Friedrich von Homburg, Käthchen von Heilbronn* [Kleist], *Macbeth, Hamlet, The Merchant of Venice, King John, Das Leben ein Traum* [Calderón] *Stella, Maria Stuart, Wallensteins Tod* [Schiller], *Maria Tudor* [Hugo], *Struensee* [Beer], *Emilia Galotti, Raffaele* [Raupach], *Herr und Sclave* [von Zedlitz-Nimmersat], *Boccaccio* [Deinhardstein], *Die Räuber* [Schiller], and

further items in the programme will be Tieck's *Blaubert, Der Arzt seiner Ehre* [Calderón], *Die Jungfrau von Orleans,* Raupach's *Henrich VI, König Enzio* [Raupach], *Alexis* [Immerman]. Should one not . . . feel a tremendous thrill at all these spirits from so many different theatres rubbing shoulders with one another within such a short period of time? Perhaps you may ask, is there any space left for something different? That has been found, or rather, genius has shown the way and *created* that space.[6]

Christian Dietrich Grabbe's essay is a strong counterblast to narratives of decline. He writes proudly of an eclectic range of European drama staged in the (then) relatively small city of Düsseldorf, where the new management had been founded through the "self-sacrificing efforts of the local friends of art," via subscriptions and shareholdings.[7] The resulting repertoire mixed the transnational and the transhistorical, staging both classics of the German national repertoire by Schiller and Kleist, with the international repertoire of Shakespeare and Pedro Calderón de la Barca, together with the contemporary popular scripts of Ernst Raupach, seen as August von Kotzebue's successor, and a prolific commercial producer of "relatively undemanding fare."[8] His excitement about the deliberate creation of a space for this rich repertoire points towards the growing role of the director as the key theater practitioner, bringing together site and text in place-making practices which had significance by combining intellectually stimulating entertainment, with moves towards both a national theater, and a nation-state. In discussing the alignment of theater and German identity pre-1870, Michael Patterson argues that the idea of a "National Theatre was therefore thought of not merely as a means of raising the quality of German theatre but also as a way of promoting German identity."[9]

Excited by the possibilities of such an eclectic, internationally circulating repertoire, Grabbe's confident voice is recoverable if we look for it. In Britain, anxieties about the pressures on the classic repertoire from new leisure cultures in the wake of industrial and urban change were most pronounced—if only by the evidence of the three Select Committee enquiries across the century. Yet despite repeated statements made to these enquiries that the geographic expansion of theatrical activity, and its generic variety, was harmful to the health and improvement of drama and theater, Shakespeare was regularly programmed on the London stage throughout the century: his plays and those of his contemporaries a staple for theater managements, and his tragedies central to their business strategy.

William Macready's diary chronicles his first working day after entering upon the management of Drury Lane:

October 7th. [1841]—Rose very early, and reached Drury Lane by a quarter past seven o'clock; found the men's names entered. Went round the work places; retired to my room, and, having first addressed my thoughts to God, began to read. Employed myself with thinking over "Hamlet" till nine o'clock.[10]

Hamlet and God. Their proximity in Macready's thoughts on his first day as actor-manager suggest that his policies were governed by the particular moral elevation which tragedy was thought to engender in the theater. The testimonial presented to Macready on his departure from Drury Lane, and in memoriam of his tenure at Covent Garden, marked Macready's work as a public educator through the performance of tragedy in the permanence of silver plate, engraved to commemorate Macready's genius and its "elevating" influence on public taste.[11]

In 1844, Samuel Phelps used the new freedoms offered by the Theatres Regulation Act of 1843 to stage the "legitimate" drama to place Shakespeare's plays at the center of his management of Sadler's Wells (1844 to 1862). In these decades he produced almost all of Shakespeare's repertoire. Charles Kean took on the management of the Princess's in the 1850s with the express intention of producing the full run of Shakespeare's scripts. Fanny Kemble's professional debut at Covent Garden was as Juliet in *Romeo and Juliet*, and her return to performance (if not the stage) was through readings of Shakespeare throughout Britain and America, a touring programme which enabled her to accumulate financial as well as cultural capital. Helen Faucit's reputation was made as a Shakespearean heroine in Macready's management; Ellen Terry and Henry Irving's stage partnership in all its conflicts, controversies, and charisma was typified by Irving's Hamlet and Terry's Ophelia, while Terry's Lady Macbeth is memorialized as a national icon in John Singer Sargent's portrait of her. It is almost too easy to rattle off a list like this: the nineteenth-century stage is dominated and haunted by Shakespeare.

As chapters in this volume argue, it is almost impossible to think about the circulation and performance of tragedy in the nineteenth century without considering its generic near-relation, melodrama. Melodrama and serious drama were usually placed in a dialectical relationship—tragedy highlighting the apparent shortcomings of melodrama; melodrama casting a fierce light on the difficulties of producing new tragedies for the contemporary world. However, while the weight of critical opinion in the nineteenth century, and orthodox historiography since then, credits melodrama for the death of tragedy (a kind of melodramatic construction in itself), it is clear that melodrama was a vehicle for the renewal and revival of tragedy at the end of the nineteenth century. By then, it is not called tragedy, but has been filtered through the generic labels of melodrama such as "romantic drama," or "domestic drama" into the general term "serious drama." Too often, as Jeffrey Cox has argued, "we replace the tragic story of the death of tragedy with a melodramatic tale of the victory of melodrama."[12] By the middle of the nineteenth century, melodrama and tragedy were interdependent, performed and viewed together within larger frameworks of understanding deriving from nation and history. Both were performed, on the same stages and by the same performers, seen by largely the same audiences. Melodrama was a dramaturgical thinking-through of the tragic mode in a modern materialist age, typified by the emergence of a mass industrializing and democratizing society. The serious drama that emerged out of melodrama by the end of the century attempted to understand tragic concepts such as Fate, *hubris*, *hamartia*, and catastrophe in terms of human agency in the material world.

Tragedy in the nineteenth-century theater thus maintained a powerful presence in a tense, uneasy relationship with melodrama, historical drama, and—later in the century—opera. Tragedy, in its reified place in the canon of dramatic literature, was often cast as the monolithic presence which authorized the aesthetic, moral, and educational place of the stage in national cultures and justified the pleasures of theater in the face of long-standing anti-theatrical prejudices. Anselm Heinrich notes the enduring influence of Schiller's advocacy of the classic theater as an essential part of individual and national *Bildung*—self-development and moral education—in both German and British movements for a National Theater to the end of the nineteenth century.[13] In his defense of tragedy, Schiller alludes to its educative effects, through a series of complex emotions:

> the species of poesy which affords us moral delight to an exceptional degree has for that very reason to employ mixed sensations and to delight us by means of pain. This

is done to an exceptional degree by *tragedy*, and its domain comprehends all possible cases where some natural purpose is sacrificed to a moral one.[14]

Schiller's idealist aesthetics are typical of theater theory, but the evidence from the theater industry suggests that nineteenth-century tragedy was increasingly a modified, transitional form.

In this account of the circulation and performance of tragedy, I am not primarily concerned with writing of the period which tried to imitate traditional forms of tragedy. There was a steady flow of such new verse-tragedies in English, French, and German, but this is not where the force of nineteenth-century theatricality—what Stephen Greenblatt calls "the circulation of social energy"—is to be found. And in another paradox of the period, some of the efforts to avert the decline of the drama by producing new works aspiring to classic tragic form, content, and intellectual seriousness probably hampered the very cause they sought to encourage—at least in the case of the British theater. Debates in the first half of the century constructed a binary opposition between "traditional" drama (which in the British theater came to be called "legitimate") and new forms of industrial modernity, chiefly melodrama. National cultural politics in Britain turned this binary into a powerful hierarchy of aesthetic value, which was closely interwoven with the attribution of moral value in a complex set of professional and industrial practices. To write in the conventions of tragedy was to aspire to powerful cultural capital, while at the same time recognizing that its power was contingent and contested, as demonstrated by the frustrations expressed in a wide variety of public discourse around the "decline of the drama."

The new writing encouraged by William Macready is a case in point. During his time as manager of Covent Garden (1836–8), and then Drury Lane (1841–3), Macready was in dialogue with various writers, including Mary Russell Mitford, who wrote *Rienzi* for him, and the poet Robert Browning. He had a long-standing working relationship and friendship with Thomas Noon Talfourd, who wrote *Ion* as a vehicle for Macready at Covent Garden in 1836, and the play was the hit of the season, going on to have a long life of revivals for several decades, with performances in France and America, including Mary Anderson starring in the title role in Boston in 1877.[15] Macready's commitment to reviving tragedy at the Theatres Royal was clear, but was stalled in traditional notions of verse drama, tragic heroism, and largely derivative dramaturgical techniques. Nevertheless, Macready premiered Browning's plays, *Strafford*, and *A Blot in the 'Scutcheon*, as part of his ambition to elevate the London stage. Browning's failure to produce tragic dramas which would be the modern rivals to the plays of Shakespeare was a great disappointment, and led the theater critic of *The Athenaeum* to speculate that if Shakespeare were alive in 1843 he would write "immortal libretti for operas, or pathetic melodramas or farces."[16] Browning's plays met with muted comment or silence. *The Athenaeum* critic tries to give Browning credit for his work, reasoning that:

> If to pain and perplex were the end and aim of tragedy, Mr. Browning's poetic melodrama, called "A Blot in the 'Scutcheon," would be worthy of admiration, for it is a very puzzling and unpleasant business.[17]

Notably, Macready did not play the hero—his part was taken by Samuel Phelps; Helen Faucit however, took her usual place as the heroine. *The Athenaeum* pronounced their acting "while not faultless, effective." In contrast, the farce that followed, John Maddison Morton's *A Thumping Legacy*, also performed for the first time, was all the more enjoyable "for the foregone horrors." *John Bull* called Morton's "screaming" farce "triumphant" while noting that Browning's tragedy was all the better for having only three acts rather than the conventional five, and that the piece was largely remarkable for "the quick situation and novel construction of the piece, taking you like a bold, unfinished sketch."[18] Other critics were equally torn between respect for Browning as a poet, and dissatisfaction with the play he offered. *The Times* forthrightly declared that although Browning had "poetical qualifications of no common order," he has

> produced one of the most faulty dramas we ever beheld. His whole thoughts seem to have been directed to the production of striking effects, and these, in some instances, he certainly has obtained, but it has been at the expense of nature and probability.[19]

The Morning Post negotiated delicately between its critical judgment of Browning's piece and the managerial ambitions of Macready's staging of the tragedy. While doubting the play's power to sustain a run at Drury Lane, the *Post* commends Macready's judgment in producing

> a work of genuine genius, conceived with an abundant and spirit-stirring passion, for which we cordially thank the writer, in these bleak and leaf-stripped days of a cold and lifeless literature.[20]

Macready was exercised in trying to produce appropriate content for the stages of the London Theatres Royal, whose special status of (theoretical) monopoly of the spoken drama called for only the best of the traditional repertoire. The irony of this approach was that in straining after legitimacy in drama through the conventions of classical poetic tragedy, Macready and Browning were in danger of turning audiences away from the very thing they wished to foster.

The specificity of legislation about *where* tragedy might be performed in Britain up until 1843 reminds us that the demarcation of "legitimate" and "illegitimate" theater happened on spatial and geographic lines, as well as aesthetic and legislative. Conventional thinking (then and now) about theatrical tragedy in the nineteenth century rarely moves far from the assumption of the playhouse, the theater building, as the site for performance. Across Europe, monumental theaters for tragedy (and latterly, opera) were built to dominate their urban locations: the architecture and space of such sites making physical connections between high art, money, and high social status.[21] Tragedy was authorized and framed within these sites of state- and capital-regulated theaters in London, Paris, and various German city-states. These frameworks of law and capital determined the production and status of tragedy as much as the aesthetic content of the scripts and performances themselves.

In this way, nineteenth-century tragedy is site-specific. As Susan Bennett and Julie Sanders argue, the concept of site-specificity enables the understanding of the "wider conceptual and jurisdictional site in which any performance takes place."[22] The reference to juridical power here is as relevant for performance in the nineteenth century as it was for the seventeenth. Attention to the site-specificity of tragedy performance, as an example of a place and space made active through practice, becomes key to the cultural politics of the theater at the start of the nineteenth century. By this time, theaters that routinely—and legally—housed tragedy in France and Britain were located at physical sites where material and symbolic capital intersected. The "conventions and techniques of the auditorium"[23] of these theaters are indeed inadequate to explain impact and effect of tragedy in the theatrical and political cultures of the first half of the nineteenth century, nor its longevity as a desirable ideal of theatrical culture. Still, by the beginning of the nineteenth century the performance of tragedy was deeply connected to particular sites, and the symbolic meanings of these sites served reiteratively to authorize what was performed within them. This is another way of understanding the power of tragedy as a cultural form—not just as a dominant theatrical genre or aesthetic mode—but as sited in specific spaces, which existed in relationship to other forms of cultural and material capital.

In the case of the London Theatres Royal, Covent Garden, and Drury Lane, the license and regulated permission to perform the "legitimate" drama was grounded in a specific practiced place (to invoke Michel de Certeau) of urban space: the sites of the theater buildings themselves. That is, tragedy in the nineteenth century was in part constituted by its legitimate performance in specific places, and through practices in those places. The Theatres Royal existed at the intersection of the legislative, symbolic, and spatial axes of Royal Patent, elite patronage of culture, and growing civic prominence in the formation of the entertainment site of London's West End. The West End itself was in the liminal space between the City of Westminster and the City of London, made distinct by its growing economic role as a center of entertainment, connected by spatial and legislative axes to both jurisdictions. Tragedy performed outside of those regulated places, the Theatres Royal, and in conformity to regulated practices of those theaters, was deemed "illegitimate" and out of place.

The performance of tragedy in Paris, although not hampered by the complex intersections of regulation and custom engendered by British theatrical regulation since 1737, was similarly situated in a building—the new Comédie Française—which occupied a powerful urban space in Paris both before and after the French Revolution. The theatrical practices linked to the revival and preservation of the canon of classic drama constituted the space of the Comédie Française, as both building and performance company, and as representative of nation and culture under Napoleon Bonaparte, and continued to do so throughout the century. The Comédie Française was seen to produce, so F.W.J. Hemmings argues, national "products of superb craftsmanship" analogous to the productions of other state supported institutions such as the State Printing Office or the Sèvres and Gobelin manufactories.[24] However, this subsidy of the company by the French state (so often held up as a model of theater practice in Britain) came with strings attached, including regulations governing the selection of new plays, and an erratic regime of state censorship. John McCormick comments wryly that "Most of the time censorship was an ongoing nuisance, which probably had far more effect on the Comédie Française than it did on the popular theaters. With each revolution censorship was abolished, and in each case was re-established within a few years."[25] Censorship may have been negligible in practice, but it meant that the Comédie Française was uniquely tied to the politics of the French state at least until the calmer times of the Second Empire in the middle of the century, when the theater was once again brought closely under government control.[26]

Before German nation-state unity in 1871, German developments were obviously less focused in a single national capital than in the federal system of city-states, where city and Court theaters created their own national legitimation based on the "internalization" of Schiller's dictum of the theater as a "moral institution" as discussed above.[27] Heinrich also notes the number of theaters founded in the period across cities of German-speaking Europe, including Hamburg, Vienna, Munich, Mannheim, and Weimar, arguing that this network of increasingly state-subsidized or publicly funded civic theaters "constituted the national theatre."[28] As a kind of imagined community—of performance and spectatorship, rather than readership—this network became part of the cultural construction of the German nation after 1870. An English visitor, reporting on Berlin theaters in 1875 for the *Illustrated Sporting and Dramatic News*, notes the plethora of theaters in the new capital, and its "multitude of theatrical amusements." According to the *Illustrated Sporting and Dramatic News* correspondent, the repertoires of the principal houses—the Berlin Opera House, the Königliches Schauspielhas (described as the Comédie Française of Berlin), the Wallner Theater, the Stadt-Theater, and the National-Theater—are strikingly European, all theaters producing a mix of the great works of the French, German, English, and Spanish repertoires. Even, the writer comments, "however bitterly the Germans may hate the French, as a nation, they have a warm and undisguised admiration for their 'hereditary enemy's' dramatic compositions."[29] However, spectators attending the Berlin Opera House were not likely to forget their own country's past imperial greatness: the opera house, built by Frederick the Great in 1745, and identified by Marvin Carlson as "the first monumental theatre of modern times,"[30] is located strategically next to the towering equestrian statue of Frederick, and opposite the Berlin university on Unter den Linden, thus creating a triptych of public expression of power and modernity.[31]

The alarums and debates over the state of the drama, its role in establishing national identity—or in the case of German theater, national unity—were largely focused in the first thirty years of the nineteenth century. This period maps roughly onto conventional literary periodization, which calls the period from the 1780s until roughly the 1830s "Romantic." There is traction in this carving up of the chronology of the nineteenth century, as it identifies a significant period of turmoil and change. Yet it also conceals other patterns and themes, and imposes a misleading sense of uniformity on the period. Conventional periodization particularly situates the mid-century period as one of little importance: as an interregnum between the excitement of Romantic revolt, and the emergence of Naturalist theater in the 1870s. In France the mid-century is the period of the Second Empire, a period of settled governance for the Comédie Française, secured by a Government grant of 240,000 francs each year from 1856.[32] This was also the period marked by the emergence of international stars such as Rachel; a young Sarah Bernhardt made her debut at the Comédie Française in 1862. Jacky Bratton notes that Clement Scott refers to these decades as the "blank period" between Macready and Irving. She goes on to ask whether that is a sustainable historiographical position, given that, in Britain at least, the middle years of the century were "the most eventful and vigorous years of Victoria's reign."[33] Jim Davis and Victor Emeljanow have already traced the formation of the London West End in the 1850s and 1860s, arguing that it is an area "demarcated less by its geography and demography than by its cultural and commercial status."[34] What becomes clear when looking at this period is the inadequacy of teleological narratives of a dormant period, of theatrical stagnation (such as Marvin Carlson's view of the German theater 1830–70), before Naturalist and social realist theater leaped forth to save the serious drama.

The professional life of Dion Boucicault encapsulates the circulation of ideas and theatrical practices in the mid-nineteenth century, and I offer him as a case study of the practices of transformation and reworkings of genre involved in the circulation of tragedy in the nineteenth century in this "blank period." Boucicault's transnational identity, iconoclastic approach to theater making, and practice of dramaturgical bricolage, position him as a typical playwright of the mid-century: "perhaps the most representative man of the theatre of the Victorian age."[35] This representativeness is important. His work exemplifies the "everydayness of experience"[36] in a standard repertory theater, and demonstrates the ways that audiences experienced a "mesh of connections" between performances in one theater through an evening (the temporal circulation of performance), and performances across a city, a nation, or transnationally (the spatial, geographical circulation of performance) in what Jacky Bratton calls "intertheatricality."[37] Boucicault is an exemplum of the dominant trend of the nineteenth-century theater industry towards globalization which Jeffrey Cox connects with melodrama, in contrast with the idea of the national drama.[38] Boucicault himself made much of his international heritage, turning it to his advantage wherever he worked. He was born in Dublin to Anna Darley and Samuel Boursiquot, a man of Irish Huguenot heritage. When in France, Boucicault emphasized his French paternity even "affect[ing] a French title for a while" and maintaining that his father was French, not Irish.[39] In America, Boucicault played his Irish self, and his plays might single-handedly be seen to cement the stage Irishman into the international theatrical imagination. As a sensation melodramatist, Boucicault is one of the few playwrights whose name has survived the general dismissal of the new dramatic writing of the nineteenth century. In this account of Boucicault's engagement with tragedy, and its performance and circulation, I discuss his forgotten play *Louis XI*, which sits somewhere between melodrama and tragedy, and somewhere between adaptation, translation, and original work. The interplay between genre, writerly production, and theatrical production, offers a framework within which to consider tragedy in its circulation and performance in the mainstream of nineteenth-century theater.

Charles Kean employed Dion Boucicault as his in-house dramatist at the Princess's Theatre, London, in 1850. Boucicault had made his reputation as a playwright almost a decade before with the hit, *London Assurance* (1841) written for Madame Vestris and Charles Mathews' company at Covent Garden. Perhaps, as Peter Thomson surmises, Kean employed Boucicault "to remind his detractors that he had an interest in modern as well as ancient plays,"[40] given that Kean hired the Princess's with a managerial aim of producing all of Shakespeare's plays.[41] Their relationship is interesting in many ways, not least because it demonstrates that even the foremost tragedian and "legitimate" theatrical producer of the mid-nineteenth century sought the kinds of services provided by an in-house playwright with a reputation for writing racy, modern commercial hits. It meant that Boucicault had a relatively secure position in which to develop his writing; while his entrepreneurial instincts may have been frustrated, his development as a playwright was surely enhanced. It was during this brief period of relatively steady employment (rumored to be paid at the rate of £700 a year[42]) that Boucicault produced the script of *The Corsican Brothers* (1852), a play that grasped audience attention for the rest of the century, and in which Charles Kean made his reputation for powerful, realist acting—just as much as in his more celebrated performances in Shakespearean roles. The inclusion of *The Corsican Brothers* into Kean's, Samuel Phelps', and then Henry Irving's repertoires, indicates the significance of Boucicault's style of drama for these actors. Boucicault's dramas offered weighty substantial roles, using contemporary language and sensibility, and complementing the canonical repertoire of Shakespearean tragedy in which these actor-managers specialized.

Kean's work on Shakespeare, and his aspirations towards a national drama of authentic and thoughtful productions of the national repertoire, has been examined in detail by Richard Schoch.[43] Remembered as the producer of historically authentic and spectacular productions of Shakespeare, he created powerful representations of the past through assiduous focus on scenography, original texts, and music. Schoch argues persuasively for the reputation and importance of Kean's work in making his theater "an agent of historical instruction"; this was "the very sign of its modernity," Schoch maintains.[44] But we must not forget that Kean's management presented contemporary drama alongside the carefully realized spectacles of authentic Shakespearean production, and that these productions garnered as much notice and praise from contemporary critics as Kean's historical productions. Kean's modernity, I would argue, lies in his position as facilitator of these kinds of hybrid dramas drawing on melodrama and tragedy written for him by Boucicault. Whatever prompted him to employ Boucicault as his house dramatist, the decision was an astute one, resulting in an output of plays significant not only for their typicality but also for the ways in which Boucicault played with dramatic form to offer original versions of expected conventions.

The collaboration between Kean and Boucicault at the Princess's was an important factor in the gradual adaptation of melodrama from the spectacle of the sensation drama, into the serious, psychological drama of the second half of the century. In 1855, at the very chronological center of the century, Kean produced *Louis XI*, one of the two plays Boucicault wrote for this season (although by this time Boucicault himself had left for America). *Louis XI* was variously credited as a translation from the French playwright Casimir Delavigne, or—in the characteristically oxymoronic language of the Victorian theater—an "original adaptation."[45] Although the title role of French King Louis XI was performed by Kean, then Samuel Phelps (1861) and Henry Irving (1878), *Louis XI* has been lost to any history of London theater in the nineteenth century, and even to most accounts of Boucicault's career. This is not surprising: as Thomson remarks in his account of Boucicault's career, it is an "odd" play.[46] My argument here is not to renovate the reputation of this play, nor claim it as a great forgotten tragedy of Boucicault's career. My point is rather that in *Louis XI* we have an example of a typical serious drama of the period, which encapsulates many of the features of site, circulation, and performance of tragedy in transition, through features of melodrama. It offers a lens through which to examine the performance practices of serious drama, and the circulation of ideas about genre—specifically, the exchanges between tragedy and melodrama—within the mainstream theater. It is significant that Kean chose to stage *Louis XI* alongside his Shakespeare repertoire, and that as a theater manager with a serious mission to renovate the respectability and instructive role of the theater through its classic forms such as tragedy, he employed a contemporary playwright—and that that playwright was Boucicault. These decisions, together with the contemporary critical success of *Louis XI* suggest a very different set of performance practices and strategies than those we inherit from the orthodox historiography of mid-century theater.

Commenting on Kean's decision to stage Boucicault's *The Corsican Brothers*, Schoch places Kean's antiquarian revivals of Shakespeare within the context of sensation drama.[47] Jacky Bratton's concept of intertheatricality is especially pertinent here. Intertheatricality, she notes, "posits that all entertainments, including the dramas, that are performed within a single theatrical tradition are more or less interdependent."[48] Neither *Macbeth* nor *Louis XI* were performed in isolation; the plays appeared under the same managerial aesthetic and on the same site. The "practiced place" of the Princess's on Oxford Street in London, a central commercial thoroughfare of the city, housed a mixed bill of pantomimes, farces, and melodramas as well as Kean's much-discussed Shakespeare revivals. Kean's audiences saw the performance of classic English tragedy alongside the "gentlemanly melodrama" of *The Corsican Brothers* and the historical drama of *Louis XI*. In this conceptual framework, the generic characteristics of the Shakespearean canon of tragedy (and history plays, played as tragedy) informed audiences' spectating experiences of *Louis XI*. Conversely, the appearance of plays such as *Corsican Brothers*, *Louis XI*, (and even *Janet Pride* in the same London season as *Louis XI*) alongside productions of *Macbeth*, *King John*, *Henry VIII*, and *Richard II* were viewed in the light of audiences' knowledge and memory of Kean as Louis XI. Tragedy and melodrama circulated generically under Kean's management; both forms united through Kean's historicism, and embodied in his radical scenographic approach. Kean's programming at the Princess's produced a set of reiterative and circulating theatrical meanings in which each production—although treated as originals—inflected and informed the performance of tragedy.[49]

Boucicault's play tells a straightforward story of the dying King Louis XI, his fear of dying, and his dynastic struggles with Charles of Burgundy. The historical accuracy of the play, noted by reviewers of both Kean's and Irving's productions, fitted well with Kean's general interest in historicism in performance. Kean's performance was much admired—the London critics almost universally praised his characterization. *The Times* wryly commented that when the play first appeared in Delavigne's version in 1832, "kings were not popular among the French dramatists," and Delavigne made the most of his opportunity to present as black a picture of Louis XI as he could. Nevertheless, *The Times* reviewer could "scarcely conceive anything more perfect" than Kean's representation of Boucicault's version of the king, judging the performance as "one of those grand works of histrionic art about which there can be no mistake."[50] *The Morning Post* was even more rapturous, hailing Kean's performance as an "histrionic triumph of the highest order," and a "sublime dramatic picture."[51] All the reviews comment on the centrality of Kean's performance, most seeing it as almost a one-man play—certainly a *tour de force* for one actor.

For Jacky Bratton, memory is an important element of intertheatricality, and it is notable that debates and discussions about tragedy, and particular performers of tragedy, circulate through memory. This was the case for Charles Kean's performance of Louis XI. It was remembered as one of Kean's best roles, and the memory mobilized when the role was performed by that other eminent tragedian of the London stage, Henry Irving, in 1878, ten years after Kean's death. We are reminded of the strength of cultural memory of Kean in the role when Kean's widow, Ellen, joined Irving in his curtain call on the first night at the Lyceum. Critic Clement Scott commented that "our lost actor would cordially have rejoiced to find the traditions and dignity of the stage were upheld in so true . . . a spirit."[52]

Irving's version was notable not just for his performance of the title role, but the scenography, which had not been a feature of Kean's production:

> The richness of costume, the care of archaeology, the beauty of scenery, the sounds of soft music, the wail of the distant hymn, the pomp of the religious ceremony—all serve their legitimate purpose.[53]

This was the "Temple of Art"—what Martin Meisel calls Irving's theater of Beauty, developed through a conscious pictorialism of staging and performance style.[54] *The Illustrated London News* commended Irving's "marvellously thorough . . . historic and pictorial rendering" of Boucicault's adaptation, and Irving's "highly artistic and deeply thoughtful performance."[55] Critical attention was focused on Irving's achievement in the death scene, almost universally described as horrid, where

> Mr. Irving saves himself from the charge of completely subordinating mental to physical expression, by the power with which he marks the progress of the mind, as well as of the body, to utter decay. . . . But, even as it is, the representation is too horrible in its reality.[56]

Scott's description of Irving's representation of Louis' death is more detailed, and less horrified. He points out that this death onstage is "no more reprehensive than the death of a hundred other heroes of tragedy" and praises Irving's playing of a "melancholy wreck, a decorated effigy."[57]

Irving's performance as Louis XI is of a piece with his revival of the other Kean/Boucicault hit, *The Corsican Brothers* and their shared practices as actor-managers intent on renovating and reviving the "National Drama" through serious attention to an eclectic repertoire. Much of this repertoire is now obscure: it was mostly representative and typical, formulaic and hackneyed if our criteria for judging value are those of the post-Victorians. However, such a repertoire should not be cherry-picked for its ground-breaking or unique scripts, which might be seen to anticipate the innovations of Naturalism and Modernist theater. We need to recognize the circulation of tragedy and the tragic in performance happening through the quotidian, the obscure, and even the "bad" theater of the nineteenth century.

In a complement to British playwrights' ransacking of French theater in the nineteenth century, one of the classics of the English tragic canon—*Hamlet*—received an extraordinary make-over as an opera in French, composed by Ambroise Thomas. Of course, adaptations and translations of English-language drama were not unusual in the rest of Europe, or across the world. The currency of Shakespeare in particular was international and polyglot. English tragedy circulated largely as Shakespeare, and Suddhaseel Sen argues that it was specifically through *Hamlet* that European theater engaged with Shakespeare.[58] This adaptation is one of many mid-century operas, notable perhaps for their representativeness, their mainstream and commercial presence, rather than their status as an innovative or striking work of art. However, entwined with this status was the growing claim for opera to be considered as the serious heir "to the legacy of tragic drama."[59] Although not considered to be a composer in the company of Verdi or Wagner, Ambroise Thomas was working at the center of the mainstream of French state-regulated culture of the mid-century Second Empire, the period in which Paris became one of the cultural centers of the world, the "paradigmatic city of modern art."[60] Thomas's first lasting success was *Mignon* (1866), followed by *Hamlet* in 1868. The combined success of these pieces placed Thomas at the core of the artistic establishment, and he succeeded Daniel Auber as Director of the Paris Conservatoire in 1871, serving until his death in 1896.

Thomas's score was developed with a libretto by Michel Florentin Carré and Jules Paul Barbier, based on the French translation of *Hamlet* by Alexandre Dumas *père* and Paul Merice made in the 1840s. This translation, famously, is a version of the play in which Hamlet the Prince does not die. Nor does his mother Gertrude, although Ophelia is shown drowning herself. The opera version was first performed at the Paris Opéra in March 1868, and brought to Covent Garden a year later, followed by revivals and productions in Europe (Palais Garnier, 1875; La Scala Milan, 1890) and America (New York, 1884). The opera is still in the repertoire today, although sporadically. The New York Metropolitan Opera production in 2010, featuring British baritone Simon Keenlyside in the title role, was the culmination of a small revival of interest in Thomas's opera, in a production originating in Geneva in 1996, and touring widely.[61] Like the Modernist reimagining of *Hamlet* by Edward Gordon Craig, twenty-first-century productions of Thomas's opera have become vehicles for reimagining the possibilities of the canon of the heyday of Second Empire Parisian opera. The most recent production, sung in the original French libretto, with German surtitles, with a radical revisioning of scenography and staging by *Inszenierung* Helen Malkowsky premiered to standing ovations at Theater Krefeld-Moenchengladbach in 2017.[62] While Thomas allegedly wrote an alternative ending for the 1869 Covent Garden production, in which Prince Hamlet dies, Malkowsky's achievement was to stage the final scene of Carré's and Berbier's libretto to show the existential burden of the Danish crown—offered to Hamlet by the Ghost (in this production doubling as a Jester)—as a heavy fate, inheriting only death and destruction. At the end of Malkowsky's staging, one comes to believe that death would have been preferable to the crown and the throne (staged as a heavy oversized chair dragged by Claudius throughout the performance). That is the triumph of this most recent production, with its emphasis on Hamlet's navigation through a nightmarishly distorted Elsinore Castle; survival is not devoutly to be wished in this stage world.

As is the practice of adaptation from one medium to another, the Thomas, Carré, and Barbier adaptation of *Hamlet* removes many of the characters and sub-plots. The opera is stripped back to the family drama: Claudius, Gertrude, Hamlet, Polonius, and Ophelia, and the voice of the Ghost of King Hamlet. Rosencrantz and Guildenstern do not appear, and neither does Fortinbras. This is not a kingdom at war, but a family in crisis. The paring down of the action and characters forces attention on the central relationships between Hamlet and his uncle, Hamlet and his mother, and Hamlet and Ophelia. The requirements of the form of opera also play a part here. Most scenes are solos and duets, where voices as well as characters are matched or contrasted. Ophélie is sung by a soprano, whose virtuoso range and technique is displayed in the fourth act of the opera—the scene of her suicide by drowning—played in the premiere by Swedish star, Christina Nilsson (Hamlet was sung by the baritone Jean-Baptiste Faure, and later by Charles Santley in the Covent Garden premiere). The opera's emotional focus is on the acknowledged love between Hamlet and Ophelia, their extended duet taking up most of the second part of Act 1. This makes Ophelia's suicide by drowning, performed onstage in an extraordinarily embroidered and virtuoso aria, all the more poignant. Physically and musically, Ophelia is far more present in this performance than in its source texts (Dumas or Shakespeare). Her death by drowning, described obliquely by Gertrude in Shakespeare's text, is played out in full operatic detail onstage in a Senecan rather than Aristotelian approach to tragic death. This was a celebrated scene from the opera, requiring extraordinary capacities of vocal technique and performance power.

In this recalibration of the focus of *Hamlet*, Thomas and his collaborators are part of a longer national relationship with the play, and various French versions of it.[63] There is a link to be made between Thomas's Ophélie and the Romantic "Ophelia mania" which hit Paris in the wake of Harriet Smithson's performances in 1827. This was the performance through which the character of Ophelia was wholeheartedly embraced by Romanticism, and in France rather than Britain. The interest in Ophelia in France was adapted and circulated into a rich visual culture of the representation of fragile feminine subjectivity through Eugène Delacroix's series of lithographs *La mort d'Ophélie* in 1843.[64] The visual cult of Ophelia found its way to Britain, with the controversial Pre-Raphaelite "Ophelia" of John Everett Millais (1851–2) culminating in J.W. Waterhouse's almost obsessive return to the moments just before Ophelia's death in three paintings from 1889 to 1910. Further French representations of Ophelia were inspired by Nilsson's performance in Thomas's opera in 1868. D.G. de Lafond describes the typical Ophelia painting in mid-century France "depicted in either period or modern costume, with disheveled hair and garlands of flowers, reflecting the styling of . . . the Swedish-born Christina Nilsson."[65] The visual links to later Ophelias can be traced through a multitude of drawings, paintings, and photographs of performers playing Ophelia/Ophélie, featuring theatrically disheveled hair (but still beautifully arranged) and holding flowers, including the widely circulated photographic portrait of Ellen Terry playing Ophelia to Irving's Hamlet in 1878, and the Australia soprano, Nellie Melba, as Ophélie in a 1910 revival of Thomas's opera. The close attention to Ophelia in these visual representations reverses the usual focus on Hamlet in stage performances. The ideological import of this translation of Ophelia from text to image, moreover, is significant: as Lee Edwards comments, "We can imagine Hamlet's story without Ophelia, but Ophelia literally has no story without Hamlet."[66] The more or less blank space of Ophelia in Shakespeare's script is filled by Thomas's score and the stripped back libretto, evolving from a century of exchange, circulation, and translation of the source text. In the case of Ophelia, and *Hamlet*, circulation through adaptation and remediation—of the content and site of performance—offers new meanings and interpretations of what was probably the major text of the English-language canon of tragedy.

The theater of the nineteenth century was characterized by mobility: the rapid circulation of theatrical practices and ideas in texts, bodies, voices, images, themes, and scenographies. Traditional modes of representation became unfixed—either from their generic conventions or from their sites of performance—after the French Revolution, and in the midst of the upheavals of industrialization and democratization across Europe. After 1848, the political urgency of cultural change abated somewhat, but the challenges to the neo-classical Enlightenment culture embodied in European political revolutions were reworked into a theatrical culture both eager to represent contemporary modernity, but anxious about the ethical and aesthetic consequences of doing so. There was a considerable risk in following through Emile Zola's exhortation to "remak[e] the stage until it is continuous with the auditorium, giving a shiver of life to the painted trees, letting in through the backcloth the great, free air of reality."[67] Part of that risk was the possibility of a loss of a culturally and ideologically powerful tradition of tragic performance which, in the theatrical cultures of Europe, carried with it the central belief in the "sweetness and light" of European civilization. Although our primary understanding of the circulation of tragedy in the nineteenth century may be geographic or spatial, performed in the site-specific places of theaters occupying significant urban space, I have also argued for an acknowledgment of the circulation of tragedy in other ways—through translation and adaptation, and for its survival in intertheatrical relationships with melodrama in the nineteenth century. As in the case of *Hamlet* and its adaptations and iterations in opera and visual culture, concepts of tragedy and the tragic survived in other sites and forms of circulation. Artists increasingly crossed genres and media to express human experience at its limits: the metaphysics of the tragic experience. And if theatrical tragedy was occluded, adapted, reconfigured, or remediated at the beginning of the nineteenth century, these transitions also produced new work, new ideas, and a powerful new aesthetic of "serious drama" by the end of the century.

CHAPTER THREE

Communities of Production and Consumption

SHARON ARONOFSKY WELTMAN

Melodrama is "simply . . . high theater," "larger than life—in emotion, in subject," says Stephen Sondheim, discussing his Broadway musical *Sweeney Todd: The Demon Barber of Fleet Street* (1979). His description applies just as easily to *King Lear* or *Oedipus Rex* or *Rigoletto*,[1] suggesting that for Sondheim there is little difference between melodrama and tragedy.[2] Indeed, Sondheim's *Sweeney Todd* is often performed by grand opera companies; Todd's vengeance run amok, his agony upon realizing that he has killed his wife, and his shocking death evoke not only the audience's horror but also their pity in an emotional experience akin to Giuseppe Verdi's *Otello* (1887). Both classical and Shakespearian tragedy focus on the great and mighty, on the reversal of fortune faced by nobility and generals. This may seem entirely different from a Broadway musical staging the vengeance of a local barber. But *Sweeney Todd* is based on a Victorian story, and tragedy in the nineteenth century was not restricted to the poetry and elevated subject matter of Sophocles, Shakespeare, or Jean Racine. Rather than uniformly the province of elite theaters such as the House of Molière in Paris, nineteenth-century tragedy also manifested in roaring melodramas at working-class venues like the Britannia in London's East End, where George Dibdin Pitt (1795–1855) first dramatized *Sweeney Todd* in 1847. Once we recognize that other genres absorbed elements of tragedy, we can enlarge the pool of tragedy's authors, actors, and fans to include more diverse populations than those associated with highbrow cultural institutions. Tragedy, often seen as declining in the nineteenth century, bloomed under the aegis of its less respectable but more popular cousin, melodrama, responding to the needs of multifarious audiences, performers, and writers.

Significant nineteenth-century British tragedies, such as *Virginius* (1820) by James Sheridan Knowles (1784–1862) and *The Patrician's Daughter: A Tragedy* (1841) by John Westland Marston (1819–90), constituted a tiny and ever-diminishing fraction of plays written over the century. As Allardyce Nicoll and Michael Booth point out, melodrama was the era's most popular form. Moreover, tragedies were often indistinguishable from historical dramas or melodramas, with the performance venue dictating its genre, in London or in Paris, because patents favored certain theaters for tragedies and comedies, the more prestigious forms. Later in the century, realistic drama developed out of melodrama, incorporating traditional tragic features such as reversal, a protagonist's death, and psychological motivations for revenge. Complex interactions within and among national, religious, and economic communities created the conditions for tragedy's metamorphosis. Consumers helped direct what dramatists produced. Performers had specific needs for playwrights to fulfill. Intrusive laws jiggered everything.

A major contributor to transnational pollination was the circulation of actors and the plays they performed. French tragediennes were fêted, with widespread adulation of Rachel Felix (1821–53) and Sarah Bernhardt (1844–1923). Their virtuosity in multiple genres did much to blur generic boundaries. But while actresses were adored, women dramatists were less noticed. In part, this is because there were fewer women playwrights than men, despite the lauded accomplishments of British Romantic-era authors Joanna Baillie (1752–1851) and Mary Russell Mitford (1787–1855) and the achievements by New Woman dramatists, such as Elizabeth Robins (1862–1952), at the century's end.[3] This is no wonder. It was extraordinarily difficult for women playwrights to succeed when, as Kerry Powell explains, "most playwrights came . . . from some other male-dominated area of employment—for example, stage management . . . or journalism and dramatic criticism . . . male clubs like the Arundel . . . the usual routes into playwriting were difficult for a woman to enter."[4] Kate Newey observes that most nineteenth-century British playwrights were already in communities that gave them alternative access to performance or publication: they were actresses, published novelists, or daughters and wives of prominent theater men.[5] The situation in France was also difficult; even the highly successful dramatist Alexandrine de Bawr advised women against writing plays because success required not only powerful backers but also establishing a physical presence backstage, opening oneself to charges of impropriety.[6]

Two nineteenth-century British women playwrights whose work was performed, published, and noticed in the papers were Caroline Boaden (*fl.* 1825–39) and Elizabeth Polack (*fl.* 1835–8), from very different backgrounds, writing for very different audiences. Although we know little about them, both came from families of authors with connections to the theater, conforming to Newey's observation. The author of several successful plays in the 1830s and 1840s, Boaden wrote the tragedy *A Duel in Richelieu's Time* (1832) for the prestigious Haymarket, adapted from *Un Duel sous Richelieu* (1832), a French melodrama by Monsieur Lockroy and Edmond Badon. Polack, the first Jewish woman playwright in Britain, wrote the 1835 melodrama *Esther, the Royal Jewess, or the Death of Haman!* for the working-class Pavilion theater in Whitechapel, a largely Jewish neighborhood. A rewriting of the Biblical story of Queen Esther, it owes something to Racine's *Esther* (1689) and the 1732 oratorio *Esther* by George Frideric Handel (1685–1759). But it also partly responds to *The Jew of Arragon, or The Hebrew Queen* (1830), a tragedy by Thomas Wade (1805–75). Notorious for undergoing massive censorship for religious content, *The Jew of Arragon* was "howled from the stage" at Covent Garden by an anti-Semitic audience; its depiction of brave and noble Jewish characters evinced "too strong a bias towards the Jews for the temper of the gallery," where the cheaper seats were.[7] In contrast, Polack's play secured more performances, apparently provoking no such resistance. While Boaden's adaptation shifts her French material from melodrama to tragedy, Polack reframes the highbrow forms of tragedy and oratorio as melodrama for the hard-scrabble mixed Jewish and non-Jewish audiences at the Pavilion.[8]

In what follows, I survey in snapshots the slippery genres of tragedy and melodrama—who wrote, produced, enacted, and watched them—at the major and minor theaters in nineteenth-century Paris and London. I examine how plays by Victor Hugo (1802–85), Boaden, Polack, Dibdin Pitt, Henri Meilhac (1830–97), and Ludovic Halévy (1834–1908) feature in this history, stressing how intersections of nationality, gender, class, and religion impact those creating and consuming theater in its various forms. I place the tragedy-melodrama continuum in a European context, focusing not only on the relationship between French and English drama, but also between grand and not-so-grand stages in both Paris and London. In my account, the generic flexibility of melodrama in this complex milieu enables tragedy to survive. But obstructive interference of the law necessitated such artistic innovation in the first place.[9]

BRITISH LAWS, CENSORSHIP, AND CULTURAL CONVENTIONS

Before 1843, because of the Licensing Act of 1737, only a few British theaters held a royal patent to perform purely spoken drama, such as tragedies and comedies by Shakespeare. In London, these were Drury Lane, Covent Garden, and (in the summer only) the Haymarket, all in the affluent West End. Legally prohibited from performing spoken drama, all other pre-1843 theaters (the majority) mounted plays including enough music—songs and underscoring—to qualify as musical entertainments, performable without a license. In the mid-to-late eighteenth century, a new French form of drama with music developed as a working-class diversion, *melodrames*. This import provided a genre with the songs and underscoring that the British legal situation required. Urban geography reflected playhouse hierarchy: many non-patent (so-called "illegitimate" or "minor") theaters resided in the East End or south of the Thames, in working-class neighborhoods.

Although the major theaters held an exclusive legal right to perform spoken drama, the genre of tragedy was never a monolithic theatrical form. Tragedy was never limited *only* to the five-act verse play performed at the few patent theaters by great Shakespearian actors such as brother and sister John Philip Kemble (1757–1823) and Sarah Siddons (1755–1831) or Edmund Kean (1787–1833) and Ira Aldridge (1807–67). In London's non-patent theaters, the taste for tragic elements found sustenance primarily in melodrama. But while the threat of a tragic outcome always looms large, melodrama makes sure that at the drama's conclusion villainy is punished and virtue rewarded. While importation of melodrama from France to England permitted non-patent theaters to perform plays without incurring steep fines, it also served its audiences in other ways. Melodramas are typically shorter (two or three acts instead of five) and written in prose rather than poetry. They often specialize in exciting stagecraft and scenes of sensational danger. They were accompanied by music and interspersed with songs. Well done, such theater is always likely to be entertaining.

Once the Theatre Regulations Act of 1843 lifted the 1737 law prohibiting London's illegitimate theaters from spoken drama, they began legally producing tragedies without fear of penalty, alongside the ever-popular melodramas. However, they now needed to submit all their plays for licensing by the Lord Chamberlain's Office, just like the legitimate playhouses. Before production could proceed, the plays could be censored—or even denied a license, usually either for potentially inciting civic unrest (working-class theater was deemed particularly likely to rile the masses) or for depicting religion. This law remained in place until abolished by a new Theatres Act in 1968. As we might expect of the author of *Sweeney Todd*, Dibdin Pitt wrote several plays turned down by the Lord Chamberlain's Office for excessive violence or political allusions. *The Revolution of Paris; or the Patriot Deputy* (1848) was judged too close to current events in France, despite Pitt's remark scribbled on the licensing manuscript that "tis stage revolution not that of Paris 1848."[10] Throughout the rest of the century, the freedom to perform spoken drama allowed Samuel Phelps (1804–78), Charles Kean (1811–68), Charlotte Cushman (1816–78), Henry Irving (1838–1905), and Ellen Terry (1847–1928) to perform Shakespeare and other dramatic authors at many fashionable non-patent theaters such as the Princess's and Sadler's Wells. The Britannia also hosted Aldridge, who was African American, in the title character of *Othello* in 1852.[11] Thus post-1843, the barriers between tragedy and melodrama became more porous; but they had always been permeable. Nearly two decades before Aldridge appeared on the boards at the Britannia, *The Standard* reviewed his portrayal of Othello at Covent Garden; while highly praising him generally, they found fault specifically with those characteristics of his acting deemed "melo-dramatic," linking his acting style with minor theaters.[12]

The blurring of generic boundaries between tragedy and melodrama is often seen as a historical shift from one to the other, although critics are also quick to make clear that such a statement is an oversimplification.[13] Booth, who led the ongoing charge to rehabilitate Victorian popular theater, baldly declared the collapse of English tragedy in the nineteenth century, blaming its ruin on the poor quality of new plays and over-dependence on Shakespeare. The Bard was by far the best and "most popular tragic writer on the Victorian stage,"[14] with performances of Shakespeare even on horseback, such as the hippodramas at Astley's Circus, legal because performances on horses qualified as being not strictly spoken drama; clearly *Richard III* fit the bill especially well. The problem for new tragedies, according to the Victorian critic and thinker George Henry Lewes, was imitation of Elizabethan forms rather than a new "nineteenth century drama . . . that will appeal to a wider audience than . . . a few critics."[15] Booth explains that "The Victorian theatre witnessed the death of English classical tragedy, a form exhausted and in ill health all through the eighteenth century. . . . [I]ts demise occurred largely because its authors looked back to a former age and were cut off from the mainsprings of modern English life and thought."[16] Yet English authors continued to write five-act verse tragedies in the antique mold throughout the nineteenth century. *Virginius*, for example, is an old-school tragedy. It dramatizes the plight of a Roman citizen whose daughter is abducted by the tyrant Appius. After an unjust trial, the father tries to free his child but kills her; by the end, he has also slain Appius, gone mad, and died. Originating the role at Covent Garden on May 17, 1820, William Charles Macready played Virginius for over three decades.

Not a tragedy (absent a heap of lifeless bodies in the final scene) but a five-act verse historical drama is Edward Bulwer-Lytton's *Richelieu* (1839), also written for Macready, who initiated his portrayal of the Cardinal at Covent Garden on May 7, 1839 and played him for many years. *Richelieu*, which exemplifies for Booth the compromise between tragedy and melodrama emerging in the first half of the nineteenth century, is best known now for bringing us the phrase "the pen is mightier than the sword" (2.2).[17] A long roster of stars performed the role at both major and minor theaters, including Samuel Phelps at Sadler's Wells in 1845. The American actor Edwin Booth—known as one of the greatest Richelieus—played the part in England in 1861, 1880, and 1882. Henry Irving at the Lyceum in 1873 revived it three times over the remainder of the century.[18] Bulwer-Lytton's choice of the French topic of Cardinal Richelieu connects directly to his playwriting craft; he "carefully studied the economical and organized structure of French Romantic drama" of authors such as Hugo, whose *Marion de Lorme* (1829, 1831) and *Hernani* (1830) were so influential.[19] But unlike Hugo, who did not see his plays as primarily historical despite the real-life characters drawn from French history, Bulwer-Lytton included footnotes in the published text of this play.

As the nineteenth century wore on, London's taste for tragedy was largely satisfied either by Shakespeare or by melodrama, with its flexibility and responsiveness to current issues such as abolition, empire, temperance, the tribulations of the ex-convict, the dilemma of sailors kept long in service, and the plight of tenants with absentee landlords.[20] Versions of *Uncle Tom's Cabin* collectively represent the most popular dramas of the century in England as well as the U.S., meriting the nickname World's Greatest Hit.[21] Tom Taylor's temperance play *The Bottle* (1847) explores the devastating effect of a man's alcoholism on his family; his *The Ticket-of-Leave Man* (1863) dramatizes the difficulty of an ex-con, innocent when everyone believes him guilty. In Douglas Jerrold's *Black-Ey'd Susan* (1829), a sailor tries to defend his virtuous wife from the unwanted attentions of his superior officer. This show was first performed in 1829 at the Surrey, a south-side minor house, for 150 nights, at Covent Garden for 400 more, then at other London theaters, remaining a staple of the stage till the end of the century.[22] Jerrold's *The Rent Day* (1832) explores the threat of unfair eviction, inspired by David Wilkie's genre paintings *Rent Day* (1807) and *Distraining for Rent* (1815). Other topics included infidelity, domestic violence, class conflict, war, imperialism, and virtually every other current topic, all grist for the mill as house dramatists like Dibdin Pitt churned out new plays to premiere every two weeks.[23] Unlike nineteenth-century tragedy, which—like *Richelieu* and *Virginius*—cultivated topics with historical or classical gravitas, melodrama often sought to tell stories that connected to "the mainsprings of modern English life and thought."[24]

As Carolyn Williams points out, during the Victorian period in England, "Melodrama replaces tragedy—not in the sense of the new driving out the old or the bad driving out the good, but in the much more powerful sense of a genre answering to new cultural and historical needs."[25] The most comprehensive way to understand the relationship between tragedy and melodrama is not so much that melodrama takes over from tragedy but that, in the words of Jeffrey Cox and Michael Gamer, "what we see now as disparate pieces—poetic tragedies, successful stage dramas, and staged spectacles—were part of a coherent, if complex, cultural configuration."[26] The audience delight in sensation meant ever more exciting and sophisticated stagecraft to mount volcanoes, fires, floods, and dramatic escapes from approaching trains and looming buzz saws. Improvements eliminated cumbersome painted backdrops that slid slowly through grooves on the stage floor, developed box sets that included complete rooms with furniture and props that approximated lifelike domestic interiors, costumes that painstakingly recreated those of the period portrayed, more restrained acting styles, well-illuminated stages in front of darkened auditoria, and a shift towards the illusion that the audience experiences a glimpse of real people's lives through an invisible fourth wall. In other words, over the course of the century, melodrama led to yet another new form, realistic theater, which also focused on middle- and working-class protagonists dealing with plausible problems such as alcoholism and domestic abuse. Theatrical realism rose to prominence throughout Europe in the century's final decades with Henrik Ibsen (1828–1906), Emile Zola (1849–1902), George Bernard Shaw (1856–1950), and Anton Chekhov (1860–1904). But it did not suddenly burst onto the scene. It grew in part out of the realism already burgeoning in melodrama. Realism, like melodrama, addresses the tragedy of everyday existence, taking the pain of regular people's lives—even ex-convicts' and evicted tenants'—seriously.

CROSSING THE CHANNEL

English, French, and German theater cross-pollinated throughout the nineteenth century. The first London play billed as a melodrama, *A Tale of Mystery* (1802) by Thomas Holcroft (1745–1809), was a translation and adaptation of *Cœlina, ou, l'enfant du mystère* (1800) by René-Charles Guilbert de Pixerécourt (1773–1844), already an adaptation of François Guillaume Ducray-Duminil's romance of the same name. The third act's scenery came whole-hog—including mountain peaks, river, bridge, and millhouse—from a 1792 production of *Die Räuber* (1781) by Friedrich Schiller (1759–1805).[27] But while Parisian melodrama influenced English melodrama, Parisian melodrama itself derived from English gothic,[28] smelted in the crucible of the French Revolution.[29] Booth explains that while the melodramas of de Pixerécourt and similar French authors were fervently anti-tyrannical, "melodrama's vision of proletarian heroes and patrician villains" is "inherited from the democratic idealism of the romantic dramas of Goethe and Schiller;" he mentions both *Die Räuber* and Goethe's *Götz von Berlichingen* (1773).[30] Meanwhile, German Romantic drama, "already influenced by English practice, returns to influence English drama in the works of August von Kotzebue" (1761–1819),[31] who gave us *Das Kind der Liebe* (1780). This play was rewritten by Elizabeth Inchbald (1753–1821) as *Lovers' Vows* (1798), remembered today mostly for symbolizing the sexually corrupting power of theater in Jane Austen's *Mansfield Park* (1814). Goethe's *Götz von Berlichingen* touts an even naughtier claim to fame in originating the so-called Swabian Salute, in which the protagonist—in true Romantic fashion defying authority—refuses to surrender in battle, proclaiming to the opposing captain that he should tell the German Emperor to "Lick me in the arse!" This play was remade as the five-act tragedy *Goetz von Berlichingen, with the Iron Hand* by Sir Walter Scott (1771–1832) in 1799, but without the now-famous battle cry.

In France, in the early nineteenth century, an ideological and aesthetic playwriting battle raged between the Classicists and the Romantics, in some ways paralleling the British legitimate and illegitimate divide. The divisions were legal as well. In 1807, Napoleon reduced the number of licensed theaters in Paris to just eight: four prestigious *Grands théâtres* and four *Théâtres secondaires*, with each playhouse restricted to specific kinds of repertoires. The rest were either demolished, used for other purposes, or empty for years.[32] But even after Napoleon's downfall, the laws about licensing lived on; likewise, the repertory division survived between the spoken comedies and tragedies that had been the sole province of the grand Comédie-Française and the melodramas permitted at the secondary theater Porte-Saint-Martin. Furthermore, the state-supported theaters like the august Comédie-Française—the House of Molière, decreed into existence by Louis XIV in 1680—maintained their high status. But something exciting was happening at the secondary theaters like the Gaîté, the Théâtre de l'Ambigu-Comique, and of course the Porte-Saint-Martin. In the 1820s, French melodrama venues were where

> the new generation of Romantic actors received their training. The acting style on the boulevard was both more impassioned and more "realistic" than that of the Comédie-Française actors. Thus ... after 1830, the actors most in demand by the Romantic playwrights were those with boulevard training: Marie Doval, Frederick Lemaitre, and Bocage.[33]

The boulevard theaters were so called because they stood on the Boulevard du Temple, nicknamed the Boulevard du Crime due to the lurid plots of the shows performed there.

The February 25, 1830 production at the Comédie-Française of *Hernani, ou l'Honneur Castillan* by Hugo brought an end to the 200-year-old French tradition requiring drama to adhere to the three Aristotelian unities of time, place, and action. The incident was called "The 'Battle of *Hernani*,'" and it was "the most famous and influential theatrical event in France in the nineteenth century."[34] Prior to this, "theatrical activity was rigidly divided: popular audiences flocked to the secondary or 'boulevard' theaters while the aristocracy and the intelligentsia supported the neo-classical tradition at the government-subsidized theaters—the Comédie-Française and the Odéon."[35] These elite institutions produced plays in the classical French style originally codified by the Académie Française established by Cardinal Richelieu himself in 1635. Hugo's manifesto in the preface to *Cromwell* (1827) systematically eviscerates any need to adhere to the unities and makes clear what he was objecting to in contemporary classical drama:

> the whole drama—takes place in the wings. . . . Instead of scenes we have narrative; instead of tableaux, descriptions. Solemn-faced characters, placed, as in the old chorus, between the drama and ourselves, tell us what is going on in the temple, in the palace, on the public square, until we are tempted many a time to call out to them: "Indeed! then take us there!"[36]

As early as 1771 Goethe was already castigating the French for imitating Greek drama with ever stricter rules, complaining, "All French tragedies are parodies of themselves."[37] Hugo moves French theater in a new direction in *Cromwell, Marion de Lorme*, and most famously in *Hernani*. Unsurprisingly, Hugo at times ran into trouble with the censors, delaying *Marion de Lorme* and requiring him to remove anything from *Hernani* that was religious or anything that could be construed as criticizing the king.[38]

In addition to rejecting the antique unities, which required audiences to watch actors react to narrated events instead of enacting them, Hugo and the French Romantics wrote action-packed plays, looser in plot, form, and language. In addition, they demanded a more naturalistic thespian style than the stiff classical mode. Hugo developed more fluid blocking, shifting away from the prior French technique in which actors largely stood still, declaiming nearly motionless in a semi-circle;[39] the new style was both more English and more melodramatic.[40] The eponymous lead of *Hernani* was so potent he spawned a fad of Hernani imitations among young Parisian men and in plays by Alexandre Dumas *père* (1802–70) and Alfred de Vigny (1797–1863).[41] In *Hernani*, Hugo not only abandoned the unities of time, place, and action but also added comedy, a hallmark of melodrama, which—as Charles Dickens so famously remarked in *Oliver Twist*—alternates dramatic and comic scenes like "the layers of red and white in a side of streaky, well-cured bacon."[42] And while continuing to write in verse (unlike melodrama), Hugo loosened the strict adherence to the Alexandrine couplets that was required of French Classicist drama. He also blended idioms and everyday word choices—as in melodrama—into a form that previously required exclusively elevated, poetical discourse. *Hernani* even includes farcical elements, with multiple men hiding in closets to avoid detection when each new man comes into the heroine's chamber. In its early scenes, the play could easily be confused with a comedy. At *Hernani*'s opening night, because Hugo knew that his new Romantic style of tragedy would prove controversial, he prepared by ensuring that the audience swelled with many of his friends and supporters, such as Hector Berlioz and Théophile Gautier. This claque of bohemians championed Hugo's innovation against the loud aspersions of the Classicists that opposed his new Romantic theatrical approach.

After the Napoleonic Wars ended, French acting troupes poured into London for engagements to present their repertoire of classical and new plays in French. Throughout the rest of the century, English audiences flocked to see them, thrilling to performances by the celebrated Mademoiselle Mars (1770–1847); the sensational Rachel (so renowned, she simply went by her first name); and the world-wide phenomenon Sarah Bernhardt. Rachel revived French classical tragedy in Paris with her powerful portrayals of female leads in plays by Pierre Corneille (1606–84) and Racine, but acting in the newer Romantic styles. Though she also performed current plays brilliantly (originating the title role of *Adrienne Lecouvreur* [1849] by Ernest Legouvé and Eugène Scribe), her most famous part was Phèdre in Racine's 1677 tragedy of that name. After Rachel's visit to London in 1840, George Henry Lewes called her "the panther of the stage" and remarked on her "irresistible power."[43] She so profoundly impressed both Charlotte Brontë and George Eliot that they created characters in their novels based on her, Vashti in Brontë's *Villette* (1853) and Alcharisi in Eliot's *Daniel Deronda* (1876). Bernhardt's fame and cultural impact was perhaps even greater. She toured not only London and the continent but also all over the world, visiting most countries in North, South, and Central America as well as Australia, New Zealand, and other countries in the South Pacific. Like Rachel, she excelled as Phèdre and many other great tragic roles such as Hamlet,[44] but her most acclaimed part was Marguerite in *La Dame aux Camélias* (1852) by Alexandre Dumas *fils*. She first played the consumptive heroine in 1880, and went on to die heartbreakingly in dozens of cities over a thousand times, including in the early film *Camille* (1916).

But it was not just these charismatic stars that the British admired; French acting in general was highly respected. In *The Eagle's Nest*, John Ruskin (1819–1901) describes the play *Frou-Frou* (1869) by Meilhac and Halévy, which he saw at the Gaiety Theatre in London on January 26, 1872, performed by a French acting troupe:

> The most complete rest and refreshment I can get, when I am overworked, in London . . . is in seeing a French play. But the French act so perfectly that I am obliged to make sure beforehand that all is to end well, or it is as bad as being helplessly present at some real misery.
>
> I was beguiled the other day, by seeing announced as a "Comédie," into going to see "Frou-Frou." Most of you probably know that the three first of its five acts are comedy, or at least playful drama, and that it plunges down, in the two last, to the sorrowfulest catastrophe of all conceivable—though too frequent in daily life—in which irretrievable grief is brought about by the passion of a moment, and the ruin of all that she loves, caused by the heroic error of an entirely good and unselfish person. The sight of it made me thoroughly ill, and I was not myself again for a week.[45]

The Gaiety Theatre in London often hosted French troupes, and it was here during her 1880 tour that Sarah Bernhardt also portrayed the unfortunate Gilberte in *Frou-Frou*. Not only do tragedy and melodrama blur, but also even "comedy" is not always easy to distinguish from tragedy. Though *The Era* listed it as a "drama," *Frou-Frou*'s title page identified it as a "Comédie" or "Comedy" in five acts, in both French and English editions of 1870.[46] The play ends with the climactic return home of the sympathetic fallen-woman protagonist, now terminally ill. Like the heroines of *Marion de Lorme* and *A Duel in Richelieu's Time*, her lover is dead because of a duel. She asks her family to forgive her adultery and abandonment. Adding to the scene's overpowering pathos, her little son runs and clings to her, crying out "Mama!" She dies, and everyone sobs, onstage and off.[47] A play that we now associate primarily with an actress's frilly, frivolous costume, from which our English term "frou-frou" derives, concludes with sorrow so poignant that Ruskin could not bear it.

CROSSING LONDON: BOADEN AND POLACK

Like Ruskin, many British theatergoers admired French acting, making Parisian touring companies performing in French a common occurrence in London. But not everyone understood the language. Successful French plays like *Frou-Frou* offered British women dramatists (as well as male playwrights, of course) a huge stockpile of material to translate and to adapt to the British stage. Sarah Lane (*c.* 1822–99), the manager of the Britannia, mounted her own adaptations of French tragedies throughout the 1870s, including *Dolores* (April 1874), taken from Victorien Sardou's *Patrie!* (1869).[48] Some estimate that at least half of the plays produced on the London stage in the nineteenth century were adapted from French, often without attribution.[49]

One play to appear in London first in French and then in translation is Monsieur Lockroy (penname of Joseph Philippe Simon) and Edmond Badon's melodrama *Un Duel sous le Cardinal de Richelieu*, first performed at the Vaudeville in Paris on April 9, 1832 and almost immediately in French at the Haymarket.[50] Caroline Boaden's three-act prose drama *A Duel in Richelieu's Time* appeared just a few months later, on 9 July of 1832 also at the Haymarket; playbills held in the British Library indicate that it was repeated every night that week because of its success, and throughout the summer.[51] *The Athenaeum* and other papers reviewed it; author and critic William Godwin noted it in his diary.[52] The chief difference between the original play and Boaden's English version is the purging of its seven songs, constitutive of melodrama. Eliminating them was not necessary. The Haymarket often mounted melodramas, even though in the summer it legally could and did produce spoken drama. Thus, Boaden's creating tragedy out of melodrama is a clear choice to shift genre, perhaps a bid for greater prestige but certainly revealing the degree to which the two forms overlap. The playbill describes *A Duel in Richelieu's Time* as "A New Serious Drama."[53] Both the French play and its English translation may have been inspired by the 1831 *Marion de Lorme* by Hugo, originally drafted in 1829 under the identical title of *Un Duel sous Richelieu* but banned by Charles X because of the poor light in which it portrays King Louis XIII, reflecting on the current king. *Marion de Lorme*'s production—intended for the Comédie-Française but ultimately opening at the Porte-Saint-Martin—was delayed till after the revolution of 1830 because, as Albert Halsall explains, "the July Revolution deposed Charles X and brought Louis-Philippe to the throne and, as well, abolished for a time State censorship of the theatre."[54]

In addition to borrowing Hugo's initial title, the temporal settings are obviously identical (both in Richelieu's time), invoking some of the same historical personages (including Richelieu). The plots, too, are very similar. Both Hugo's *Marion de Lorme* and the French and English versions of *A Duel in Richelieu's Time* involve violent death, illegal duels, secret liaisons, men of honor unwittingly pledging their lives to protect the lives of their rivals in love, and women of dubious sexual morality surviving their lovers with nothing to look forward to but a life of regret and pain. (This is, by the way, a punitive rewriting of these historical women's actual biographies.) All three plays provide magnificent roles in the unlucky heroines, Marion de Lorme and the Duchess Marie de Rohan-Monbazon, whose passionate speeches thoroughly moved their audiences. The plays push hard to depict the caprice of those in power, the folly of dueling, and the agony of a fallen woman. The most significant difference between *Marion de Lorme* and both the French and English versions of *A Duel in Richelieu's Time* is the very last scene. The conclusion of Hugo's play places supreme emphasis on protesting Richelieu's tyranny: the bereaved Marion de Lorme, pointing to Richelieu's approaching carriage, cries out to those assembled both on stage and in the audience, "Look, all of you! Feast your eyes on the man of blood!"[55] Although in the plays by Lockroy and Boaden the mechanism for the final loss of life and love is again the state's oppressive interference, the concluding tableau is exquisitely melodramatic, by which I mean it narrows its focus to the domestic tragedy of a wife spurned and grieving. Seeing her husband covered by the blood of the man she loves (who has just killed himself to evade capture by Richelieu), Marie de Rohan-Monbazon falls to her knees; her betrayed husband declares, "Eternal separation, and never-ceasing remorse be your portion," as he throws her the incriminating evidence—a letter and portrait—that Richelieu had sent him to provoke his jealousy and foster bloodshed and desolation. Rather than exposing the cruelty of Richelieu, the attention here is all on the failed marriage, the illicit couple's indiscretions, and the wife's punishment, despite her earlier heroism in first successfully saving her husband's life by interceding with the Cardinal. She ardently tries to save her lover's as well. Unlike *Marion de Lorme*, by the end of *A Duel in Richelieu's Time*, the potential for protesting a system of oppression inherent in the earlier scenes castigating King Louis and Cardinal Richelieu is forgotten.[56]

The Athenaeum devotes more than a third of a page to Boaden's *A Duel in Richelieu's Time*, pronouncing the play "perfectly and deservedly successful." The only complaint specifically highlights the drama's status as a tragedy, which the critic sees as generally a weak point for this theater: "The Haymarket is not the stage for tragedy or tragic dramas; and we regret that Miss Boaden did not reserve her work for Drury Lane or Covent Garden, where its elements would have been in their element."[57] *La Belle Assemblée* also declared Boaden's new drama "deservedly successful," though not as quite as deserving as another play on the bill, also translated from French.[58] *The Literary Gazette* announced its being received with "great applause," but did not even bother mentioning Boaden's name,[59] a snub that Newey identifies as a pattern among reviewers of plays by women dramatists. Another is rebuking plays for immorality, worse when, as *The New Monthly Magazine* ruefully states, it is "the work of a lady," not to be tolerated despite being "clever and effective" since it is also "offensive to good taste and injurious to good morals."[60]

Caroline Boaden was the daughter of the prominent British playwright and theatrical biographer James Boaden. Her brother John Boaden also wrote plays. It is precisely such immersion in a theatrical family that, Newey argues, provided nineteenth-century women dramatists the support that could help them break through walls that would necessarily keep so many out of the profession.[61] This connection gave Boaden an entrée into the Haymarket, which produced no fewer than six of her plays, both comedies and tragedies, between 1825 and 1838. She performed the role of Lady Teazle in Richard Brinsley Sheridan's *The School for Scandal* at the Haymarket in 1827, compounding her relationship with the Haymarket's theatrical community. Coming from a very different community on the other side of town, Elizabeth Polack may have enjoyed similar support from a family also connected to the theater and authorship. Though even less is known about Elizabeth Polack than Caroline Boaden, James Picciotto's *Sketches of Anglo-Jewish History* (1875) identifies Polack's grandfather as the man who supported the celebrated opera singer John Braham (*c.* 1774–1856) when he was a boy. Picciotto's comments also indicate that her aunt was likely Maria Polack, whose novel, *Fiction without Romance; or,*

The Locket-Watch (1830), made her "one of the first English Jews to publish a novel depicting the struggles concerning Jewish modernity among Anglo-Jews."[62] Joel Samuel Polack, author of two highly regarded books on New Zealand published in 1838 and 1840, may have been Elizabeth's brother.[63] Like the Planchés, the Kembles, and the Boadens, the Polacks sound like a family who perhaps would boost—or at least not deter—a daughter, niece, or sister who wanted to write plays professionally, despite the social pressure against it. But regardless of Polack's family background, writing for the far less prestigious Pavilion in the largely Jewish working-class neighborhood of Whitechapel may have paradoxically helped her success; Heidi Holder argues the East End was more welcoming to women dramatists, where "the ideology of 'separate spheres' . . . was virtually absent . . . and women's public role was more flexible."[64] It certainly was the right venue to present her Jewish-themed melodrama *Esther, the Royal Jewess, or the Death of Haman!* (1835).

Although based on a Biblical story and wrapped up in the Jewish holiday of Purim, Polack's play also has an important antecedent in a French classical tragedy. Racine's three-act verse play *Esther* dramatizes the familiar Bible tale of the secretly Jewish queen of Persia, Esther. When she learns of the perfidious plans of Haman, the chief advisor to King Ahasuerus of Persia, to murder all the Jews, she bravely goes uninvited to the king (the penalty is death if he were to choose not to admit her) to reveal her Jewish identity, thus preserving the Jewish people. Her virtuous Uncle Mordecai, who saves the king's life and counsels Esther wisely, becomes the new chief advisor to the king. The Jewish holiday of Purim celebrates the Biblical Esther's success. From a Jewish perspective, it is hard to see why Racine's play relating the Persian Jews' rescue and the heroine's happy survival is subtitled *tragédie*, except that the villain Haman is a man of high office who tumbles to a dishonorable and grisly death. As we have seen, the term "tragedy" is far more fluid than we typically think.

Thomas Brereton translated Racine's play into English as *Esther, or Faith Triumphant: A Sacred Tragedy* (1715), which Handel then adapted into a full oratorio, *Esther* (1732), his first in English. Handel's oratorios regularly appeared on the London concert stage well into the nineteenth century, especially during Lenten season,[65] when the law prohibited non-musical theatrical performance on Wednesdays and Fridays. Braham—the great tenor whom Polack's grandfather helped—performed in concerts including selections from Handel's *Esther* in the 1820s.[66] It seems likely that Handel's oratorio and its sources, as well as traditional Jewish Purim plays performed in homes and around synagogues, would have been well within Elizabeth Polack's ken. Because Polack's play is also a musical form (that is a melodrama, necessary because it was written for performance at an illegitimate theater pre-1843), it too could be performed during the Lenten season without penalty, and this helps to explain its premiere during Lent in 1835.

Esther, the Royal Jewess would likely draw a large Jewish crowd celebrating Purim from the neighborhood, as it opened and repeated in the week leading up to the Purim holiday.[67] That it specifically targeted a Jewish clientele is clear from the scrim that lowers in the final scene with the word "Purim" on it while the actress playing Esther directly addresses the audience wishing them a "happy Purim!"[68] But plays with Jewish-themed content at the Pavilion attracted non-Jews and well as Jews.[69] It was reviewed in issue 172 of the anti-Semitic paper *Figaro in London*, which suggested that even its readers were interested in attending plays at the Pavilion. Moreover, the play textually invites non-Jews into its ethos: just before wishing the audience a happy holiday, Esther declares, "May the sacred tree of liberty never lose a branch in contending for religious superiority; but all be free to worship as he pleases. Let that man be for ever despised who dares interfere between his fellow man and his creed."[70] She rallies the crowd in favor of universal religious tolerance, in effect not only admonishing Christians to accept Jews and Jews to accept Christians but also everyone to respect everyone else's faith.

Polack's play physically brings together a diverse crowd inside a commercial theater (the Pavilion) in a mixed neighborhood (Whitechapel) for a play that is about Jewish people living productively in ancient Persia (as a stand-in for contemporary England). The Jews find a home there, despite the hate-mongering of the powerful, high-ranking official, Haman. The happy marriage of the Persian king and Jewish maiden-cum-queen becomes a national allegory in Frederic Jameson's terms for the positive possibilities for Jewish assimilation into British civic life without conversion.[71] Recognized as worthy by King Ahasuerus (standing in for King William), an upright Jewish man—Mordecai—rises to the highest level of government because he merits promotion, just as English Jews in the 1830s were agitating for the opportunity to move into professions, public service, the vote, higher education, and the right to hold office. They were slowly gaining rights: to become a barrister (1833), to serve as Sheriff of London (1835), and to attend university (1837).[72]

In Racine's *Esther*, the hatred Haman foments infects the king and causes him to fear Jews; Esther's revelation begins to undo that damage. In Polack, the king remains entirely ignorant of Haman's malevolent plans; he never expresses any animosity toward Jews or any other group. Racine's Ahasuerus suffers nightmares about what evil the Jews might do to him,[73] but Polack's Ahasuerus has dreams in which Father Time reveals "the hidden sorrows of thy people," meaning the Jews, underscoring they are every bit his people and as much under his care as any other Persians.[74] Unlike Hugo's (and even to an extent Boaden's) impetus to expose weak monarchs in a revolutionary context, Polack's concern is to depict a benevolent kingship that will help to smooth the path of Jews to full civic rights and to show the non-Jewish audience members that their Jewish neighbors are just regular folks who could contribute as full citizens. In her brilliant study of illegitimate theater in London, Jane Moody twice identifies Polack's play as a tragedy, perhaps influenced by memories of Racine and Brereton or thinking of the precipitous fall of the mighty Haman.[75] Yet despite the word "death" in the title and the demise of the second titular character, *Esther, The Royal Jewess, or the Death of Haman!* shifts from tragedy to melodrama as Dickens describes the genre, replete with humor and music as well as anguish and sensation, written in prose. It aims at uniting the multifarious theatergoers of the Pavilion and at integrating Jews into the state.

SWEENEY TODD

Beginning this essay about variations in production and consumption of nineteenth-century tragedy with a discussion of Sondheim's twentieth-century *Sweeney Todd* may seem surprising. But its Victorian origin helps us to think through the generic fluidity of melodrama and tragedy. It demonstrates that working-class authors like Dibdin Pitt wrote for working-class theaters like the Britannia (dubbed The People's Theatre, and admired by George Bernard Shaw),[76] which attracted the working-class clientele Dickens described in "Amusements of the People."[77] Dibdin Pitt tailored his play *Sweeney Todd* (at the time entitled *The String of Pearls: or the Fiend of Fleet Street*) to the Britannia's audiences and its acting company.[78] As a role for Sarah Lane, the Britannia's leading lady (as well as co-manager),[79] Dibdin Pitt added to his adaptation a pert serving girl who outwits Sweeney

Todd and every other villain; besides Todd, there is a hypocritical preacher (from the source novel) and a group of ruffians (created just for her to foil). The popular Lane specialized in soubrettes, so this energetic character's addition was vital to the play's initial success with the Britannia crowd who idolized her, an example of how each theater company's composition dictated what sorts of roles the house dramatist must create.[80] Another character inserted into Dibdin Pitt's 1847 *Sweeney Todd* was a second young servant hero, a freed mute slave boy named Hector, played by a prominently featured company dancer, Madame Roby. Hector saves the life of the romantic lead (his employer, a sailor) and works closely with Lane's character to bring Todd to justice. The sailor—who explains that he had freed the lad from slavery when he was just a baby—makes strong abolitionist declarations. Including anti-slavery speeches and a valiant former slave who rescues a British tar makes Dibdin Pitt's original *Sweeney Todd* an abolitionist and patriotic play, signaling the anti-slavery views among working-class artists and patrons of the Britannia in March 1847. The production occurred during the final weeks of Frederick Douglass's twenty-month tour of the British Isles, including a famous speech in May 1846 at nearby Finsbury Chapel, also in the East End. The two servant roles—specific to the Britannia's talents and audience's interests—never reappeared in the play's later post-American emancipation versions, either in its initial publication in 1883 or after.[81]

Although, as in many tragedies, the titular character Sweeney Todd dies in the final moments of all versions of the play, Dibdin Pitt's Todd is such an utter villain that—as with Haman—the audience rejoices in his just deserts. Unlike Sondheim's musical, no heartbreaking backstory or justifiable revenge plot awakens audiences' sympathy for Todd. He murders his clients for their valuables; he dumps them into his neighbor Mrs. Lovett's cellar for her to make them into meat pies without any thought about rectifying class inequities or avenging crimes committed by those in power, vital components of Todd's intent in Sondheim.[82] Both Dibdin Pitt and Sondheim play on collective fears of vulnerability in trusting strangers with our necks as we lie back (or imagine lying back) in the barber chair for a shave and on our dread of contamination to the urban food supply, where people have no control over the quality, origin, or even species of meat. Rather than tragedy's traditional catharsis evoked by strong feelings of pity and awe, Sondheim's musical adds a hefty dose of horror inspired not only by the English tradition of melodrama terror but also by the Grand Guignol theater,[83] which opened in Paris at the fin de siècle and flourished for over sixty years. The notoriously graphic violence onstage there meant that the house physician might be called up to fifteen times to attend to fainting or vomiting members of the audience[84]—perhaps a physical manifestation of Aristotle's decree that tragedy should purge emotion.

The disturbingly ritualistic reiterated murders in Sondheim are already present in Dibdin Pitt's melodrama, provoking terror that provides satisfaction in Todd's sensational death scene, which culminates in his visions of the damned taking him away while he swears his repentance.[85] Just as wickedness is punished, virtue is rewarded. Although many unnamed extras end up in pies, all the meritorious main characters emerge happily uneaten at the play's end. Filled with pathos, terror, spectacle, humor, and song, this is a melodrama. And yet, the tempered elements of tragedy remain, and they matter. In Dibdin Pitt's *Sweeney Todd*, on a stage populated not with monarchs but sailors, barbers, opticians, servants, apprentices, and pie-makers, we recognize Todd's extraordinary successes both in the barber's art and the killer's ingenuity; we loathe him morally, but—like Richard III—we appreciate his shrewdness in wrongdoing. As in old-fashioned tragedies, his achieving great heights yield to a precipitous fall, sudden ignominy, and death. But melodrama shifts the tragic register from shock and sorrow to terror and satisfaction in the deserved destruction of villainy.

Dibdin Pitt's holograph prompt books held in the Templeman Library at the University of Kent contain notes that reveal his strategy in adapting his sources to appeal to East End audiences in contrast to those more prestigious venues in the West End. He alters plots, language, and duration to create melodramas. He does so even though *Sweeney Todd* (or rather *The String of Pearls*) was mounted at the Britannia in 1847, after it became legal to produce purely spoken tragedies there. In order "to suit the taste of the Audience" at the hard-working Britannia, he would write shorter plays of around two acts, as he explains, making it "more highly coloured" with "more MeloDramatic Effect" than West End playhouses would produce.[86] Dibdin Pitt lived in the Britannia's vicinity of Hoxton. As Davis and Emeljanow show in *Reflecting the Audience*, not only the house dramatist but also the acting company of working-class theaters were generally also working class, living near the theaters that employed them. These actors were so needy that appreciative fans threw onto the stage not only artificial flowers, but also "sausages, tobacco pouches, comforters, rounds of beef, and trousers."[87] The actors knew their audiences because they were one of them. To a significant extent, the communities of production and consumption were the same.

CONCLUSION

Hugo's *Hernani* and *Marion de Lorme*, Boaden's *A Duel in Richelieu's Time*, Meilhac and Halévy's *Frou-Frou*, Polack's *Esther, The Royal Jewess*, and Dibdin Pitt's *Sweeney Todd* illustrate the complexity of tragic genres in the nineteenth century: the intersection of tragedy, comedy, and melodrama; of supposedly high and low forms; of Biblical subjects and current events; of Paris and London; of gender, class, and ethnicity; of intricate networks of authors, actors, and audiences. Tragedy blossoms far more broadly in popular genres than in the five-act verse dramas housed at Drury Lane and the Comédie-Française. By paying attention to how tragedy inhabits and is altered by melodrama and other forms, we can include women, minorities, and working-class writers among the producers of plays that substantially incorporate tragic elements. We can mightily expand the audience. My goal is not to prove that tragedy gave way to melodrama in the nineteenth century; that has been said by Booth and adjusted by others such as Williams, Cox, and Gamer. Instead, my aim here has been to demonstrate the agility of the genre of melodrama in providing a vehicle for a wide variety of authors and audiences to employ elements of tragedy. This flexible musical form focused on timely problems, giving birth to realism in the late nineteenth century and contributing mightily to the emergent Broadway musical in the twentieth. Given melodrama's maneuvering of both tragedy and comedy and its dependence on music as constitutive to the form, it is not surprising that a villain-driven Victorian melodrama like *Sweeney Todd* ultimately yielded Sondheim's tragic musical masterpiece.

CHAPTER FOUR

Philosophy and Social Theory

JONATHAN SACHS

Tom McCarthy's novel *Satin Island* (2015) begins in Turin, at the Torino-Caselle airport on an evening when a rogue airplane has grounded all flights over Europe. As the protagonist, U., waits, he checks his phone, clicks through news sites and social media, looks up random information on the internet, wanders around, browses duty free luxury offerings, glances at the omnipresent television screens, and watches other people do exactly the same thing. Increasingly, as the night wears on, these screens are dominated by news of an oil spill, "aerial shots of a stricken offshore platform around which a large, dark water-flower was blooming."[1] U. watches the fascinating blur of images and then:

> The man sitting beside me, noticing the rapt attention I was paying these pictures, tried at one point to spark up a conversation. Tutting disapprovingly in their direction, he opined that it was a tragedy. That was the word he used, of course: *tragedy*, like a TV pundit. . . . He addressed me in English, but his accent was Eurozone: neither French nor Dutch nor German but a mish-mash of all these and more, overlaid with ersatz, business-school American. I didn't answer at first. When I did, I told him that the word *tragedy* derived from the ancient Greek custom of driving out a sheep, or *tragos*—usually a black one—in a bid to expiate a city's crimes.[2]

U., of course, is right. Tragedy is thought to originate in scapegoating perpetuated as an urban ritual and it takes its name not only from the Greek word for sheep, but also from the singing that was part of that ritual. As a poetic genre, tragedy was subsequently formalized as part of the City Dionysia, the annual Athenian festival in honor of the god Dionysius, and then later defined by Aristotle as "a representation of a serious, complete action which has magnitude, in embellished speech, . . . [represented] by people acting and not by narration; accomplishing by means of pity and terror the catharsis of such emotions. . . . So tragedy as a whole necessarily has six parts . . . plot, characters, diction, reasoning, spectacle and song."[3]

Aristotle's definition is generic: tragedy is a form of poetic expression that conforms to certain rules and expectations. The attempt to formalize an understanding of the genre, though, moves it from its original ritualistic purposes and reveals already a rift between tragedy as a literary and philosophic concept and tragedy as an experience, in this case as a ritualistic response to events in the polis, as an extraordinary event nonetheless enmeshed in ordinary experience. As an urban ritual, tragedy can be understood as proximate to the concerns of social theory: it is meant as a shared activity to bring a community together, as a performance witnessed collectively but also through what Aristotle famously calls catharsis, a shared emotional response, a joint experience of pity and terror that purges such emotions individually and collectively. In U.'s case, however, the invocation of tragedy has the opposite effect. Following U.'s response, the man "turned back to the screen and watched it with me for a while as though this shared activity now formed part of our dialogue, of our new friendship. But I could feel he was upset not to have got the response that he expected. After a few minutes, he stood up, grasped the handle of the bag on which his tie was resting and walked off."[4]

The stifled exchange raises a series of questions: to what extent does the origin of a concept limit and bind its potential contemporary meanings? Is tragedy possible in modernity, or is it something that had meaning only at earlier historical moments in a clearly delineated set of conditions?[5] What do we make of the disconnect between specialist uses of tragedy as a philosophy or a literary genre and more common understandings of tragedy as the name for a particular kind of devastating social experience or catastrophic contemporary event? At bottom, these are questions about the relation between tragedy in common everyday parlance and tragedy as a specialist term for literary and philosophical analysis—between, in other words, tragedy as an experience, tragedy as a literary genre, and tragedy as an idea. In this sense, U. stands for tragedy as a closely delineated and narrowly defined problem of literary and philosophical import, one that has little to do with contemporary experience. The man beside him, however, understands tragedy as part of contemporary life not limited to theater and philosophy.

As the tensions between tragedy as a social ritual and Aristotle's definition of tragic form suggest, these questions shadow the long history of tragedy, but arguably they become more acute in the nineteenth century, especially in response to the experience of the French Revolution. Tragedy as a genre turns on extremes of passion, recklessness, daring, and suffering. It focuses commonly on kings and rulers, and always on exceptional individuals in special circumstances. Can ordinary individuals, nobodies really, be the subject of a tragedy? What happens to an elevated genre like tragedy in an age of democratic revolutions? On the one hand, the very exceptionalism of tragedy would seem to make it less viable for an emergent modernity ostensibly predicated on equality and the right to political participation; on the other hand, from fifth-century Athens forward, tragedy as a genre has been commonly understood as acutely attuned to the irresolvable conflicts that arise in societies undergoing transitions of political authority. According to Raymond Williams, "tragic experience ... commonly attracts the fundamental beliefs and tensions of a period, and tragic theory is interesting mainly in this sense, that through it the set of a particular culture is often deeply realized."[6] The excesses of tragedy, in other words, would seem perfectly consistent with an age of revolution. This seeming paradox of tragedy's relevance to the nineteenth century moves in at least two directions. We find it first in the emergence of a philosophy of the tragic in German idealism at once inclusive in its generalizing of tragedy as fundamental to the human condition and exclusive in its carefully delimited sense of what counts as tragic. Second, it exists in the possibility that tragic experience is open to everyone and therefore offers a master trope for understanding collective social experience and historical process more generally.

These two directions can be taken as emblematic of the two main concepts of this chapter's focus, philosophy and social theory. After a brief discussion of tragedy and ordinary experience, the chapter considers a philosophical tradition that developed from the later eighteenth century forwards, most notably (but not exclusively) by Friedrich

Wilhelm Joseph Schelling, Georg Wilhelm Friedrich Hegel, Arthur Schopenhauer, and Friedrich Nietzsche, in which new ideas about tragedy emerge as a problem of metaphysics and aesthetics. Most of the chapter focuses on this tradition because the philosophy of the tragic that develops through and against German idealist thinking is the nineteenth century's single most important contribution to tragedy and thinking about the tragic. The chapter then turns to other nineteenth-century understandings of tragedy that look more explicitly at the relation between tragedy and nineteenth-century social theory. Thinkers like Percy Shelley and Karl Marx understand tragedy as closely related to historical events and political experience; indeed it is through an understanding of tragedy that they develop their prescriptive social theories and seek to make sense of historical process more broadly. Tragedy works to shape a broad range of experiences and hence works as an expedient and effective instrument for social critique.

THE PROBLEM OF VERNACULAR TRAGEDY

Although this chapter treats first philosophy and then social theory, the two categories are not unrelated, and we will see repeatedly how the philosophical can be an under-explained resource for the political and vice versa. Indeed, the German idealist concept of the tragic, with its sustained focus on the problem of freedom, emerges directly from the problems of French Revolutionary politics. The development of a philosophy of the tragic by Schelling, Hegel, and others can thus be understood as a response to the French Revolution's pressing questions about the possibility of human agency and the relationship between freedom and necessity. But as the tragic becomes formalized as a particular kind of experience, as a philosophical condition of existence as much as a literary genre, what happens to the more vernacular sense that anyone can be the subject of tragedy and the related possibility that tragedy can be a means to grasp contemporary social experience and historical process? We are back to the episode from *Satin Island* and the tension between a visceral, almost instinctive colloquial tendency to label adverse events as "tragedy" and a more formal, even philological, insistence that tragedy is something very particular and not universal.

U.'s rejection of a vernacular sense of tragedy, his refusal to believe that a philosophical concept like tragedy can have any relevance to the seemingly random disasters of ordinary life like an oil spill, is precisely what critics like Raymond Williams and, more recently, Terry Eagleton, push against. For these critics, a concept of tragedy that is unable to accommodate vernacular experience and colloquial usage is unduly narrow—this despite how common it is "for men trained in what is now the academic tradition to be impatient and even contemptuous of what they regard as loose and vulgar uses of 'tragedy' in ordinary speech and in the newspapers."[7] In resisting such narrowness, Williams insists that the so-called tragic "tradition" is not singular but plural, that "Tragedy is . . . not a single and permanent kind of fact, but a series of experiences and conventions and institutions."[8] For Eagleton, the impossibility of a substantive definition that can accommodate all acknowledged examples of tragic art means that scholars should give credence to everyday invocations of tragedy even if commonly used only to refer to something as very sad. Like Williams, Eagleton suggests that the tensions around the participatory politics of the nineteenth century that develop from the later eighteenth-century revolutions may themselves be a precondition for universalizing potentially tragic experience. This is because the changes that follow from these events extend the possibility of democratic self-determination and self-actualization to a widening range of people.[9]

For Marxist critics like Williams and Eagleton, it is the gulf between the desire for freedom, the possibility of agency, the movement of progress, and the actual realization of these desires that can be considered tragic. Tragedy, in other words, is the schism between the promise of improvement and the inevitable misjudgments, errors, and failures that so often occur in pursuit of that promise.

How can Williams' and Eagleton's twentieth-century assessments of tragedy—or U.'s twenty-first-century notion, for that matter—help us to understand what is at stake over a century earlier? The answer requires thinking in more detail about the philosophy and social theory of tragedy after the French Revolution. As Williams observes,

> Since the time of the French Revolution, the idea of tragedy can be seen as in different ways a response to a culture in conscious change and movement. The action of tragedy and the action of history have been consciously connected, and in the connection have been seen in new ways. The reaction against this, from the mid nineteenth century, has been equally evident: the movement of spirit has been separated from the movement of civilization. Yet even this negative reaction seems, in its context, a response to the same kind of crisis.[10]

Williams suggests here that both a limited and a capacious sense of tragedy are part of the same nineteenth-century crisis, namely the joining of the action of tragedy and history in response to cultural change. U. and the tie-less Eurozone traveler may have more in common than they think.

SCHELLING

With its democratic, often populist and inclusive quality, and its attempt to make the world anew on an improved model, the French Revolution establishes the modern understanding of tragedy. That revolution's limitations and inevitable failures, in turn, help clarify the tragic aspects of modernity itself. But this does not mean that the understanding of tragedy that follows the French Revolution is simply an attempt to translate the events of that revolution into tragic terms. On the contrary, one of the foundational effects of the Revolution was the development of a tradition of tragic thinking that turned away from an explicit sense of politics and towards the abstraction and sublimation of politics into metaphysical and aesthetic terms. Crucial here is Peter Szondi's insight that "Since Aristotle, there has been a poetics of tragedy. Only since Schelling has there been a philosophy of the tragic."[11] For Schelling and the German idealist tradition of tragic theory that follows in the wake of the French Revolution, the central issue raised by tragedy is the link between freedom and necessity, an ontological problem that takes on a decidedly political inflection following the French Revolution.

In his reading of Sophocles from the final letter of the *Philosophical Letters on Dogmatism and Criticism*, Schelling's philosophy of the tragic shifts focus away from Aristotle's idea of catharsis, or the effect that tragedy has on its audience, and towards the phenomenon of the tragic itself. These letters, written in 1795 when Schelling was twenty years old, attempt to reconfigure the Kantian debate about metaphysics as a problem of freedom. For Immanuel Kant, one can prove neither absolute necessity nor absolute freedom because to do so would require an elevated, God's-eye view of the world. Schelling works through the problem by deftly navigating between the philosophical systems of Baruch Spinoza, whom he associates with dogmatism, and Johann Gottlieb Fichte, as the representative of criticism. In Schelling's reading, Spinoza grounds dogmatic philosophy in necessity or nature. It proceeds from the absolute object, or non-I, such that the subject seeks knowledge of the absolute before which he is passive. Dogmatism, in other words, radically minimizes subjectivity and freedom. In contrast, Fichte's critical philosophy proceeds from the subjective, the absolute-I, unconditioned by an object, and posits everything in the subject as part of a striving "for immutable selfhood, unconditional freedom, unlimited activity."[12] As Schelling wrote to Hegel, "the real difference between critical and dogmatic philosophy appears to be that the former proceeds from the absolute (which has yet to be conditioned by an object), while the latter proceeds from the absolute object or non-I."[13] Between the extremes of dogmatism and criticism, then, Schelling seeks to carve out a third possibility, one that locates freedom in the experience of art and that in his view arises not from philosophical systems but from life itself. In the tenth letter, he begins by insisting that freedom is threatened by an objective power (as dogmatists would have it), but that this power must be resisted, fought against even in certain defeat, and that the possibility of freedom "must be preserved for art even after having vanished in the light of reason; it must be preserved for the highest in art."[14] At the core of what Schelling means by art is the tragic, that which can move beyond the seemingly irreconcilable extremes of philosophical thought.

Schelling attempts to work through these contradictions between freedom and necessity in his reading of Sophocles' *Oedipus Rex*:

> Many a time the question has been asked how Greek reason could bear the contradictions of Greek tragedy. A mortal, destined by fate to become a malefactor, and himself fighting *against* this fate, is nevertheless appallingly punished for the crime, although it was the deed of destiny! The ground of this contradiction ... lay in the contest between human freedom and the power of the objective world in which the mortal must succumb *necessarily* if that power is absolutely superior, if it is fate. And yet he must be *punished* for succumbing because he did not succumb *without a struggle*. That the malefactor who succumbed under the power of fate was punished ... was the recognition of human freedom; it was the *honor* due to freedom. Greek tragedy honored human freedom, letting its hero *fight* against the superior power of fate. In order not to go beyond the limits of art, the tragedy had to let him succumb. Nevertheless, in order to make restitution for this humiliation of human freedom extorted by art, it had to let him *atone* even for the crime committed by fate ... It was a *sublime* thought, to suffer punishment willingly even for an inevitable crime, and so to prove one's freedom by the very loss of this freedom, and to go down with a declaration of free will.[15]

The passage suggests a recipe for the tragic grounded in the structure of tragedy itself. The metaphysical problem of freedom and necessity is not new, Schelling implies; the Greeks find in the figure of Oedipus a formulation for the simultaneous impossibility and necessity of free will. Oedipus does not merely succumb to the force of necessity, but he is punished for succumbing, for attempting to struggle in the first place. The will to freedom turns against him, but in that turning against comes the recognition of freedom itself. But—and here is the paradox that for Schelling best captures the tragic—this manifests the greatness of Oedipus, his sublimity: he is willing to "suffer punishment ... for an inevitable crime, and so to prove one's freedom by the very loss of this freedom, and to go down with a declaration of free will." It is in tragedy, then, that the contradictions of philosophy become bearable; and it is tragedy that offers a defense of freedom unavailable in philosophy. In seeing beyond the contradictions of freedom, tragic art can encompass the elusive identity between freedom and necessity. For Schelling, aesthetics rather than metaphysics offers a locus where the contrast between subject and object can be overcome through their own dissolution.

But, as Miriam Leonard clarifies, "the inability to convert the ontological insight of tragedy into an ethics of human freedom has a two-fold dimension."[16] First, because the discovery of freedom in tragic contradiction rejects metaphysics in favor of the realm of art, it offers no possibility for action, for ethics. Art may have better resources than philosophy for choosing freedom, but ultimately all it can do is resist and go down fighting. But if the impasse between aesthetics and ethics means that tragedy offers no model for action, a further problem is that antiquity has now given way to modernity. A titan like Oedipus makes modern man look small and timid: Greek reason and Enlightenment reason are of a different order. The tragic recognition of the nature of freedom—of the incompatibility of art and action, and the impossibility of reconciling art and philosophy—thus becomes a symptom of the breaks and fissures that separate modernity from the antique past.

This is not to suggest that Schelling's understanding of tragedy is historicist: tragedy will not return us moderns to the insights of Greek reason. Instead, tragedy reveals the contradictions of reason as exposed not just in Schelling's own age but in all ages. For Schelling, therefore, tragedy describes best the human condition—it is not simply a literary genre or the historical manifestation of Greek culture or reason. This is why, for Szondi, Schelling initiates the philosophy of the tragic in the identification of tragedy *as an ontology*, as the human condition itself. Schelling would later develop these ideas in his lectures on *The Philosophy of Art* (1802–4), in which he claimed that "The essence of *tragedy* is . . . conflict between freedom in the subject and . . . necessity, a conflict that does not end such that one or the other succumbs, but rather such that both are manifested in perfect indifference as simultaneously victorious and vanquished."[17] Such indifference to both freedom and necessity is central to Schelling's concept of the beautiful, which he further articulates as differently manifested in the dialectical development of three literary genres: epic for an original innocent unity; lyric for the conflict resulting in dispersion; and drama (or tragedy) as the subsequent reconciliation of unity at a higher level. Tragedy, then, restores the indifference in conflict central to the beautiful; once again the conflicts of reason are reconciled within the aesthetic. In Schelling's dialectic, as Szondi notes, "The site of the conflict is not an intermediate zone that remains external to the struggling subject; rather, it has been transferred into freedom itself, which, now at odds with itself, becomes its own adversary."[18]

HEGEL

Schelling's dialectical account of tragedy would prove central to Hegel's subsequent account. For Hegel, the tragic is a synonym for both ethics and metaphysics and a mark of the irreconcilability of the conflicts and contradictions between these two categories. In Hegel, "the tragic and the dialectic coincide"[19] because the contradictions of tragedy become the contradictions of the self, and hence initiate a dialectical self-consciousness. Tragedy, in other words, is a name for the contradiction that requires dialectical thinking. This is one difference between Hegel and Schelling, and it implies a more important distinction between them—namely that for Hegel, the tragic is a less individualized experience than it is for Schelling. Schelling locates the tragic in the figure of Oedipus, who then comes to stand for the individual human condition. Hegel, in contrast, links the tragic to an entire people and the mechanics and structures of Greek tragedy can, in his account, thus be used to make sense of the Greeks and their culture. If Schelling brings Oedipus and the question of the tragic into philosophy, it is Hegel who makes the individual Oedipus into a sign of the philosophical itself. For Hegel in the *Lectures on the Philosophy of History* (1822–30; published 1837), Oedipus's naming of himself in answer to the riddle of the Sphinx is the origin of philosophy as both a geographical movement from the Levant to the Aegean, and as a historical progression from Egyptian wisdom to Greek reason. When Oedipus solves the Sphinx's riddle with "man," he thereby exposes human self-comprehension, and the essence of human nature becomes thought, which comes from self-consciousness. The freeing of man into thought is thus particular to Oedipus but also generalizable to humankind. As for Schelling, Hegel's Oedipus also provides an answer to the question of human freedom since the birth of philosophy, associated with self-consciousness, produces human liberation. The philosophical subject, the "I," emerges in the confrontation with the object. But if Oedipus, for Hegel, initiates the philosophical quest and launches the dialectic in his self-consciousness, what is the upshot of linking philosophy with the fate of Oedipus?

In part, the answer lies in recognizing the limits of human subjectivity. This is a fundamentally tragic question, for just as the fate of Oedipus reveals the limits of his own freedom as a real problem, so does the conflict for Hegel expand outward to more abstract questions of political freedom and the problem of the law generally. In Hegel's earlier writing, tragedy represents a self-divided ethical world that finds reconciliation in love. The law, which is based on the firm opposition between the universal and the particular, has no place here since the firmness of its foundational opposition offers no possibility of the tragic. As the young Hegel characterizes tragedy:

> Tragedy consists in this, that ethical nature segregates its inorganic nature (in order not to become embroiled in it), as a fate, and places it outside itself; and by acknowledging this fate in the struggle against it, ethical nature is reconciled with Divine being as the unity of both.[20]

As for Schelling, tragedy here turns on the struggle and eventual reconciliation with external necessity. The implication again is that the tragic creates a solution to metaphysical questions about the relationship between freedom and necessity, a way through the impasse between the two, where the dualistic formalism—the rigid oppositions between law and individuality, the universal and the particular—of Kant and Fichte always get stuck. But what distinguishes the passage is the distinct relation between the individual and the collective, the way that Hegel consolidates the abstract and the real. Hegel, as Szondi explains, "seeks to replace the abstract concept of ethics with a real one that presents the universal and the particular in their identity, for their opposition is caused by formalism's process of abstraction."[21] Here, and elsewhere, the opposition between "inorganic nature" and living individuality ("ethical nature"), between the universal and the particular, is drawn into an identity that can only be characterized through dynamic opposition and self-division—in other words, a tragic identity. It is therefore not surprising that in the work from which the above passage is taken, an early essay on "The Scientific Ways of Treating Natural Law" (1802–3), Hegel reads the sacrifice required to constitute individuality, or ethical nature, through the conclusion of Aeschylus' *Oresteia*. Here, the conflict between Apollo, as the living ethical imperative, and the Eumenides, who stand for the inorganic part of ethics, is staged in front of the Athenian people. In the reconciliation brought about by Pallas Athena the Eumenides win honor as divine powers and, "By interpreting the tragic process as the self-division and self-reconciliation of the ethical nature, Hegel makes his dialectical structure immediately apparent for the first time."[22] These ideas are also developed in Hegel's writings from 1798–1800 on the spirit of Christianity, in which he links the genesis of fate to the spirit of Christianity and sees ethical life developing through the self-division between ethics associated with Christianity and the law associated with Judaism as resolved dialectically in love. For the young Hegel the tragic process is akin to the dialectic of ethics.

But this will change as Hegel develops both his dialectical thinking and his understanding of the tragic. In the lectures on *Aesthetics* (1818–29; compiled 1835), composed twenty years or so after the essay on natural law, he suggests that

> The original essence of tragedy consists then in the fact that within such a conflict each of the opposed sides, if taken by itself, has *justification;* while each can establish the true and positive content of its own aim and character only by denying and infringing the equally justified power of the other. The consequence is that in its moral life, and because of it, each is nevertheless involved in guilt.[23]

The passage marks an essential change in Hegel's thinking about the tragic, which no longer belongs to the idea of the divine. While the ethical remains self-divided, the contours of this division are now determined by the contingent circumstances that surround the particular conflict. According to Szondi, "Unlike Hegel's earlier definition of the tragic, the one he presents in the *Aesthetics* does not appear to be immediately drawn from a philosophical system; rather, corresponding to its position in an aesthetic theory, it strives to encompass the full range of tragic possibilities."[24] If Schelling identifies the tragic with the solution to the specific contradictions of Greek reason, then when Hegel invokes the tragic—or when his conceptual engagement reveals the place of the tragic in his dialectical thinking even when it is not explicitly invoked—he offers no contextualization for his discussion or explanation of the tragic. Perhaps this is because throughout Hegel's thinking there is a sustained interchange between tragedy as a historical phenomenon and tragedy as metaphysics. If idealist philosophy, as we saw with Schelling, makes tragedy ontological, Hegel's insistent attention to the actual, phenomenal world makes that ontology into a problem. Just as the tragic and the dialectic coincide for Hegel and become the means through which each can be explained, so the tragic becomes for Hegel a vehicle for discussing the life of spirit, but spirit here is neither metaphysical nor phenomenal. It is rather suspended between historical reality and metaphysical abstraction, a further indication of how for Hegel the tragic, like identity itself, has inner movement. This is nowhere revealed more fully than in the dialectic of spirit from the *Phenomenology of Spirit* (1807).

Hegel offers no definition of the tragic, nor do the terms "tragic" or "tragedy" occur in the *Phenomenology*, but it is here that he uses Sophocles's *Antigone*—elsewhere called "the most magnificent and satisfying artwork . . . of all the masterpieces of the ancient and modern world"[25]—to illustrate the stage of "true spirit" in his development of the dialectical process of spirit. True spirit, for Hegel, is ethics divided into two essences, divine law and human law. The fulfillment of divine law is in woman and the sphere of the family, while human law is realized in man and the sphere of the state. *Antigone* shows the fundamental conflict between the two. For Szondi, "Contrary to the *Aesthetics* and in agreement with the early treatise on natural right, the *Phenomenology* places the tragic (of course without naming it as such) at the center of the Hegelian philosophy and interprets it as the dialectic governing ethical life, the spirit in its stage as true spirit."[26] But the key difference here is that the law is now drawn into the tragic, for *Antigone*'s tragic conflict sits precisely at the intersection of the rigidity of law, represented by Creon standing also for the spirit of Judaism and formalist ethics, and love, embodied by Antigone. In Hegel's account, both are justified in their actions and both have the potential for ethical pathos. The dialectic, whose place in Hegel's thought is fundamentally knitted with the development of the tragic, now includes the sphere of the law because the dialectic itself, like the tragic, now encompasses all aspects of thought and life. There is, then, nothing from which the dialectic—or the tragic—can be excluded. The dialectic and the tragic then transcend their emergence as historical-theological phenomenon in Christian fate and as the means for restoring ethical theory as confronted by the rigid formalism of Kant and Fichte; they become "the law of the world and the method of knowledge."[27]

SCHOPENHAUER

If for Hegel the dialectic, and by extension the tragic, is the law and binding force that holds the world together, then for Schopenhauer, what he calls the "will" occupies that centrality. The will, in other words, is the source of all phenomena. By will, Schopenhauer refers to something that is at once particular and composed of its individual instances, but also something exterior to those instances that can be known through awareness of its individual manifestations, something akin to an impulse to life. As such, the body itself is will, or perhaps more accurately the expression of a will to life, a blind striving beneath the level of conscious thought and deliberate action directed toward preserving life and creating new life. The tragic process for Schopenhauer is the will's coming into self-knowledge, or the objectification of the will.

Schopenhauer understands this objectification of the will as a progression from the less to the more complex, which he organizes hierarchically beginning with the inorganic and moving through to plants, to animals, and finally to man. In and of itself, the will works like a blind instinct, an unconscious life-drive; but, as one moves to more complex forms of objectification, through "the addition of the world as representation developed for its service, the will obtains knowledge of its own willing and what it wills."[28] By the world of representation, Schopenhauer means the world as it is for our experience: the world of appearances in contrast to the underlying reality of the thing in itself, or the world as will. The goal of art is to communicate knowledge of the will beneath representation, and the aesthetic emerges in Schopenhauer's philosophy as the key to this process. It is through art that the will best comes to know itself and through aesthetic contemplation that willing ceases and the world is transformed into a timeless reality of ideas. Central here is Schopenhauer's understanding of tragedy.

For Schopenhauer, in *The World as Will and Representation* (1818–19 first publication; 1859 final edition) tragedy turns around the destruction and repudiation of the will. Whether the tragic conflict is framed as a confrontation between man and the gods or between man and man, tragic conflict in Schopenhauer's reading reveals the diverse expressions of the will and shows them fighting against each other. Tragedy, in other words, breaks through representation to expose the will and, more specifically, the battle of the will against itself:

> It is the antagonism of the will with itself which is here [in tragedy] most completely unfolded at the highest grade of its objectivity, and which comes into fearful prominence. It becomes visible in the suffering of mankind which is produced partly

by chance and error; and these stand forth as the rulers of the world, personified as fate through their insidiousness which appears almost like purpose and intention. In part it proceeds from mankind itself through the self-mortifying efforts of the will on the part of individuals, through the wickedness and perversity of most. It is one and the same will, living and appearing in them all, whose phenomena fight with one another and tear one another to pieces.[29]

Crucial here is that the knowledge conveyed by tragic conflict, the exposure of "one and the same will," is completed not within the tragic drama itself, but in the knowledge that tragedy broadcasts outwards, in its effect on spectators and readers. The knowledge delivered by tragedy comes from the will itself, from the inner being of the will's more complex manifestations—"the highest grade of its objectivity"—and works to preserve both the individual and the species. But if knowledge is subordinate to the will, it can also break out from that servitude, it can disentangle itself from the aims of will and establish "a clear mirror of the world."[30] This is the experience of art—and, especially, the experience of tragedy, which realizes the possibility contained in art that the knowledge that should serve the will can turn against it. Tragedy showcases the will's self-destruction, which enables one to abolish the will within oneself. This, for Schopenhauer, is how one reaches the ethically good and achieves even a kind of mystical salvation: "everything tragic, whatever the form in which it appears, the characteristic tendency to the sublime, is the dawning of the knowledge that the world and life can afford us no true satisfaction, and are therefore not worth our attachment to them. In this the tragic spirit consists; accordingly, it leads to resignation."[31] The spectator of tragedy thus comes to recognize that life, the supposed object of the drive or instinct of the will, is "not worth our attachment" and we are led away from will towards resignation. Tragedy, in other words, performs the dialectical inversion whereby its presentation of the will in its most naked and evident form—the will itself as sole hero of the tragic action—teaches us how the will can turn against and destroy itself, and in extinguishing itself, the will offers us the knowledge and clarity that comes from resigning the very will itself.

NIETZSCHE

The centrality of tragedy in Schopenhauer's theory of the world as will and representation shadows Nietzsche's more famous theory in *The Birth of Tragedy* (1870–1). Continuities of Schopenhauer's will and representation can be seen in Nietzsche's ideas of the Dionysiac and the Apollonian respectively. Within Nietzsche's account of tragedy's emergence, the fierce and driven force of Schopenhauer's will becomes the Dionysian world of revelry, while the visibility and self-knowledge of representation, the world in its appearance, becomes the Apollonian world of images. Moreover, just as for Schopenhauer metaphysical concepts become aesthetic concepts—as only art can show the path towards transcending the force of the will or at least sublating it in resignation—in Nietzsche's *The Birth of Tragedy* metaphysics also appears in the form of aesthetics, with Nietzsche similarly insisting that the tragic can be explained only with recourse to aesthetics. "Let the serious minded people take note," Nietzsche exclaims, "art is the highest task and the truest metaphysical activity of this life."[32]

It is through this emphasis on aesthetics that Nietzsche, who came late to tragedy and the question of its relation to the modern world, marks his difference from Hegel.[33] The very opening of *The Birth of Tragedy* announces its turn to aesthetics and suggests that its aim is to show "with the certainty of something directly apprehended (*Anschauung*), that the continuous evolution of art is bound up with the duality of *Apolline* and the *Dionysiac* in much the same way as reproduction depends on there being two sexes which co-exist in a state of perpetual conflict interrupted only occasionally by periods of reconciliation."[34] Not for Nietzsche, the tragic dialectic. Indeed, Leonard reads this opening as marking an explicit series of contrasts with Hegel: an emphasis not on the development of spirit but rather of art; a concern with "something directly apprehended" and with felt, phenomenological experience rather than a combination of the immediate and the abstract; a shift from dialectic reconciliation and advance to a duality of perpetually conflicting irrational forces. Thus for Leonard, "In his vocabulary of duality, conflict and reconciliation . . . Nietzsche takes over the structure of Hegel's insights into the functioning of tragedy but diverts it to a new end."[35]

Instead of seeing tragedy as the solution to a metaphysical impasse, like Schelling and Hegel, for Nietzsche the birth of philosophy comes from the death of tragedy, and it is Socrates—as "archetype of *theoretical* man," as representation of the development of rational thought and individuation and an associated optimism that Nietzsche sees as the core of dialectics—who destroys the tragic aesthetic. As Nietzsche states:

> One only needs to consider the consequences of these Socratic statements: "Virtue is knowledge; sin is only committed out of ignorance; the virtuous man is the happy man;" in three basic forms of optimism lies the death of tragedy. For the virtuous hero must now be a dialectician; there must now be a visible connection between virtue and knowledge, faith and morality; the solution by transcendental justice in the plays of Aeschylus is now debased to the shallow and impertinent principle of "poetic justice," with its usual *deus ex machina*.[36]

We can read Nietzsche's dismissal of tragic hero as "dialectician" as a jibe at Hegel. It is also a dismissal of Euripidean tragedy, which Nietzsche understands as undoing the earlier tragedians' balanced reconciliation between the Dionysian chorus and the Apollonian world of images. As with Schopenhauer's insistence that all tragic conflicts are manifestations of the larger singular will, Nietzsche understands all tragic heroes prior to Euripides as mere stand-ins for the original tragic hero, Dionysius. And in the Dionysian fate of being torn to pieces as the essence of all various manifestations of heroic tragic conflict, Nietzsche reads a symbol of the broader process of individuation itself. If Schelling and Hegel want to use tragedy to show the formation of the subject, Nietzsche finds the ultimate metaphysical truth of tragedy under the sign of Dionysius in the rent dispersion of the individual and in the disintegration of subjectivity more generally. Hegel's tragedy constitutes the subject, in other words, while Nietzsche's tragedy obliterates the subject, but both seek in tragedy a metaphysical unity standing beyond the realm of conflicting forces.

The rending and self-destruction of the Dionysian subject in Nietzsche's version of tragedy is also the fate of the will in Schopenhauer, and here we can further grasp the resemblance between Schopenhauer's representation and Nietzsche's Apollo: both concepts understand individuation as moving away from an originary wholeness and unity, the Dionysian for Nietzsche and the will for Schopenhauer. We can see Schopenhauer's influence when Nietzsche invokes the "Will" in his description of the perfection of tragedy:

> These two very different drives exist side by side, mostly in open conflict, stimulating and provoking one another to give birth to ever-new, more vigorous offspring in whom

they perpetuate the conflict in the opposition between them, an opposition only apparently bridged by the common term "art"—until eventually, by a metaphysical miracle of the Hellenic "Will," they appear paired, and in this pairing, finally engender a work of art which is Dionysiac and Apolline in equal measure: Attic tragedy.[37]

Art here encompasses the metaphysical, but the passage shows also how even as Nietzsche moves from Hegel to Schopenhauer in his understanding of tragedy, that understanding remains rooted in metaphysics. But despite considerable similarities and conceptual overlap between Nietzsche and Schopenhauer, there remains a significant difference between Schopenhauer's theory of tragedy and that of Nietzsche. For the former, the will's exposure of itself in the tragic process produces a turning away from itself and a resignation of the will in those who see or read tragedy. But for Nietzsche, as Szondi explains, "Dionysius emerges from his dismemberment in the process of individuation as one who is powerful and indestructible, which is precisely the 'metaphysical consolation' that tragedy offers. Nietzsche confronts Schopenhauer's negative dialectic with a positive dialectic that is reminiscent of Schelling's interpretation in the *Letters*."[38] For Schopenhauer, art holds up a clear mirror to the will and allows the process of resignation to begin. Through art one escapes the will and resigns the drive for life and the world of representation. For Nietzsche, tragedy teaches simultaneously that individuation is "the primal source of all evil" and that art is "the joyous hope that the spell of individuation can be broken, a premonition of unity restored."[39] Nietzsche thus finds in tragedy both the apogee of an idealist philosophical tradition seeking to overcome distinctions between subject and object, freedom and necessity, in the achievement of a renewed wholeness and a challenge to that very tradition in repudiating the idealist attempt to subordinate art and aesthetics to philosophy, abstraction, and the world of ideas. In developing a theory of tragedy that fundamentally rethinks idealist philosophy, Nietzsche further confirms tragedy's centrality to the idealist metaphysics of nineteenth-century philosophy.

TRAGEDY AND SOCIAL THEORY

Nietzsche's understanding of tragedy, then, attempts to move beyond the philosophical preoccupations of idealist metaphysics by championing aesthetics and the sphere of art as the frame for understanding tragic conflict and resolution. As we have seen, however, he does not manage entirely to shake off the preoccupations of that idealist tradition. One fundamental carryover is in the relationship of Nietzsche's interpretation of tragic art to the project of German rejuvenation through philosophical renewal. Nietzsche's program may reject metaphysics in favor of art, but his aesthetic manifesto, especially in its case for Richard Wagner, aspires also to become a program of national renewal, such that "the matter with which we are concerned is a grave problem for Germany, a problem which we now place, as a vortex and turning point, into the very midst of German hopes."[40] In suggesting that Wagner's works can renew German national hopes, Nietzsche raises questions about the relationship between tragedy and social theory: does social and political experience shape tragedy, and might tragedy also help to shape social and political experience? Can dramatic production, and tragedy as its supposed highest form, reform national life? We are now in a position better to appreciate the bearing of these general questions on the nineteenth-century understanding of tragedy specifically.

When Nietzsche proposes that opera, or dramatic art more generally, can revitalize a nation in his case for Wagner, he recalls Shelley's earlier "Defence of Poetry" (1821;

published 1840). There, tragedy had served as a barometer for the health of national life and the locus of national renewal. As Shelley claims, "The drama at Athens or wheresoever else it may have approached to its perfection, coexisted with the moral and intellectual greatness of the age."[41] Shelley praises Greek tragedy for its cathartic effects but also for the "self-knowledge and self-respect"[42] that it promotes in its audience. His focus, like Schopenhauer's, is on the enriching and imaginative effects tragedy has on its spectators. But when he considers the importance of drama, Shelley shifts his attention from its effects on individual spectators to its effects on the nation collectively. Shelley insists, in other words, that the state of drama itself reflects the state of the nation, which is why for Shelley, "in periods of the decay of social life, the drama sympathizes with that decay. Tragedy becomes a cold imitation of the form of the great masterpieces of antiquity."[43] We should note here the ease with which Shelley slips from drama in the first sentence to tragedy in the second. The movement underscores that when Shelley talks about "drama" he is referring to tragedy in particular. He uses the terms interchangeably. More important here is the link Shelley establishes between the vitality of tragedy and republican politics. This explains Shelley's understanding of the Restoration of Charles II as a time of the "grossest degradation of the drama," as a period when "all forms in which poetry had been accustomed to be expressed became hymns to the triumph of kingly power over liberty and virtue."[44] Again, the example that Shelley offers, Addison's *Cato*, shows that we can read "tragedy" into Shelley's reference to "drama."

For Shelley there is a direct link between the production of tragedy and social life. Each serves as a measure of the other. As Shelley explains:

> The drama being that form under which a greater number of modes of expression of poetry are susceptible of being combined than any other, the connexion of poetry and social good is more observable in the drama than in whatever other form: and it is indisputable that the highest perfection of human society has ever corresponded with the highest dramatic excellence; and that the corruption or the extinction of the drama in a nation where it has once flourished, is a mark of the corruption of manners, and an extinction of the energies which sustain the soul of social life. But, as Machiavelli says of political institutions, that life may be preserved and renewed, if men should arise capable of bringing back the drama to its principles.[45]

Poetry, and tragedy in particular, not only can promote the social good, but also is the greatest measure of whether that good is being promoted. It is an index of the health of a nation's social life—and in 1820, the time of Shelley's writing, England was not in his view healthy. Calls for the extension of the franchise and other political reforms had been met with brutal repression, notoriously at St. Peter's Field, Manchester in August 1819 and Shelley feared more political violence. In this context, it is important to recognize that for Shelley the relative health of tragedy is, in addition to being a benchmark of national well-being, also a potential source of renewal. In contrast to Machiavelli, whose *Discorsi* locate the potential for national renewal in the reform of political institutions, Shelley suggests that when the health of a nation declines, it can be restored through the renewal of dramatic excellence. Again, for drama, read tragedy, and we can see clearly that Shelley sees the production of tragedy as a direct means for advancing what he calls "social good" and for returning society to its "highest perfection." Shelley's "Defence" then is not so much a social theory of tragedy as an insistence that tragedy itself functions as social theory and that tragedy itself performs vital social work.

Shelley's work has often been linked to that of Marx but Marx of course does not insist that the world can be changed through drama.[46] Nonetheless, Marx does, like Shelley, use tragedy as a metaphor for historical process as such. Indeed, at points in Marx's work the narrative form of tragedy offers a way of emplotting what might otherwise appear as discrete historical events. In this Marx follows Hegel, who finds in the dialectical movement so central to tragedy a register for understanding historical progress. Like Hegel, Marx uses tragedy to grasp historical process, perhaps most famously in the oft-quoted opening to the *Eighteenth Brumaire* (1852). There Marx declares "Hegel remarks somewhere that all facts and personages of great importance in world history occur, as it were, twice. He forgot to add: the first time as tragedy, the second as farce."[47] While Marx follows Hegel in characterizing history as tragedy and in transforming tragedy into a philosophy of history, as the account of the farcical 1848 revolution develops in comparison to the tragic revolution of 1789, Marx introduces his own particular concerns with the relationship between tragedy and revolution.

"Men make their own history," Marx insists,

> but they do not make it just as they please; they do not make it under circumstances chosen by themselves, but under circumstances directly encountered, given and transmitted from the past. The tradition of all the dead generations weighs like a nightmare on the brain of the living. And just when they seem engaged in revolutionizing themselves and things, in creating something that has never yet existed, precisely in such periods of revolutionary crisis they anxiously conjure up the spirits of the past to their service and borrow from them names, battle cries and costumes in order to present the new scene of world history in this time-honoured disguise and this borrowed language.[48]

Marx here understands revolution through dramatic terms and concepts. He imagines the French Revolutionaries playing their parts in a staged play, using stage names, wearing theatrical costumes, and borrowing also phrases and language to heighten the sense of drama inherent in their action. The implication here is that such drama shadows historical action and marks it as inauthentic. Marx's remarks thus carry the insinuation that to make history through dramatic performance might just be mere drama and, more, mere self-delusion.

But before we dismiss the performative language as a mark of inauthenticity, we should recall Marx's distinction between tragedy and farce, for it suggests that Marx structures his distinctions between the earlier and the later revolution around the classical hierarchy of genres. All drama is not alike: tragedy is a higher form than farce, and there is something more powerful and perhaps more real in modeling revolution through the forms of tragedy. As Marx explains, "unheroic as bourgeois society is, it nevertheless took heroism, sacrifice, terror, civil war and battles of peoples to bring it into being. And in the classically austere traditions of the Roman Republic its gladiators found the ideals and the art forms, the self deceptions that they needed in order to conceal from themselves the bourgeois limitations of the content of their struggles and to keep their enthusiasm on the high plane of the great historical tragedy."[49] Tragedy, here and elsewhere, gives revolution form and shape, it is the "art form" through which revolution can be grasped. Though Marx is dismissive of the "bourgeois limitations" of the first French Revolution with its seeming "unheroic" struggles, it is tragic form that elevates those struggles and that revolution to "the high plane of the great historical tragedy." Tragedy is the genre through which revolution can be understood; moreover, it elevates revolution and moves what could be dismissed as a petty struggle to a higher plane entirely. This "resurrection of the dead," this dredging up of the ancient generic example glorifies the revolution, revealing its "spirit" and "magnifying the given task in imagination."[50] Marx's reference to spirit here inevitably recalls Hegel, but Marx takes Hegel's conflict of ethical forces and translates them into social and historical terms. What for Hegel was a spiritual process, Marx has made a social one.

What then is distinctive about the philosophy and social theory of tragedy in the nineteenth century? The major innovation—a distinctly complex question that this essay has set out in abbreviated form—is the emergence of a philosophy of the tragic as the events of the French Revolution impacted ongoing philosophical debates about freedom and necessity. But if the philosophy of the tragic can lead to rarified views about the distinctness of tragedy, it doesn't always need to: tragedy is also a part of nineteenth-century social experience and consequently important for social theory as well as philosophy. In Marx we can recognize the use of tragedy to understand not just the broader tendencies of historical process that we see also in Hegel and Shelley, but the particularity of actual historical experience. This intermeshing of tragedy and experience—which might even be understood to lend substance to the increasingly regular use of "tragedy" by the contemporary news media in its various forms to describe any sad or adverse event—is new in the nineteenth century. As Hannah Arendt insists:

> The modern concept of revolution, inextricably bound up with the notion that the course of history suddenly begins anew, that an entirely new story never known or told before, is about to unfold, was unknown prior to the two great revolutions at the end of the eighteenth century. Before they were engaged in what then turned out to be a revolution, none of the actors had the slightest premonition of what the plot of the new drama was going to be. However, once the revolutions had begun to run their course, and long before those who were involved in them could know whether their enterprise would end in victory or disaster, the novelty of the story and the innermost meaning of its plot became manifest to actors and spectators alike.[51]

In declaring the importance of the American and French Revolutions of the later eighteenth century, Arendt suggests that they begin a new story, but she promptly shifts into a different generic frame, and, like Marx, uses drama and dramatic terms for understanding those revolutions. Revolution becomes drama, and everyone equally becomes a spectator.[52] Her comments suggest not only what is new about the uses of tragedy in the nineteenth century, but they also set the stage for understanding historical process in the twentieth century and, indeed, into the twenty-first.

CHAPTER FIVE

Religion, Ritual and Myth

JEFFREY N. COX

Stranger: Are you religious?
Lady: I am nothing.
Stranger: All the better, then you can become something.
—August Strindberg, *To Damascus*, Part I[1]

As the nineteenth century opened upon the era we normally label as "Romantic," the intricate links between tragedy and religion had been seriously frayed if not severed. Of course, the historical ties between belief and tragedy were complicated and remain contested: for example, while Jon Mikalson has argued that the gods in Greek tragedy are theatrical devices, divorced by the form from being seen as the gods of Athenian religious cults, Christiane Sourvinou-Inwood has responded by contending that these plays were in fact ritual performances, having varying but real connections with the audience's religious practice.[2] We find similar debates about early modern tragedy. Still, no one doubts that within these plays, whatever their links to everyday beliefs, the divine underwrites the tragic world. And from at least since George Steiner's *Death of Tragedy* (1961), we have seen drama from the Romantic period forward as lacking that necessary providential grounding. If tragedy had traditionally offered a struggle between a heroic human and the gods or God, tragic drama in the Romantic period came to be located elsewhere, in a struggle with history or with society or, perhaps most interestingly, with a post-providential world that might appear meaningless or absurd. The challenges to traditional beliefs—from the French Revolution's disestablishment of the Catholic Church to the work of Charles Darwin and beyond—meant that the presence of religion, particularly in tragedy as the key form of "serious" drama, was bound to be controversial and ideologically laden; and, of course, many playwrights we identify as Romantics and their inheritors had their own religious doubts and heterodox visions.

Defenders of religion had perhaps always doubted the propriety of treating matters of faith in literature, of offering sacred truths in the guise of fiction. Samuel Johnson's comments in his *Life of Cowley* are representative:

> Sacred history has been always read with submissive reverence, and an imagination overawed and controlled. We have been accustomed to acquiesce in the nakedness and simplicity of the authentick narrative, and to repose on its veracity with such humble confidence as suppresses curiosity. We go with the historian as he goes, and stop with him when he stops. All amplification is frivolous and vain; all addition to that which is already sufficient for the purposes of religion seems not only useless, but, in some degree, profane.[3]

This squeamishness about representing religion in literature becomes particularly pronounced when the text is to be spoken from the stage. Part of the "antitheatrical prejudice" exhaustively examined by Jonas Barish arose from concerns, expressed from Plato to the Puritans and beyond, that the fictional show of the theater mocked and distorted the truth that passes show.[4] In England, the theatrical censors during the Romantic period, particularly John Larpent but also George Colman the Younger, sought to ban religion from the stage, even positive representations.[5] We see Larpent removing quite trivial religious references from plays, as when he insists on striking the word "Halleluiah" sung at the close of Act 4 of Matthew Gregory Lewis's *The Castle Spectre* (Drury Lane, 1797), which was then replaced by "Jubilate."[6] When James Boaden came to stage Lewis's *The Monk*, he ran into greater difficulties, even after removing all of the novel's supernatural trappings: Michael Kelly, the play's composer, notes that "many thought it indecorous to represent a church on stage"; Boaden himself reports that the Duke of Leeds objected to having an actor portray a man of the cloth, "avow[ing] that his *religious feelings* hardly allowed him to tolerate the powerful effects, which he saw produced upon the stage."[7] Michael Gamer has summarized the critical concerns regularly expressed about putting religion and the supernatural in the theaters, with "Anglican critics condemning representation of spirits as a blasphemous turn to the idolatries of popery; and rationalist critics dismissing them as invasive, unenlightened barbarism."[8]

The representation of the supernatural on the English stage was a particularly vexed issue because, as Gamer's analysis suggests, either one saw the supernatural and thus perhaps the sacred as belonging to an earlier unenlightened time, an infamy to be erased, or one offered the supernatural as a glimpse of the numinous that could not be confined by standard theological frameworks. If ghosts are a fiction, why not the Holy Ghost? If supernatural spirits smack of popery or evoke pre-Christian superstitions, perhaps they point to a power outside of, say, Anglicanism. The controversy over how to stage ghosts is one sign of these concerns, with even the precedent of Hamlet's father being insufficient to protect Boaden from criticism when he introduced a ghost in *Fontainville Forest* (Covent Garden, 1794), his adaptation of Ann Radcliffe's *Romance of the Forest* (1791), not to mention when George Colman included an animated skeleton in *Blue-Beard* (Drury Lane, 1798).

Depictions of the supernatural were linked in the critics' minds with portrayals of morally questionable characters and with what were seen as espousals of atheism. In *The Monthly Mirror*'s review of *The Castle Spectre*, for example, we find, alongside concerns about the propriety of introducing a ghost, additional objections to the villain-hero Osmond's "*Atheism*" and to his use of religious language: "The licenser, if he had known the intention of his office, would have *struck his pen* across such expressions as '*Saviour of the world*,' '*God of Heaven*,' etc."[9] This supposed atheism is often linked to what is called the "German" drama, a term reviewers used to discuss both translated plays by Johann Wolfgang von Goethe, Friedrich Schiller, and particularly August von Kotzebue, and the gothic drama as a whole. *The Rovers; or, The Double Arrangement*, a wonderful satire on the "German" drama published in the *Anti-Jacobin*, argues that these plays require a new "SYSTEM comprehending not Politics only, and Religion, but Morals and Manners, and generally whatever goes to the composition or holding together of Human Society; in all of which a total change and Revolution is absolutely necessary."[10] Such moral revolutions and the gothicized villain-heroes who espouse them are found throughout the drama of the Romantic period and beyond. For example, while Samuel Taylor Coleridge, in his attack upon Charles Robert Maturin's *Bertram; or, The Castle of*

St. Aldobrand (Drury Lane, 1816), would also object to German morals and gothic supernaturalism and while William Wordsworth, in the preface to *Lyrical Ballads*, would attack "sickly and stupid German Tragedies," both of them in their tragedies present characters in the mold of Lewis's Osmond. In *The Borderers*, Wordsworth's Oswald, whom we are told is overcome with "A sudden blankness" when he hears "the name of God," tries to lure Marmaduke into relying upon "an independent Intellect," to exploring "a region of futurity, / Whose natural element was freedom," freedom from morality and religion in particular.[11] Ordonio, in Coleridge's *Remorse*, explains that "Nature had made him for some other planet . . . In this world / He found no fit companion;" in his isolation, he has found "Something within [that] would still be shadowing out / All possibilities."[12] Both characters find that their radical intellectual independence leads them to justify murder, as Wordsworth and Coleridge explore a kind of atheist's tragedy.

One way to try to treat religion in a less contested way was to historicize it. One tradition of historical tragedy in the nineteenth century did so by representing the end of the medieval period and the beginning of the early modern era as a crisis in religious authority, institutions, and belief. From Goethe and Schiller to Henrik Ibsen and George Bernard Shaw, plays evoke the rise of Protestantism and the collapse of a unified European Catholicism to suggest we are living in a time of religious uncertainty, perhaps in a post-providential moment. Goethe and Schiller returned time and again—in *Goetz von Berlichingen* (1773) and *Egmont* (1788), in *Don Carlos* (1787) and *Wallenstein* (1800)— to the wars of religion and the rise of nationalism as the Church and the Holy Roman Empire no longer have the power to order life, in a preview of the French Revolution's abolition of the monarchy and disestablishment of the Church. Shaw, revisiting after Schiller the story of Joan of Arc, makes explicit the historical implications of such moments. The debate in scene 4 of *Saint Joan* (1923) has Bishop Cauchon interpret Joan's message as posing the same threat as Mohammed, offering a heretical reinterpretation of the Judeo-Christian tradition that emphasizes individual conscience, while the Earl of Warwick accuses her of espousing a kind of blood-and-soil nationalism that would unite individuals with their king. As Warwick sums it up, "These two ideas of hers are the same idea at bottom. It goes deep, my lord. It is the protest of the individual soul against the interference of priest or peer between the private man and his God. I should call it Protestantism if I had to find a name for it." Cauchon responds, "To her the French-speaking people are what the Holy Scriptures call a nation. Call this side of her heresy Nationalism if you will."[13] The old order—that had provided the social structure to define the hero as Chaucer's man of "high estate" and the providential order to place limits on heroic action—goes up in the flames that engulf Joan at her death.

Other playwrights stage the earlier power of church and state to expose their corruption and to suggest the political and religious oppressions of the present. As Stuart Curran among others has noted, *The Cenci* (1819) was surely the British Romantic play most likely to succeed on the London stage; yet, Percy Bysshe Shelley's play never could be submitted by a theater for licensing because the censor would certainly have blocked its performance for its depiction of religion, not to mention incestuous rape.[14] Set in Renaissance Italy, *The Cenci* explores an interlocked set of patriarchal oppressors: God, the Pope, and Count Cenci as lord and father. While the play focuses on the crimes of Cenci and their consequences, it is clear that state and ecclesiastical power stands behind his outrages; more than one character even speculates that God the Father stands as Cenci's ally. The first scene makes palpable the interconnections of these Blakean Nobodaddies.[15] Cardinal Camillo explains to Count Cenci that the Pope has accepted a bribe to cover up a murder Cenci has committed. We learn that the cardinal has claimed "that you have half reformed me," so that Cenci has no qualms about telling him about his various sexual and violent actions.[16] Camillo's response is to hide behind his religion: "Hell's most abandoned fiend / Did never, in the drunkenness of guilt, / Speak to his heart as now you speak to me; / I thank my God that I believe you not" (1.1.117–20). We learn later that the Pope, to whom one of Cenci's sons appeals for help, stands with the father against the son: "In the great war between the old and young / I, who have white hairs and a tottering body, / Will keep at least blameless neutrality" (2.2.38–40). Believing himself as God's scourge on earth (4.1.63), Cenci sees his saintly daughter as "A rebel to her father and her God" (4.1.90).

After Beatrice arranges the murder of her father, she is condemned by an ecclesiastical court that uses torture on witnesses. Camillo once more appeals to the Pope who again asserts his sympathy for the devilish father. In the face of this unremitting hierarchy of male power, Beatrice imagines a hellish universe: "If there should be / No god, no Heaven, no Earth in the void world; / The wide, gray, lampless, deep, unpeopled world! / If all things then should be ... my father's spirit" (5.4.57–60). While in her last moments Beatrice turns from this vision of eternal oppression to embrace female solidarity, the play indicts a society where male power is seen as entrenched from the domestic hearthstone to the heavens. To free herself, Beatrice would effectively have to kill not just her father but the entire system of "fathers," from priests and cardinals to the Pope (*il Papa*, in Italian) himself.

Alfred de Musset depicted a similarly oppressive world in *Lorenzaccio*, also set in Renaissance Florence at another moment of transition and of threats to the old order. The play takes place after the fall of the Republic and centers on the rise of the Medicis, a new kind, even *nouveau riche* kind, of dynasty though still backed by church and state, the Holy Roman Emperor and the Pope. While Alexandre de Medicis is more interested in sex than violence, he still relies upon brutal power: "It does no good for the Florentine families to cry out, or for the people and the merchants to protest: the Medicis govern by means of a garrison ... a bastard, half a Medici, a boor that heaven created for a butcher boy or a farm hand, corrupts our daughters, drinks our wine, smashes our windows."[17] In revolt against his society, Lorenzaccio understands that he battles political and religious power and even God himself: "When I was going to kill Clement VII, a price was put on my head in Rome. Now that I've killed Alexandre, naturally there's a price on my head all over Italy. If I were to leave Italy, I'd be hunted all over Europe, and at my death the Good God wouldn't fail to post my eternal condemnation at every crossroads of the universe" (5.6.617–23, 91). The play closes by reasserting the powers that be, as a new Medici is crowned and as it becomes clear that the real power in Florence will be the perpetually plotting Cardinal Cibo.

The world of Ibsen's *Brand* (1866), set in eighteenth-century Norway may seem far from the Catholic and Italian settings of *The Cenci* and *Lorenzaccio* or the early modern moments in *Egmont* or *Don Carlos*. Still, Ibsen offers perhaps an even more daring account of the demise of the power of traditional religion, for he has Brand stand against modern Protestantism rather than stage Catholicism. The issue is set forth in the first act when Brand comes upon his old schoolmate, Ejnar, who declares that his love for Agnes lies beyond the conventions of religion: "Without a priest, our lives were declared free / Of sorrow, and consecrated to happiness."[18] Ejnar proclaims his faith in God, but he wants to pursue that faith outside the strictures of an organized church and to see God as embracing beauty and love. Brand, a "mission preacher," comes, like Nietzsche's madman, to proclaim the death of Ejnar's God as a projection of human desires:

Brand: . . . I am going to a burial feast.
Agnes: To a burial feast?
Ejnar: Who is to be buried?
Brand: That God you have just called yours.
Agnes: Come, Ejnar.
Ejnar: Brand!
Brand: The God of every dull and earth-bound slave
Shall be shrouded and coffined for all to see
And lowered into his grave. It is time, you know.
He has been ailing for a thousand years.

—1, 59

While Ejnar's God allows him "to flirt, / And play and laugh," while only paying "lip service to your faith" (1, 59), Brand puts forth a new vision of God embodied in his catchphrase, "All or Nothing." Refusing to comfort his mother or protect his son, Brand rejects any notion that God is "humane" (3, 101). God, for Brand, is exactly the inhuman, the incomprehensible. In the final act, he rejects all the representatives, secular and religious, who stand for a traditional, consoling God—the Mayor, the Provost, the Schoolmaster. He leaves behind the physical church of his parishioners to enter into the Ice Church of the lunatic, Gerd. There he dies in an avalanche, Gerd shrieking in terror and Brand still asking, "If not by Will, how can Man be redeemed?" (5, 157). The answer, perhaps echoing the end of *Faust*, is "He is the God of Love." As in *The Cenci*, a hope appears, but the play has been dominated by a sense that the old religion is dying without a new one having been born. Whether depicting the destructive power of religion or tracking the historical decline of that power, these plays suggest that tragic drama exists in a world no longer defined by conventional religion.

This questioning of traditional beliefs does not mean that religion and myth do not appear in nineteenth-century plays. Quite to the contrary: moving beyond the confines of conventional systems of faith, these playwrights embrace a medley of mythical and religious systems, sometimes experimenting with alternatives to traditional religion, sometimes suggesting through comparative mythology and religion that all belief systems are human creations open to critique. I opened this essay with a quotation from Strindberg that suggests that a complete break with organized religion, a lack of conventional belief, enables the individual to "become something." Nineteenth-century tragic drama can be seen as leaving behind traditional religious structures that underwrote earlier tragedy in order to become something new. Byron, for example, offers in *Manfred* (1817) what he called "a mixed mythology of my own," what the *Literary Gazette* saw as a "heterogeneous assemblage of mythology."[19] Traditional Catholicism is embodied in the figure of the Abbot, who in Byron's original version is mocked and dragged off by the demon Ashtaroth. While his dignity is restored in the final version of the play, the Abbot's religion has no hold on Manfred. Neither do the devils who come, as in various Faust dramas, to haul him off to hell; like the Abbot, these are repulsed by Manfred who asserts, "The hand of death is on me—but not yours."[20] On *Manfred*'s sources, the *Critical Review* noted, that Byron drew "at once from the Grecian, Persian, and Gothic mythology," particularly in the body of the play.[21] Thus, in Act 2, we get Nemesis and the Three Destinies or Fates from classical mythology. The Witch of the Alps appears earlier in Act 2 as a supernatural spirit of a natural place, while Arimanes arrives at the end of the act to suggest a turn to Zoroastrianism. This kind of comparative religion run wild ends up by suggesting that no providential order, no mythological system, is sufficient to describe the complexity of human life. The struggle of Manfred and his fellow Romantic tragic heroes is to discover an order for life that does not depend upon conventional notions of heaven and hell, good and evil.

Strindberg himself shows the strong pull towards some system of belief or myth. He may have left behind the pietistic Lutheranism of his mother, but he clearly engages the Christian tradition in plays such as *Easter* (1901) and the three-part *To Damascus* (1898, 1904). In the latter play, one immediately notes the allusion to Paul's conversion, to the stages of the Cross, and to the tradition of medieval mystery and morality plays, particularly, *Everyman*.[22] Blending Emmanuel Swedenborg, the eighteenth-century Swedish scientist and mystic who also influenced Blake, with Catholic imagery, Strindberg offers a pilgrimage towards a possible hope and faith but certainly not a conventional one. And it is not only to the Judeo-Christian tradition that Strindberg turns. *A Dream Play* (1910), drawing on Hinduism, tracks the journey of Indra's Daughter who is incarnated on earth in order to understand human life. She re-enacts what she defines as a primal fall:

> In the dawn of time, before your sun gave light, Brahma, the divine primal force let himself be seduced by Maya, the World Mother, that he might propagate. This mingling of the divine element with the earthly was the Fall from heaven. This world, its life and its inhabitants are therefore only a mirage, a reflection, a dream image . . . But in order to be freed from the earthly element, the descendants of Brahma sought renunciation and suffering.[23]

Having come to understand human life as suffering, the Daughter returns to heaven. The Castle that has stood throughout the play as an emblem of our entrapment in life bursts into flame as a giant chrysanthemum blossoms, perhaps as a symbol of rebirth. Again, the final scene of Strindberg's *Ghost Sonata* includes in its set a *"large seated Buddha, in whose lap rests a bulb from which rises the stem of a shallot . . . bearing its globular cluster of white, starlike flowers."*[24] The play ends with the Student praising "You wise and gentle Buddha, sitting there waiting for a Heaven to sprout from the earth," before offering a prayer that combines Buddhist and Christian imagery. This religiously eclectic play closes on an image of Böcklin's painting of *The Island of the Dead* (five versions, 1880–6), with its combination of classical and Christian imagery. Where Byron in *Manfred* uses a form of comparative religion to suggest that all religions are, if not false, incomplete, inadequate, Strindberg suggests that all religions are one in their gesturing towards some sort of hope on the far side of suffering.

It is perhaps the return to classical myth that is strongest in nineteenth-century drama, from Goethe and Schiller to Shelley and Algernon Charles Swinburne. The range and complexity of these efforts needs to be noted. Schiller, for example, in *The Bride of Messina* (1803)—set in Sicily "perhaps around the year 1060"[25]—attempts a direct recuperation of Greek tragedy, offering a Greek chorus and seeking to create a tragedy of fate. In his prefatory essay "On the Use of the Chorus in Tragedy," however, he notes that "I have represented the Christian religion and Greek mythology as intermingled, and have even suggested Moorish superstition" (11–12). Even as he evokes the formal restraints of Greek drama, Schiller still engages in the same eclectic sampling of religion we find in quite different plays by Byron or Strindberg. While Schiller, Byron, and Strindberg juxtapose varying religious from pagan mythology to Christianity to Islam and Hinduism, Shelley blends the classical with contemporary history. In his preface to *Hellas* (1822), he notes that, while he directly imitates Aeschylus' *Persae* in order to offer a *"goat song"* that he imagines being "recited on the Thespian wagon to an Athenian village at the Dionysiaca," he must rely upon "newspaper erudition" to depict the "events of the moment" in the Greek fight for independence.[26] His satiric *Oedipus Tyrannus, or Swellfoot the Tyrant, A Tragedy in Two Acts* (1820) claims to be "translated from the original Doric," but is, in fact, a riff on Sophocles in order to comment on the political fight between George IV and his queen.[27] *Prometheus Unbound* (1819) may not refer so directly to the news of the day, but Shelley completely reworks both the form and vision of his precursor, Aeschylus, in order to offer a revolutionary vision for his time.

Goethe's *Iphigenia in Tauris* (three versions, 1779, 1781, 1786) stands as a particularly strong reworking and rethinking of Greek tragedy and myth. Goethe does not attempt as did Schiller to recreate the Greek chorus, but he does adhere to the so-called unities. At the same time, he does as did Shelley completely reimagine his Greek source, in this case the tragedy by Euripides. Before the play opens, Iphigenia's father Agamemnon has agreed to sacrifice his daughter in order to appease the gods who have becalmed the Greek fleet, blocking their progress to Troy. In fact, Artemis has rescued her and secreted her in a temple in Tauris, considered by the Greeks as a barbarian land and defined in the play by its custom of sacrificing any strangers who land upon its shore. The king of the Tauridians, Thoas, respects Iphigenia and has allowed her to suspend the bloody sacrifice, but he now wishes to marry her, threatening to return to the old custom if she refuses. Iphigenia's brother, Orestes, who has killed their mother, Clytemnestra, for her murder of their father, arrives in disguise at Tauris with his friend Pylades. Orestes has come under the command of Apollo who has said he will free Orestes from the Furies that pursue him if Orestes will return to Greece the statue of Apollo's sister, Diana, from the temple at Tauris.

The play seems to be moving towards a moment when Iphigenia must sacrifice her brother, continuing the pattern of familial murder that has marked the Tantalids. She relates the story of her family's repeated claims to greatness and repeated catastrophes in the first act, as she tells Thoas of Tantalus, welcomed the table of the gods, only to be cast down by them, of the violent horrors of Pelops, Atreus, and Thyestes, and then of Agamemnon's sacrifice of her. The Tantalids in seeing themselves heroic equals to the gods have blinded themselves to the bonds and boundaries of human relationships, those of host and guest and of family. The "Parzenlied" or "Song of the Fates" that closes the fourth act provides a generalizing account of the Tantalid curse that places all humankind in a bind:

> In fear of the gods let
> The race of man stand!
> Dominion they hold
> In hands everlasting,
> With power to use it,
> As they may see fit.
>
> One whom they exalt
> Should fear them twice over.
> On the cliffs and on clouds
> Are chairs set out ready
> At tables of gold.

> If discord arises,
> The guests may be cast,
> Abused and dishonored,
> To depths of the dark
> And there wait in vain,
> Amid gloom and in fetters,
> For judgment with justice.
>
> Those others, however,
> Sit endlessly feasting
> At tales of gold.
> And striding from mountain
> Across unto mountain,
> They scent from the chasms
> The smoking breath
> Of the stifling Titans
> Like a thin cloud of odor
> Up-wafting from sacrifice.
>
> These rulers avert
> The eyes of their blessing
> From whole generations,
> Declining to see
> In the grandson the grandsire's
> Once well-beloved features
> Now mute but eloquent.[28]

Here, the gods—able to act only as "they may see fit"—oversee an order that exists completely independent of human values, human sympathy, and human understanding. They rule without any concern for those below them, as they enjoy an endless feast, scented with the tortures of the Titans. When, as was the case with Tantalus, they raise up a human being to their level, it is only—shredding any sense of host-guest relations—to cast him down, bringing a curse down on his family. In this vision, there are only the heights inhabited by the gods and a completely fallen world populated with those they destroy.

Given this frame, we might imagine the play hurtling towards a crisis in which Iphigenia must either kill her brother or turn against Thoas, who has been her benefactor and who now loves her; she can re-enact the horrible intimacy of familial murder or the violation of host-guest bonds at the core of society. At a similar point in Euripides' play, when Iphigenia has plotted with Orestes and Pylades to escape on a boat only to be driven back to shore and a battle with the Tauridians, Athena appears onstage to order Thoas to stand down and to instruct Iphigenia and Orestes to take the statue of Artemis to her own land, to Athens. Goethe, having imitated Euripides and having offered a vision of tragic fate grounded in Greek myth, has his characters completely rewrite the oracle, freeing them from the curse of the past and, in fact, ushering in an era of humane values freed from control of the gods. While the Tantalids have lived a life of deceit—with Atreus, for example, serving Thyestes his own children, disguised as dinner—and while Pylades urges Orestes to continue to deceive the Tauridians, Orestes insists upon revealing himself to Iphigenia, "between *us* / Let there be truth" (3.1080–1). Orestes, who has been told by

Apollo that he must return Diana's statue to be freed from the Furies, finds that he is in fact cured in the arms of his sister. Where Apollo had ordered him to use violence and cunning to return the statue of his sister, Diana, Orestes realizes the true meaning of the oracle is that he has been returned to his sister, Iphigenia. He understands "the error which a god / Cast like a veil about our heads when he / Bade us set out upon our journey here" (5.2108–10). It is the human Iphigenia, not a fickle god who can "give back all things" (5.2124). In particular, Iphigenia replaces the gods' pattern of banishing guests with whom they disagree with a "guest-right." Rather than the Tauridian sacrifice of strangers to gods there will be a humane order of hospitality:

> O do not banish us. A friendly guest-right
> Must rule between us: that way
> We are not cut off forever. For you are
> As dear to me as ever was my father
> And this impression is fixed in my soul.
> And if the least among your people ever
> Brings to my ear the cadence of the voice
> I am so used to hear from you, or if
> I see the poorest man dressed in your manner,
> I shall receive him *like a god*, I shall
> Myself prepare a couch for him, myself
> Invite him to a seat beside the fire,
> Inquiring new of you and your fate.
>
> —5.2152–65; emphasis added

Writing to Schiller, Goethe called his play "devilishly humane,"[29] and that is because he has reworked Greek myth much as, say, Blake reworks Milton, finding liberation in the strictures of past traditions. If we treat each other not as the gods have treated us but as if we were all gods, then we can put an end to the violence of the Tantalids, the violence of Greek myth itself.

Taking a different reading of the classical tradition, Swinburne in writing his own version of Greek drama in *Atalanta in Calydon* (1865) sought to move beyond the "devilish" humanism of Goethe or, more directly, Shelley:

> I think it [*Atalanta*] is pure Greek, and the first poem of the sort in modern times, combining lyric and dramatic work on the old principle. Shelley's Prometheus is magnificent and un-Hellenic, spoilt too, in my mind, by the infusion of philanthropic doctrinaire views and "progress of the species;" and by what I gather from Lewes's life of Goethe the Iphigenia in Tauris must also be impregnated with modern morals and feelings. As for Professor Arnold's Merope the clothes are well enough but where has the body gone? So I thought, and still think, the field was clear for me.[30]

Using a chorus, long lyric "arias" by the main characters, and some quick dialogue exchanges, Swinburne sees himself as recreating a "true" Greek drama, and, in part, he sees himself as doing this by avoiding "modern morals and feelings," any Shelleyan sense of progress. Terry Myers has shown how Swinburne picks up passages from *Prometheus Unbound* in order to refute them, with Althæa, who dominates the play, in particular rejecting the Shelleyan ideals of hope and love.[31] In *Prometheus Unbound*, we are told that "All things are subject" to "Fate, Time, Occasion, Chance, and Change" except "eternal Love";[32] Prometheus and Asia, drawing on love and the hope it brings, are able to break free from the fated world of violence ruled by Jupiter just as Iphigenia can find a way beyond the Tantalid curse. In *Atalanta*, there is no escaping from the "chance / The gods cast lots for and shake out on us."[33] While Meleager hopes that love, particularly his love for Atalanta, can defeat the "high-seated violences," the "Wild evil, and the fire of tyrannies" that mark human life (450–2), Althæa warns "Love thou the law and cleave to things ordained" (454). She does not argue that what the gods have ordained is good or just from a human perspective: "the gods love not justice more than fate" (644). Love, far from providing a way beyond violence, is seen as violent and as leading to violence. In the choral account of the birth of Aphrodite, we learn that "they knew thee for mother of love, / And knew thee not mother of death" (760–1). Meleager's passion for Atalanta leads him to kill his uncle in her defense, which in turn leads to Althæa fulfilling her fate by causing the death of her son. As he dies, Meleager begs Atalanta to "stretch thyself upon me and touch hands / With hands and lips with lips" (2300–1). She responds: "Hail thou, but I with heavy face and feet / Turn homeward and am gone out of thine eyes" (2310–11). Love offers no respite from the destruction willed by the gods, as the chorus closes out the play:

> Who shall contend with his lords
> > Or cross them or do them wrong
> Who shall bind them as with cords?
> > Who shall tame them as with song?
> Who shall smite them as with swords?
> > For the hands of their kingdom are strong.
>
> —2312–17

Swinburne clearly feels that to revive Greek tragedy he must return to an absolute sense of fate, to a world controlled by the inscrutable dictates of the gods. He believes he can reach back beyond the Romanticism of a Goethe or a Shelley to a true classical vision. Yet, this "Greek" play repeatedly echoes the Bible, and critics have noted the influence of contemporary thinkers, including Schopenhauer, on the vision of the play. Robert Greenberg also argues that Swinburne's later classicizing play, *Erechtheus* (1876), turns from the grim fatalism of *Atalanta* to allow for hope, for progress.[34] It may even offer a kind of modern ecological vision. Swinburne strives to be "pure Greek" in his form and his embracing of fate, but his vision still engages the Romantic re-imagination of Greek tragedy.

There is, then, a great deal of engagement with religion and myth in nineteenth-century tragedy; but in the end the project of these playwrights, as I have argued elsewhere, is to discover a form of tragedy that does not rely upon religion or myth, upon a providential order or an existence governed by fate.[35] While I have tried to suggest the various ways in which these plays take up religion and myth, the most striking turn in nineteenth-century drama is towards a new kind of tragic drama that arises when the protagonists come to understand that they must define themselves in a world no longer governed by the divine. The religious eclecticism of many of these plays and the historicizing of religion in others suggest in different ways the inability of traditional religious ideas to organize the world of modern tragic drama. In fact, these tragic dramas relocate tragedy exactly in a fall from a providential, hierarchical world that defined traditional tragedy. If traditional tragedy depicted the struggles of a heroic human, trying to make sense of her or his world during a time of crisis, against a divine order that might provide sense but not a human one, then these plays pit a would-be hero, striving to create any order in a chaotic world, over against a world that might be incapable of being ordered. Oedipus seeks to find the solution to the plague imposed on Thebes just as he had previously solved the riddle of the Sphinx. He posits himself as the one who can heal his society. But the order of the gods, as embodied in the oracle, has other plans: Oedipus is the cause of the plague, not its solution. His heroic attempt to avoid destruction, his struggle to find a human path beyond the devastation willed by the gods, results only in death and destruction. Hamlet confronts a world that is out of joint and he understands it as his cursed duty to set it right. Seeking to reclaim his place in his society, he would offer himself as its heroic savior, but he finds that his role is to purge his world of all those who contribute to the sickness at the heart of his society, including himself. He willingly goes to his death, believing that God has ordered it, as there is providence even in the fall of a sparrow. By the nineteenth century, in the place of *Oedipus*, we have Schiller's *Bride of Messina*, which demonstrates the difficulties of reviving classical notions of fate. In the place of Hamlet we have Musset's Lorenzaccio.

Lorenzaccio is one of the more memorable of the would-be Hamlets in the nineteenth-century drama. Where Hamlet exists in a world that, while in crisis, supports his heroic role as the king's son, the "observ'd of all observers," Lorenzo de Medici lives, as we have seen, in a world corrupted by the oppression of the Pope and the Emperor. Where Hamlet dons a mask to navigate his troubled world, Lorenzo appears to us first in his disguise as Lorenzaccio because he has no heroic identity to conceal, only an identity he would create. Or, as I have put it elsewhere, "[t]here is no way for Lorenzo to establish a heroic identity within his decadent society.... Musset's departure from the model of *Hamlet* points to the crucial difference between the traditional figure like Hamlet who *is* a hero and the Romantic protagonist who wants *to become* a hero."[36] While many critics have noted the similarities between Musset's play and Shakespeare's, in the end the meaning of the play lies in the *distance* it takes from the traditional model of tragedy.

Schiller's *Bride of Messina*, as we have seen, is his closest imitation of Greek tragedy. The play opens, as in Sophocles' tragedy, with a city in crisis; here, Messina has been ripped apart by civil war between Isabella's two sons, Don Manuel and Don Cesar, who have allowed childhood rivalries to erupt in violence at the death of their father. Like Oedipus, Isabella, claiming to be "Obedient to Necessity" (1.1.1), offers herself to the chorus, and thus the city, as the solution to their problem. But, where his problem is that he cannot escape an inevitable order determined by the gods, hers is that she can see no order to her world. Isabella stands forth like Oedipus to solve the violence afflicting her city. She has also, like Oedipus, tried to provide her life with a human shape by rejecting an oracle. He, of course, learns that he is fated to murder his father and marry his mother, so he leaves the only home he has known, not realizing that he has been raised by adopted parents; his attempt to evade the gods leads him back to Thebes, murdering his father on the way and taking his mother, the queen, as his wife. Isabella's husband, meanwhile, has received an oracle from a Moorish seer (2.2.1318–19), who interprets a dream as indicating that Manuel's and Cesar's sister, Beatrice, will lead to their destruction: the image is of them as two laurels and her as a lily between that bursts into flame and sets them on fire. Isabella, by contrast, consults a monk "well loved of God" (2.2.1348) who reads the dream as indicating the daughter will bind together the two warring brothers through the "heat of ardent love" (2.2.1352). Isabella takes his words as coming from the "God of Truth," while the Moor is seen serving the "god of lies" (2.2.1354–5), and hides

Beatrice in a convent. It is not clear if Isabella makes her choice on the basis of religious preference or self-interest.

We see here the result of the mixed religious world Schiller has self-consciously constructed. There is no clear divine order here. As in *Iphigenia*, there is only human interpretation. There may be a great deal of language invoking the fated world of Greek tragedy, but the world of Messina is closer to that of gothic romance, where the "call of blood" leads Manuel and Cesar, as they separately discover Beatrice without knowing who she is, to fall in love with her. If this play took the form of a romance, the characters would realize that their interest in one another is filial rather than erotic, and they could end the play being shuffled offstage to marry appropriate mates. Here, Cesar, who has only glimpsed her from afar, comes to learn that Beatrice loves Manuel and, before any explanations can be made, he murders his brother in jealousy. At the close of the play, he commits suicide in order, he claims, to end the curse. Isabella, unlike Oedipus, stands at the close of the play having lost complete control of the action. Her heroic attempt to make herself and remake her world has not just failed; it has become irrelevant. She is neither the heroic human who saves her society nor the one cursed by the gods who still struggles to make meaning of an inhuman world. The active character at the end of the play is the fratricide, a villain-hero, a figure akin to Byron's Cain in historical dress.

Byron's *Cain* (1821) and *Heaven and Earth* (1821) do exactly what Samuel Johnson and the British government's theatrical censor wanted to prohibit: the direct representation onstage of stories from divine scripture. While neither appeared in the theater of the day, it comes as no surprise that *Cain* provoked shocked protest and that *Heaven and Earth* did not appear under the imprint of Byron's usual publisher, John Murray, but rather in Leigh Hunt's journal *The Liberal*. In these plays, Byron imports the era's religious eclecticism and skepticism directly into Biblical stories. *Heaven and Earth*, labeled as a "mystery" rather than a "tragedy" and offering apocalyptic disaster in the place of the fall of an individual hero, takes up a passage in Genesis, offered as the play's first epigraph, where we learn "that the sons of God saw the daughters of men that they were fair, and they took them wives of all which they chose."[37] On the eve of the Flood, Samiasa and Azaziel appear to claim Anah and Aholibamah, descendants of Cain. Anah is loved by Noah's son, Japhet, a descendant of Seth who will be saved from the flood. After Noah warns the women that they are repeating the sins of Cain and Raphael proclaims that the angels are re-enacting the revolt of Lucifer, the two couples fly off to escape the Flood, as "*The waters rise; Men fly in every direction; many are overtaken by the waves; the Chorus of Mortals disperses in search of safety up the mountains; Japhet remains upon a rock, while the Ark floats towards him at a distance*" (3.929). While ostensibly a straightforward account of God's destruction of the world by water as a result of man's sins, the underlying framework of the play seems to roam from conventional monotheism. For example, we learn that Noah believes that the light cast by the arrival of the angels comes from "the moon / Rising to some sorcerer's tune" (1.140–1). Japhet, lovesick, goes "to the cavern, whose / Mouth they say opens from the internal world / To let the inner spirits walk the earth" (2.41–3), and he is greeted there by a troop of undefined spirits who rejoice at the coming destruction of humanity. The religious eclecticism of *Manfred* seeps into the play and allows for the characters to dispute the nature and power of the divine, with the descendants of Cain and those of Seth having quite different visions of their God and with the Angels and the women whom they choose arguing that love is more important than obedience to God's will: as Aholibamah proclaims, "where is the impiety of loving / Celestial natures" (1.9–10); for his part Samiasa contends that he worships God by

"Adoring him in this least of works display'd" (3.525). The lovers choose what they are told will be eternal exile and revolt rather than remaining to "Survive in mortal or immortal thrall" (3.628). The play may swerve from tragedy in allowing the central characters to escape, but their love can exist only on some world other than the "chaos-founded prison" that is earth (3.813).

Byron wrote a tragic drama for Anah's and Aholibamah's progenitor, Cain. In one of the boldest takes on religion in the period, Byron suggests that we might live in a world where God is dead. *Cain* opens on "The Land Without Paradise," with the pun putting the action outside of Eden but perhaps also in a world without redemption.[38] Cain appears as a kind of Old Testament version of Beckett's Vladimir and Estragon, waiting for a sign that God is still engaged with the post-lapsarian world. Cain rejects his parents' acquiescence in their punishment, their demand that he "Content thee with what *is*" (1.1.45), their willingness to worship a God that Cain sees as all powerful but not necessarily good (1.1.64–80). With God refusing to show himself, Cain is open to the overture from Lucifer who attempts to recruit Cain into his revolt. Lucifer claims to bring a truth that will set Cain free, but it can only be attained through a loss of love: "Choose betwixt love and knowledge—since there is / No other choice: your sire hath chosen already / His worship is but fear" (1.1.426–8). Adah, Cain's sister and wife, urges him to choose love, arguing that they can find a new paradise in one another: "Why wilt thou always mourn for Paradise? / Can we not make another? . . . / where'er thou art, I feel not / The want of this much regretted Eden" (3.1.37–40). But, as Lucifer tells Cain, the love he bears for Adah, while necessary at a time when the only mates are siblings, will in later times be labeled as incestuous, as Manfred knows. Lucifer argues instead for an absolute independence of the self, grounded in a willingness to know even the most terrifying of things. Taking Cain into the Abyss of Space (2.2), Lucifer shows Cain that earth with its Paradise is in the infinity of space like the firefly in a nighttime sky. He also rejects the supposedly unique story of man's fall and potential redemption, arguing that this is but one moment in a long history, as he shows him, in Hades, "What thou dar'st not deny,—the history / Of past, and present, and of future worlds" (2.1.24–5). In the place of a providential order, there is deep time and an everlasting universe of things. Against, this apparently meaningless world, Lucifer would pit the independent intellect, the self:

> *One good* gift has the fatal apple given—
> Your *reason*:—let it not be over-sway'd
> By tyrannous threats to force you into faith
> 'Gainst all external sense and inward feeling:
> Think and endure,—and form an inner world
> In your own bosom—where the outward fails;
> So shall you nearer be the spiritual
> Nature, and war triumphant with your own.
>
> —2.2.459–66

Inhabiting a kind of Sartrean world where hell is the other, Lucifer urges the absolute self as the only source of meaning.

Still, Cain longs for something more. He returns from his voyages with Lucifer to join his brother Abel in making a sacrifice to Adam's God, with Abel sacrificing a lamb and Cain offering the fruits he has raised from the soil. His prayer (3.1.245–79) is a plea that God reveal himself. When the flames from Abel's altar rise to the heavens and a wind comes to scatter the fruit of Cain's sacrifice, Abel is convinced that God has shown him favor and indicated his displeasure with Cain; but Cain, much like Orestes and Iphigenia reinterpreting Apollo's oracle in Goethe's play, contends that the return of the fruits of the soil back to the earth is appropriate. There is no divine revelation, only human interpretation. Still trying to provoke God to reveal himself, Cain moves to destroy Abel's altar, offering himself as a sacrifice if necessary. Of course, it is Abel who dies, as Cain strikes him with a brand from the altar. It is only now that an *"Angel of the Lord"* (3.1.467) appears to mark Cain's brow, to define him as the first murderer and a permanent exile.

While Byron offers *Cain* and *Heaven and Earth* as "mystery" plays, quite different from the historical tragic dramas he penned in, say, *Marino Faliero, Doge of Venice* (1821) or *Sardanapalus* (1821), the radical thrust of these plays is still to convert the religious stories into history. The Flood in *Heaven and Earth* appears apocalyptic, but human history will go on, and the angels and their lovers will find a world elsewhere. Cain is made to see that the life he knows, where he could find in his love for his sister Adah a counterweight to Lucifer's isolated rationality, will, in the course of history, be labeled as incestuous. He departs from the play to enter into a history of suffering without redemption, East of Eden. There is no recourse to God for Cain, and, by extension, we must make our way in the Land without Paradise, the time without an end; we live in historical time and not in the great three beat story of fall, redemption, and end of days. From Schiller and Goethe to Byron and Shelley, Musset and Georg Büchner, Shaw and Bertolt Brecht, history is the heartland of modern tragic drama. Schiller, in particular, had relocated tragic drama in the struggle to make sense of history, with the fact that history is always shaped by forces greater than any one individual supplying something akin to the power of fate without it having any providential plot behind it. Religion and myth play vital roles in the tragic drama of the era, but in the end they too are historical formations, limited attempts to make sense of things that will pass with the passage of time.

CHAPTER SIX

Politics of City and Nation

MICHAEL MEEUWIS

We know from Benedict Anderson that the nineteenth century was the age of the nation-state.[1] From the census, one of the century's typifying inventions, we know that these nation-states formed alongside the widespread move into cities. Rural life now served the domestic culture of the city. Thomas Hardy's Tess is perhaps the most famous literary character who contemplates the "whirl of material progress" in which milk from her Wessex dairy participates. "Londoners will drink it at their breakfasts to-morrow, won't they?" she exclaims: "Strange people that we have never seen."[2] Milk establishes that Tess's world and that of the city are one and the same. Her subsequent tragedy is inflected by the fact that she cannot be singular. For Hardy the onward move of society, its constant new growth, will keep producing repetitive tragedies—as his conclusion, with Angel Clare married to a "budding" replacement for Tess, confirms.[3] I rehearse these familiar narratives in order to consider them from a new angle: specifically, that of the tragedies written specifically to address the imagination of these newly consolidated populations organized into cities and states. New nineteenth-century stage tragedy is cluttered by domestic objects and the networks that support them. These are fated to outlast the action of the tragedy itself.

This enduring clutter reframes these tragedies' human elements, particularly with regard to tragic *waste*. An object-oriented network looks at waste differently: as part of the system, and as a necessary support rather than the distinct negative *telos* A.C. Bradley invokes when he describes one aspect of tragedy, historically, as a depiction of "the waste of good."[4] Rather than invoking irreconcilable loss or abjection, object culture makes nineteenth-century tragedy more efficient: less is lost when a tragedy occurs amidst a stable object-world. I link this reframing of waste to the demographic trend in nineteenth-century political theory that relentlessly mapped and quantified populations and spaces. Statistical mapping meant that no human action could be truly abject: a suicide became a statistic, a murder a cause for social concern. Like the ever-more-detailed interior walls that appeared in later-century maps of major cities, stage properties set stable frames around tragic actions, limiting the abjection of what could be within.

Plays in performance are by necessity closer to contemporary domestic object-worlds than are plays in reading. Other essays in this volume address how nineteenth-century closet tragedies depict the "intellectual independence" of strongly individuated protagonists finding themselves at odds with their societies. Placing these same tragedies on a stage with living actors adds a new component: a web of object relations that threaten or even overthrow the psychological individuation of human subjects. Things often direct tragic denouements. Virginia, the daughter of a dead Roman nobleman, returns to the stage as an urn in James Sheridan Knowles' *Virginius* (1820); an obstreperous lamp lights the tragic unveilings of Henrik Ibsen's *Ghosts* (1882).

Indeed "theater" itself became a different kind of commodity in the late nineteenth century: one produced by national and even internationally circulating syndicates, rather than by small companies.[5] Industrial expansion meant that more tragedies were performed; indeed, more of nearly every genre was performed as theaters multiplied, usually through syndicates reproducing metropolitan tastes throughout individual countries and the continent as a whole. Similarly, the vast expansion of print culture, bringing with it new widely accessible translations of Greek and Roman texts in most European countries, meant that wider audiences could read classical tragedy.[6] Renaissance tragedies, too, were now more generally available. Audiences who wanted to find abject characters could find them somewhere, even if the drive to standardization that defined most syndicate-driven, nineteenth-century theaters meant that they were as likely to encounter them in the pages of a book.

Standardization also meant that—in these cities that also supported the theaters—the lives of their citizens became more alike than ever before. This was true both within and between nations as certain experiences became increasingly common to all city-dwellers, regardless of country. From this newly heightened similarity came the Marxian perspective of class progression and struggle as standardized across all nations.[7] Consumer culture realized this similarity in the lives of these newly standardized millions. The bourgeois of London and Paris, or the workers of Strasbourg or Belgrade, might aspire to the same brand of soap—these aspirations set by their class level, rather than nationality. The "vast apparatus of humans and things" that Ian Hodder describes supporting urban domestic object culture, which included Tess's dairy, was coming into being.[8] This apparatus creates what Hodder terms "entanglement," wherein intensifying human effort is required to sustain objects that both enhance and drain the efforts of human civilization, leading in some cases to "entrapments in particular pathways from which it is difficult to escape."[9]

This inability to consider a tragic action as purely a one-off event is, I suggest, one of the defining and distinguishing aspects of tragedy within the century. Dominated by ideologies of collective progress, nineteenth-century stage tragedies emphasized the role of the individual *within* the collective. Whether free trader or socialist, nineteenth-century social theorists emphasized benefits to groups of people. Even when Schopenhauer denies the possibility of collective human progress, he at least responds to the idea.

Onstage objects also gesture towards units of understanding larger than those of individual human life. In nineteenth-century tragedies, objects are usually more stable, less susceptible to harm, than tragic protagonists. This is even more the case in plays intended for performance, which draw their props from a theater's limited inventory of furniture. Recurring across multiple plays and many performances, these objects at once bestow on society a present, extant shape—invoking normal everyday life, in other words. The action of the tragedy need not necessarily change this. The presence of these objects, then, emphasized the potential lack of significance of tragic events and characters: specifically, the limited ability that they had to enact meaningful social change. Consumer culture limited the ability of tragic abjection to blow a hole in social norms—and the subsequent expectation of change that this invited. While, as Matthew Buckley writes, during the times of the French Revolution, tragedy overflowed the theaters, shaping the actions of those involved in contemporary politics, in the later part of the nineteenth century the conservative pushback that these objects performed showed society as ultimately more powerful than tragic change.[10] Tragedy, then, addressed the compromises written into a collective progress seen as inevitable.

The existentialism of the 1950s reframed tragedy around the alienated, individuated outsider. When Gilles Deleuze and Félix Guattari pronounce Sophocles' Oedipus a "Greek Cain," they emphasize that wider tendency within the long history of tragedy towards designating one individual as an outcast, making them a figure of energy and interest but also an outcast from their society.[11] In contrast, a statistical understanding of a population invites a unity of comparison between everyone within it. This was the understanding of population that Thomas Malthus, among others, had invited. Within such a statistical understanding of a population, no individual could become entirely abject: every death or even suicide is given a statistical presence, and so made part of an overall tendency. I term this tendency *efficiency:* the way that tragedies made use of all of the parts of society, showing them to be part of a shared teleology. Tragic efficiency gestures towards what Hodder terms the apparatus of things: towards the shared networks of humans and objects that supported domestic life. The presence of these objects meant that these plays highlighted those tendencies in tragedy that emphasized the reconstitution of society following the death of the tragic protagonist, rather than those that emphasized the protagonist's ultimate abjection.

These props mapped the tragic mind onstage in the way that liberalism mapped populations offstage: making it stable, consistent, and representable, but no longer unique or singular. This shift took place alongside the development of that new consistency of interior self-understanding that characterized the liberal nineteenth-century state in much of the world. Ever-more-detailed maps and ever-more-expansive urban planning made the physical boundaries of household dwellings legible within the national imaginary. As Pamela Gilbert writes, nineteenth-century governance established the "ruthless equivalences of all bodies and sites," doing so without making "class or moral distinctions."[12] New stage tragedy, too, claimed no special case for the action it depicted, whether the dignity reserved for particular classes or the privacy of the unusual mind of a tragic protagonist.

In this chapter I read four plays, all premiering in America and Europe, in order to establish this effect across the global repertory of new stage tragedy. Sheridan Knowles' *Virginius* (1820), Georg Büchner's *Woyzeck* (1836–7), Leopold Lewis's 1871 translation of Erckmann-Chatrian's 1867 *Le Juif Polonais,* and Henrik Ibsen's *Ghosts* (1882). All make objects central to their plots. A similar dramatic crux appears repetitively in all four of these plays. At a key moment in their action, characters find themselves unable to make a decision about how to act. This dilemma is resolved by the onstage presence of a domestic object, which focuses the tragic protagonist's will into action—but also, simultaneously, indexes that action to a wider domestic object culture that, in turn, betokens the link between tragedy and the wider nation. I argue that, by focusing their intention through such an indexed object, these characters integrate their will with that of society.

All of these plays make object-dense domestic interiors a synecdoche for the nation. The entanglement that Hodder notes was true at the level of the state as well as that of the individual, as more of the nation's total daily activities were spent sustaining complex object-worlds. In *Virginius*, Virginia's body dies, but through her sacrifice the sort of household in which her urn can be displayed—and polished, dusted, and remarked upon—survives and prospers. Nothing is wasted, save for individual human consciousness. *Ghosts*, in contrast, shows society's forward movement as both inevitable and destructive at the same time. Society will continue to produce human waste—indeed will do so routinely, a byproduct of progress. Making the urban bourgeois interior will consume rural life, if necessary; and indeed might consume the lives of anyone living in such interiors. Individuals become like the sea creatures who make up a coral reef, leaving behind some small trace of themselves within a larger accretion of matter.

Liberalism and nineteenth-century tragedy both imagine a world without exceptional spaces or events. Tragedy's major nineteenth-century theorists treat it as a fact of existence: one from which nothing, finally, is excluded or made abject. So, Schopenhauer's universal tragedy, "the terrible side of life . . . the wail of humanity, the reign of chance and error, the fall of the just, the triumph of the wicked," makes prince and pauper alike subject to its rules.[13] Tragedies are not the result of extraordinary circumstances, like the will of the gods towards a single family. Whether in Georg Wilhelm Friedrich Hegel's optimistic account of tragedy's final reconciliation—bad for the individual, good for human progress overall—or Arthur Schopenhauer's direful account of all human life as profoundly negative, "tragedy" became a shared condition rather than the unique sufferings of a single person.[14] As Jonathan Sachs writes in chapter four of this volume, tragedy becomes the story of "an entire people" rather than a one-off action. For Franco Moretti, in effect splitting the difference, "tragic form is the paradoxical outcome of the violence required by the formation of the nation state"—which is to say, conversely, that state-formation puts tragedy's constitutive violence to some sort of use.[15] All of these theorists announce a balance between destruction and regeneration. I argue that these tragedies show object culture stabilizing this balance. Objects and the networks that support them limit what tragedy destroys to selected individuals, while at the same time providing other people with the tools for progress to continue on around them. Milk delivery will continue regardless of what happens to Tess; put another way, Tess's fate is at least in part to be reconciled into the aggregate.

TWO KNIVES: BUILDING THE BOURGEOIS OBJECT-WORLD IN *WOYZECK* AND *MISS JULIE*

Considering nineteenth-century tragedy as a whole, I find it striking that two of its defining works both represent the acquisition of objects as moments when a character becomes eligible to participate in the action of a tragedy. Georg Büchner's *Woyzeck*, although never performed during the playwright's lifetime, was written with the products of a newly "commercial" German stage in mind.[16] Within the play's provincial world, at the fringes of urban bourgeois society, objects initiate animals into humanity. A carnival barker, for example, addresses his audience: "Gentlemen! Gentlemen! Observe this creature God has created. A nothing, a mere nothing at all. But see what he has achieved; he walks upright, has a coat and trousers, carries a sword. The monkey is a soldier."[17] The "monkey" in rural nature becomes the "soldier" commanded by the authority of the nation-state centered on the city. Objects transform the unformed animal into the classified human: in a nearly literal sense they harness human animals into social service.

The soldier Woyzeck himself largely concurs with the barker's view. His initiation into object culture curbs his tendency towards the wild leaps of either imagination or madness that characterize his early scenes in the play. Addressing society, he describes poverty as being bereft of objects, and so bereft of social ends: literally of things to do with one's life. He describes himself to his Captain as standing outside bourgeois culture, looking inwards. His description suggests that he conflates bourgeois "virtue" and bourgeois objects: "Yes Captain, Virtue—I don't have that problem. We ordinary people don't have any virtue, we just follow our natures. But if I was a gentleman and had a hat and a watch and a long overcoat and could talk nicely then I'd like to be virtuous. It must be nice to have virtue, Captain, but I'm a poor man" (6). Objects create the actionable dilemmas on which "virtue" rests. "Virtue" is a shared inner and outer condition: a socially recognized mode of outward action that shapes interior "nature." Woyzeck fights not to change society but simply to enter into it by laying hold of some of the material objects that direct it.

    Woyzeck's fragmentary nature and enigmatic ending leave its human trajectory unclear. This is in part because the order of the scenes is uncertain, reconstructed as they are from Büchner's unfinished draft. But the protagonist's opacity of motive is on some level a profounder uncertainty still. We cannot say for certain what drives him, whether military discipline, the medical interventions undertaken by the Doctor, poverty, some underlying mental idiosyncrasy—or some combination of these factors. In the midst of all of this, objects present clarity. For much of the play, Woyzeck simply tells others how he does not understand himself: his dark visions, his frustrated wishes. Objects, however, provide the play with a definite tragic *telos*; and provide Woyzeck himself with a means of shaping his inchoate wishes into concrete ends. In the play's most significant onstage action, Woyzeck kills the prostitute Marie after he acquires a knife. The Jewish merchant he buys the knife from informs him that "You can get your death cheap—but not for nothing. What do you say? You'll have an economical death" (18). Acquiring the knife changes Woyzeck's death from a one-off, isolated incident into something "economical": part of a larger system. As a murder weapon, it forms Woyzeck's entrée into the world of "virtue" problems—it crystallizes his interior torment into social action, to tragic ends. Without the knife, Woyzeck is unable to act; after he acquires it, he is both a murderer and part of an "economy." The knife entangles Woyzeck in something that is larger than him, and that will outlast him.

    A similar process of object entanglement structures August Strindberg's *Miss Julie* (1888). Strindberg, too, wrote for performance: *Miss Julie* was intended to be the opening play of his new Scandinavian Experimental Theatre in Copenhagen. While Woyzeck and Marie stand at the fringes of bourgeois society, the valet Jean and the mistress he seduces into suicide stand in the midst of an object-clogged household. The pantomime scene performed by the maid Christine is the most famous example of this, as she "*Finds Miss Julie's handkerchief, which the latter has forgotten; picks it up and smells it; then, spreads it out, as though thinking of something else, stretches it, smooths it, folds it into quarters, etc.*"[18] Here the handkerchief interrupts Christine's seeming ability to "think about something else": to imagine something outside of mere object relations. She cannot resist entanglement. We see something similar in Jean's great speech clarifying the impossibility of a relationship with Julie, centered as it is on his master's boots:

> There are still barriers between us—there always will be, as long as we're in this house. There's the past, there's his lordship—I've never met anyone I respected as I do him—I only have to see his gloves on a chair and I feel like a small boy—I only have to hear that bell ring and I jump like a frightened horse—and when I see his boots standing there, so straight and proud, I cringe. (*He kicks the boots.*) Superstition—ideas shoved into our heads when we're children.

—210

Jean considers the possibility that we can escape this object-based class coding, but his employers are equally entangled. Like Woyzeck, Julie concretizes one of her most significant actions—her probable suicide—via the knife that Jean ritualistically sharpens for her. Rather than showing Jean escaping object fetishism, then, the play shows Julie succumbing to it. Both servant and master are subservient to the domestic object culture that orders their lives.

TRAGIC FURNITURE: THE CASE OF ENGLISH STAGE TRAGEDY

Why did the nineteenth-century tragic stage show characters thinking and acting in this object-led way? I next consider this question in light of English social and theatrical history; following Karl Marx, I take the case of one country's bourgeois development to extrapolate some general conclusions about Europe as a whole. Tragedy itself, in particular the possibility of tragic abjection, sits oddly with that mode of middle-class social climbing and aspirational emulation that marked, say, English bourgeois society, particularly during the so-called "High Victorian consensus" that began in the 1840s and continued in some form through to the end of the century.[19] The Victorian theater industries offered a product that modeled stable, emulative social success: one could attend the theater to see an exemplary mode of daily life demonstrated, and subsequently model what one observed there in one's own daily life.[20] The performed repertory of nineteenth-century drama on the nineteenth-century English stage was not, by and large, tragic. As Michael Booth writes, "The larger-than-life world, the metaphysical matrix and values of classical tragedy, were no longer within reach of playwrights living in a growingly materialistic, non-metaphysical England of bustling progress and rapidly changing values."[21] Whether flat-out farce, melodrama, or sensation drama, the most-performed new plays of the century tended towards happy endings and the regeneration of the societies they depicted. Even when classical tragedy was performed, Christian redemption was ultimately offered as a compensation hovering over the events occurring onstage. Thus, as Edith Hall and Fiona Macintosh write, "The identification of the Victorian conscience, founded in Christianity, with Antigone's virtue is crucial."[22] The century's dominant tendency wanted tragedy to be efficient: to redeem something or to produce some positive effect.

In England, theater in the years between 1800 and 1900 became an industry with an increasingly large hold over the life of the nation as a whole—and, so, a need to offer a consistent product to a wide range of people. As Tracy Davis notes, "Always London-centric in its aesthetic influences, production became by the end of the century almost totally centralized in the metropolis."[23] Though new tragedies were being written continuously, they appeared less frequently on this industrially standardized national stage.[24] Those that did achieve popular success, however, became long-term fixtures: Sheridan Knowles' *Virginius; or The Liberation of Rome* kicked around the stage for most of the nineteenth century. First performed in 1820, *Virginius* received at least one performance in 1830, 1840, 1846, 1848, 1850, 1853, 1854, 1856, 1862, 1868, 1880, 1881 (an "elaborate revival"[25]), and 1897; short films followed in 1909 and 1912. Harry Ritchie suggests that, in its first appearance, *Virginius* confirmed "the supremacy of a new style based on 'domesticity' and 'humanity,'" as practiced by the actor William Charles Macready.[26] It did so by uniting various classes—plebeians and commoners alike—around the emblem of a virtuous dead daughter. Most pertinent to this essay, the play shows domestic properties as finally more durable, more lasting, than the lives of human individuals.

In this, the play speaks more to the mode of domestic tragedy introduced by George Lillo's *The London Merchant* (1731) than, say, Shakespearean tragedy.[27] While in the 1820s the Greek tragic mode on the London stage predominantly "dramatized struggles against tyrants, perceived to be a broadly topical theme" owing to the contemporary Greek independence, this play's Roman mode seems much more concerned with the threat to domestic unrest still floating in the background due to the French Revolution.[28] Richard Hengist Horne notes that the play presents "Roman tunics, but a modern English heart. The scene is the Forum, but the sentiments those of the 'Bedford Arms.'"[29] *Virginius* shows the transformative, insurrectionary force that Matthew Buckley locates in the tragic genre during the French Revolution being recuperated in the name of the bourgeois and the orderly.[30] It also, significantly, makes the urban household the center of the nation—a move fundamental to how the whole of the nation, urban and rural, was imagined.

As Horne suggests, *Virginius* identifies domestic virtues, rather than the formal political process, as the crux of nation-building. Further, the play realizes these virtues through household property. This category often, ambiguously, includes people. The Roman masses, supernumeraries who flutter in and out throughout the play, are flighty and easily swayed. As the play opens, a hated Decemvirate, a ten-person panel, runs Rome. As Dentatus, a veteran soldier, claims, "No man's property is safe from them. Nay, it appears we hold their wives and daughters but by the tenure of their will."[31] Throughout the play "wives and daughters" are figured as domestic property. Indeed the Roman "liberation" to which the play's title gestures, proposes to end these infractions over private property, as well as a more general social atomism. And the play's final tableau shows private property as secure—indeed establishes that people are more secure as property than as living humans.

Knowles' Virginius might seem a vastly different character from Woyzeck. However, both plays present these figures as psychologically opaque during the onstage killings that are their most significant actions. The patrician Virginius's daughter, Virginia, has died at her father's hand. This follows the legal claim of the villainous Appius Claudius that Virginia was in fact the product of one of his household slaves, and so his property—Virginius kills her rather than allowing her to be taken and sexually possessed. The play's last scene opens with "Virginius discovered on one knee, with Appius lying dead before him": he has, it seems, strangled Appius in a fit of insanity (84). Virginius has not himself been able to summon the will to strangle his adversary; rather, the play's introduction notes, "it would have been indecent to represent him in the attitude of taking the law into his own hands. I therefore adopted the idea of his destroying Appius in a fit of temporary insanity, which gives the catastrophe the air of a visitation of Providence"(4). So this central action is not taken by the character himself, but rather by a "Providence" that is larger than him. "His senses," onstage characters note, "are benumbed": an audience surrogate at his eponymous play's climax, he requires some striking image to restore him to his senses—an image that will be provided by a household object (84).

Trying to rouse him from this fit, characters place the urn holding Virginia's cremated body in his hand, constructing the play's final tableau: "*Virginius looks alternately at Icilius and the Urn—looks at Numitorius and Lucius—seems particularly struck by his mourning—looks at the Urn again—bursts into a passion of tears, and exclaims, 'VIRGINIA!'—Falls on Icilius's neck*" (85). Around the urn, this concluding tableau presents an image of close male relations: Icilius is Virginia's former betrothed; Numitorius is Virginius's brother-in-law; and Lucius is Icilius's brother. This scene gives a version of the male familial bonds that would have formed, had Virginia not been killed. The urn stands for her absent body. It returns Virginius to his senses, provoking his "passion of tears"; it causes him to fall on another character for support, integrating him into the reconstituted social structure of this final tableau. The potential abjection of a Virginius struck numb by his actions is corrected by this final return to full emotional participation within the scene and society more widely.

Out of context, the presence of this urn might seem to gesture towards bathos or even camp. A contemporary reviewer was struck by its oddness: "we scarcely know whether to admire or condemn. The idea is striking, but . . . it is a little absurd to see Icilius carrying this urn about, from the house of Virginius to the dungeon in which the insane father is found gazing on the dead body of Apius. Does Mr. Knowles think that a funeral-urn is like a 'pouncet-box,' to be held 'betwixt the finger and the thumb,' or transported in a side-pocket?"[32] As this reviewer suggests, part of the incongruity of the urn lies in the way that it domesticates the space of the dungeon, bringing to it the ordering unit of the family. I see this tableau as analogous to what a statistical society promoted: a way of arranging humans around an implied norm centered on the household. Virginia's role as a living human creature is, for the purposes of this restorative tableau scene, secondary: the urn recovers the potentially abject space of the dungeon for the play's dominant logic of the family unit.

While the embodied presence of the actors was linked to the local conditions of any one particular performance, the urn could be moved from place to place and used from performance to performance. It gestured towards a stability that superseded any individual performance. The urn could be moved around the world, bringing its original domestic context—however incongruous—wherever it appeared. The urn would seem the same, performance after performance; the same urn might even be used across a myriad performances. Virginia's urn comes closer to this movable, iterable commodity of the play itself—repeated across a myriad settings—than any individual actor's performance could.

In the play, characters' intentions are transmuted into household objects and, through these objects, outlast the characters themselves. Near the beginning, Virginius is informed by Servia, one of his household slaves, that Virginia has been adding Icilius's name into a variety of domestic objects:

> You'll find this figuring where'er you look:
> There's not a piece of dainty work she does—
> Embroidery, or painting—not a task
> She finishes, but on the skirt, or border,
> In needle-work, or pencil, this, her secret,
> The silly wench betrays.
>
> —15

Virginia engrafts her mind and interiority into these exterior objects, which the other members of the household learn to read. As Jon Plotz writes of female monogramming, "Any object monogrammed with her initials or her family name seems an almost physically attached extension of herself."[33] These handicrafts are Virginia's trapped agency, representing her romantic intentions: her desire to knit Icilius into her family. In this sense, the urn that triggers the play's final tableau fulfills this agency, even in Virginia's absence.

By this token, the play proleptically reduces how wasteful Virginia's death is. In life, she makes domestic ornaments; in death she becomes one. In either case, she fills out the physical culture of the home. She is even called "a piece of furniture in the house of a friend of mine, that's called Virginius" (14). Virginius, too, describes Virginia making the other members of the household more furniture-like. The sight of his daughter, he claims, produce in their eyes "a stream of liquid living pearl / To cherish her enamell'd veins" (66). Indeed, enameling was one of the processes characteristic of nineteenth-century furniture making. Although violence can deprive the household of its members, it does not halt its slow accumulation of decorative objects. In this way, the century's forward material progress may be seen to leave a trace even in tragedy, showing a world of stabilizing things that can potentially stand in for those lost to tragic violence. *Virginius* captures what would become a particular middle-class worldview, which contrasted the heavy permanence of objects (the stuff-filled world of the bourgeois home) with the seeming impermanence of human life. Dead family members might frequently be replaced with memorial objects; yet the household survived, with these mourning objects continuing to rouse the other members of the family to affective awareness.

Virginius's killing of his daughter in the Roman Forum repeats this pattern of a domestic object driving a senseless character to act—in effect, standing in for his motivation. As the stage direction relates: "*Virginius, perfectly at a loss what to do, looks anxiously around the Forum; at length his eye falls on a butcher's stall, with a knife upon it*" (69). As, at the moment preceding his strangling of the villain, Virginius is "at a loss" for how to act, the play suggests that this moment, and so the character's indecision, be prolonged and, thus, made legible for the audience. The selection of a butcher's knife in particular suggests efficiency and economy: a good butcher makes the fullest possible use of an animal carcass. Onstage characters draw attention to the possible uses of the corpse: "Defend the body, freemen, / There's a spark / Remaining still, which / May yet rekindle liberty, and save / Expiring Rome!" (70–1). The agency Virginia inscribed into the household's furnishings might burst free, performing the work of family cohesiveness on the national level, knitting Rome back together, as she had hoped to knit Icilius into her family. And even in death, Virginia's agency does not leave the household. Rather, she is dragged back onstage, where her remains form part of the final tableau.

Virginius remained one of the warhorses of the nineteenth-century popular English stage. The object culture it depicted recurs in another noted nineteenth-century tragedy, *The Bells* (1871), which provided Henry Irving with one of his signature roles. The French original *Le Juif Polonais* (1867) by Émile Erckmann and Alexandre Chatrian was successful enough to warrant an 1869 opera adaptation. As a nearly word-for-word translation of the French original, *The Bells* speaks for material on both the French and English popular stages. The action of this play, too, is heavily mediated by onstage objects. Mathias, the Burgomaster of a small Alsatian town, has some years previously murdered a character known only as the Polish Jew, a wealthy seed merchant. Through this murder the play enacts nineteenth-century tragedy's move from the rural to the urban. The killing takes place by a lime kiln far from the city; the Burgomaster's house literalizes the bourgeois space that this killing creates. Mathias's first action in the play is to give his daughter a hat as a wedding gift, announcing the trapped agency that it contains: "It is my wedding present, Annette. The day of your marriage I wish you to wear it, and to preserve it for ever. In fifteen or twenty years hence, will you remember your father gave it to you?"[34] Throughout the play, memory—and, in Mathias's case, guilt—is built into the objects that make up his household, and indeed will continue to do so after his death. Yet another character's dilemma about how to act is caused and resolved through the mediation of an object from the play's onstage dimension.

As with *Virginius*, objects—and bodies that death has converted into objects—have a hard time leaving the stage. Mathias, for example, hears bells whenever the Polish Jew's name is mentioned, and subsequently falls into a state similar to a stroke. Instigated by this sound, the backdrop lifts up at the end of the first act to show the scene of the murder as Mathias imagines it. The raised backdrop and the realist details of the revealed scene make Mathias's mind legible. And during the psychological episode that comprises most of the third act of the play, Mathias imagines himself on trial for the murder, within a courtroom attended by a full complement of officials. These officials reflect explicitly on the way the play's object culture functions. In particular, the President of the court explains: "this noise of Bells arises in the prisoner's mind from the remembrance of what is past. The prisoner hears this noise because there rankles in his heart the memory of that he would conceal from us. The Jew's horse carried Bells" (22). This speech foregrounds the way that objects contain the agency of the characters. The bells serve as a sort of objective correlative for Mathias's guilt, his inability to forget the murder.

Mathias's final series of actions before his death stage a lengthy interaction with the objects related to the Jew's murder. He concludes his guilt-ridden recounting of the murder by miming his interaction with objects found on the Jew's body, and then finally the body itself:

> Quick, quick! The girdle! I have it. Ha! (*He performs the action in saying this of taking it from the Jew's body and buckling it round his own.*) It is full of gold, quite full. Be quick, Mathias, be quick! Carry him away. (*He bends low down and appears to lift the body upon his back; then he walks across stage, his body bent, his step slow as a man who carries a heavy load.*)
>
> —25

Mathias is made both to wear the Jew's girdle and to bear the weight of his corpse. The body is efficient: even in death, it still causes characters to act, in this case fulfilling Mathias's burden of guilt over the murder. Yet this play, like *Virginius*, finally shows the action of the murder as reconciled into the reconstitution of society in the play's conclusion. There is no sign that Mathias's angst-ridden recounting of the murder has disturbed the members of the town or of his household. The Burgomaster's guilt dies with him—but the material benefits of the action that caused that guilt are recuperated into his household and community. No one else is privy to the courtroom of his mind. His daughter's wedding will take place as planned. The Jew's capital—and the physical objects that carried it—are now reintegrated into society.

GHOSTS AND GLOBAL DOMESTIC TRAGEDY

Tracing object culture in nineteenth-century tragedy takes us practically everywhere in tragic performance—even into bordering genres. Giuseppe Verdi's tightening of William Shakespeare's plot in his opera *Othello* (1887), for instance, emphasizes the role of the handkerchief, with Othello even falling into a faint after exclaiming "Il fazzoletto!" ("The handkerchief!"). Even more pointedly, Richard Wagner assigns leitmotifs—repeated short musical tags—to key objects on which his plots hinge. Human characters also receive leitmotifs. In this way, things like the love potion and magic casket in *Tristan and Isolde* (1865) are given a musical presence similar to that of the human characters. Snappy bits of music, Wagner's leitmotifs can unfasten themselves from the score: thus, one can find oneself humming the leitmotif assigned to Siegfried's sword in the *Ring Cycle* operas (1848–74), the object's presence fully detaching itself from the musical setting in which it first appears. Also, in these operas, objects last far longer than individuals: Siegfried's sword, and finally the ring itself, outlast anyone who possesses them.

Wagner's dramas provided a mythic cast to a mundane fact: that domestic economies servicing household goods were now directing the daily lives of individuals to a vast and variegated degree. From a similar perspective, Ibsen's *Ghosts* is a play about how lamp oil causes syphilis. Oil, and the maritime sexual economy that it calls into being, acts like the ring in Wagner's operas. It is the underlying cause of everything, which survives the destruction of the text's central household. Within the narrative, non-musical drama more specifically, objects provide similar foci for action in tragedies written to travel around a wider world stage: that is, dramas that were portable between the bourgeois theater-going worlds of different nations. The very performance history of *Ghosts*, the fact of being first produced by a Danish-speaking theater company in Chicago, reflects the world-wide bourgeois milieu—and the trade that supported it—that the play itself addresses.

The Alving family is haunted by the dead Alving patriarch, who lived a dissolute life both before and after his marriage. This dissolution includes fathering an illegitimate child, Regina, by a woman who was paid off to marry the dissolute carpenter Engstrand, and contracting syphilis, which has been passed on to his son Oswald. The play's action involves the slow revelation of both of these facts: properties in the play activate behaviors that lead to previous generations' mistakes being repeated. These activating objects sustain a society in which the destruction of the good is routine. The work thus opens with an odd prop: Engstrand is attempting to gain access to the Alving house, while Regina, the Alvings' maid, stands *"with an empty garden syringe in her hand"* and *"bars his entry"* (27). The syringe, used to spray pesticides on garden plants, contributes to the play's heavy ironies, suggesting an impossible struggle to live free of biological intrusions. Contemplating the relation between ideology and practice in Ibsen, Toril Moi has suggested the importance of "housework" as an index of characters' attitudes, often presenting a critique of certain characters' selfish, impractical idealism: "Ibsen's deliberate foregrounding of cooking and cleaning is not just a critique of . . . idealism. It is also a metatheatrical statement, which tells us that the last thing Ibsen wants to write is grand tragedy, whether classical or romantic."[35] In particular, the grandness that this tragedy does not present is the grandness of some final, shattering abjection. Instead, it presents a world of stable objects that activate particular social roles, which are played out by the humans who use them. Like *Virginius*'s butcher's knife, this syringe offers a role for Regina to perform, one that replicates the wider performance of pan-European bourgeois domesticity. Further, it suggests that a certain amount of disease control has always been built into the system of domesticity. Regardless of the fate of any one character, someone will keep the garden tended. This small realist detail frames the play within a larger domestic world not on the brink of collapse: a bourgeois world organized around these domestic objects will continue to exist, with a potentially endless series of individuals performing the roles that these objects trigger.

A conversation early in the play sets it as occurring within a modern, statistical state, that is, one whose spaces and population are depicted as part of a contiguous whole, imaginable as part of a system of other nations. Mrs. Alving, whose ship captain's husband's infidelities are responsible for the play's central degeneration plot, discusses progressive thinking with Pastor Manders, an index for conventional social morality:

Mrs Alving. Well, they sort of explain and confirm many things that puzzle me. Yes, that's what's so strange, Pastor Manders—there isn't really anything new in these books—there's nothing in them that most people haven't already thought for themselves. It's only that most people either haven't fully realised it, or they won't admit it.
Manders. Well, dear God! Do you seriously believe that most people—?
Mrs Alving. Yes, I do.
Manders. But surely not in this country? Not people like us?
Mrs Alving. Oh, yes. People like us too.

—37

An impasse in motivation—a "puzzle"—has been solved for Mrs. Alving by some of the domestic objects, in this case the books that feature prominently in the play's initial stage direction. The books link the Alving household to the spread of knowledge through the nineteenth-century world, what even Pastor Manders calls "these intellectual movements in the great world outside about which one hears so much" (38). But of course it is not just books and ideas that link this pan-national bourgeois "great world." A garden syringe, and the gesture of using it, would be just as recognizable to audiences in the bourgeois households of Chicago or London. Mrs. Alving imagines people all over the world having essentially similar ideas, which these books simply "explain and confirm": "there's nothing in them that most people haven't already thought for themselves" (37).

Mrs. Alving calls these books a potential trigger—to change, to social action. Yet this trigger is never activated, and the play never explicates what these ideas are. Even the orphanage that Mrs. Alving has endowed does not come as a result of them: as Pastor Manders notes, the orphanage she created with her late husband was founded "at a time when your attitude towards spiritual matters was quite different from what it is now" (38). Part of the waste of good in the play is that whatever possibility for progress the books contain remains latent, never explicated in any detail—never, we might say, made as concrete as the garden syringe, or the brothel that Engstrand proposes to build in the first act. Instead, it is the objects that cause characters to repeat the mistakes of previous generations that seem to have the most traction over social life.

These stage properties seem to drive the action by evoking the presence of dead characters. Around these objects, the play's society demonstrates what Joseph Roach calls "surrogation": the tendency of characters within society to take on the roles of dead or absent people, sustaining social continuity.[36] They do so in an attempt to find "satisfactory alternates" for the departed, suggesting a desire for the function of the social roles that they played (38). And indeed from his first entrance, smoking his father's "big meerschaum pipe," Oswald evokes a complex desire to live as his father did, even without fully comprehending the debauches that this had entailed (43). Yet as Katherine Kelly notes, "Ibsen portrays Osvald as potentially complicit in his fate": "he drinks, smokes, sleeps till all hours, complains of the boredom of provincial life, and fondles the maidservant," repeating many of his father's behaviors.[37]

It is when he is following what the pipe suggests to him that Oswald's motivations are most legible to the other characters. Repeating his father's behavior makes other characters notice him—it makes Oswald a more compelling figure than he is when acting on his own. His desires seem to have been produced by a moment of close connection with his father, which the pipe has recalled: a moment when "he picked me up and sat me on his knee and let me smoke his pipe. 'Puff away, boy,' he said, 'puff hard.'" (44–5). This speech grips the interest of the other characters in a way that his other actions do not. As Pastor Manders notes, "When Oswald appeared in that doorway with that pipe in his mouth, it was just as though I saw his father alive again" (44). In other words, Oswald enacts what Woyzeck imagines: that one becomes noticeable as a human through objects. His pipe smoking evokes in others the respect that his father—once the king's chamberlain—had received. But this also fits within the play's larger pattern of ghostliness—objects' ability to resurrect the behavior of the dead—having more social currency, more attraction of the attention of others, than the creation of change. Oswald's tragedy, then, partly lies in that he is not strong enough to break away from following his father's actions if presented with the right triggers; and partly in that his society seems to prefer him to follow those triggers.

The most significant object in the play is probably the lamp that accompanies Mrs. Alving, Oswald, and Regina onstage throughout the second and third acts. In a long, lamp-lit sequence that extends through the play's second and third acts, Mrs. Alving reveals the true nature of her marriage—particularly her husband's infidelities—and initiates what may be Oswald's final mental breakdown. Oswald has spent the preceding scene discussing his disavowal of the family's situation, telling his mother: "I'm not thinking about anything. I *can't* think about anything. (*Softly.*) I take good care not to." He links his lack of mental illumination, his inability or unwillingness to think clearly about his situation, to the weather: "how—how dark it is in here! . . . And this incessant rain. It goes on week after week; sometimes for months. Never to see the sun! In all the years I've been at home I don't remember ever having seen the sun shine" (75). Oswald has been permitted not to face facts, leaving the household in a state of drift—or, worse, in the state of regression that his potential incest with his sister Regina would bring about.

The lamp concretizes Mrs. Alving's decision to reveal the darkest of all the family's secrets. Oswald's speech, and the state of disavowal it attempts to justify, gives Mrs. Alving the idea to finally reveal everything, an intention that she expresses by ordering Regina to bring the lamp in:

> *Mrs Alving.* Yes, bring in the lamp.
> *Regina.* Yes, madam, at once. I've already lit it. (*Goes.*)
> *Mrs Alving* (*goes over to Oswald*). Oswald, don't hide anything from me.
> *Oswald.* I'm not, mother. (*Goes over to the table.*) Haven't I told you enough?
> *Regina enters with the lamp and puts it on the table.*
>
> —75

The lamp creates an effect similar to a sustained tableau: an onstage arrangement of the three characters that stresses their connections around the same object. That Regina has "already lit" the lamp suggests she has intuited that something requiring illumination is about to happen. Thus the lamp gestures to the long pre-existing relationship between Regina and Mrs. Alving: the concealed relationship of Regina's hidden paternity, the subsequent years of commanding a servant that have resulted in Regina being able to intuit what her mistress wants.

The extent to which we see the lamp as purely figurative may depend on whether we consider the play as read or as repetitively performed. The lamp is of course on a certain level metaphorical—and the illumination it offers presents the promise of social change, or at least an uncovering of the hypocrisies of social convention. However, like all of the play's other objects, the lamp is also tied, by its nature, to an outside economy. Whatever sort of oil the lamp is burning, the household itself could not produce it itself. Whether this lamp burns whale oil or a petroleum-based product, it would have necessarily drawn on the conduits of maritime trade that sustained Captain Alving's career—but also his dissolute lifestyle. Distributing the energy that now illuminates the Alving household, in other words, was responsible for the circumstances that the lamp is required to illuminate. Like the books in Mrs. Alving's garden room, the lamp offers no possibility of an illumination that will break the domestic system that has created the play's problems. Instead, it points towards the continuation of these problems, as the circumstances that created them are repeated elsewhere.

Mrs. Alving's decision to put out the lamp triggers what may be Oswald's final breakdown. Here again the lamp concretizes her behavior. The decision signals her return to offering Oswald comforting delusions:

> *Mrs Alving (leans over him).* You've just imagined these dreadful things, *Oswald*. You've imagined it all. All this suffering has been too much for you. But now you shall rest. . . . Point at anything you want and you shall have it, just like when you were a little child. . . . And, Oswald, do you see what a beautiful day we're going to have? Bright sunshine. Now you can really see your home.
> *She goes over to the table and puts out the lamp. The sun rises. The glacier and the snow-capped peaks in the background glitter in the morning light.*
> *Oswald (sits in the armchair facing downstage, motionless. Suddenly he says).* Mother, give me the sun.
>
> —97

This scene shows a final triumph of object culture over redemptive illumination. Mrs. Alving promises Oswald a pleasant and palliative immersion within the object-world of the home: "Point at anything you want and you shall have it, just like when you were a little child" (97). However, within the terms of the play's consistent metaphor linking light and self-conscious awareness, Mrs. Alving's action is too late. The sun, suggesting an illumination more general still than oil-based lamplight, has come out: Oswald knows the truth, and his mind snaps. Mrs. Alving suggests that she realizes this when she states that "Now you can really see your home": the sun's illumination breaks over a house in which everything is known (97). Not simply the rural, but even the universal, is subsumed into the household's objects.

Caught between these irreconcilable perspectives—between comfort and knowledge—Oswald seeks what characters have had throughout these plays: a domestic object that will serve as an objective correlative for his feelings. Oswald responds to his mother's offer to "Point at anything you want;" yet what he is drawn to look at is the sun and the illumination that it promises. Within the limited understanding that follows his attack, his request to his mother to "give me the sun" shows him straining to integrate both of these perspectives. He wants the reassuring, and limited, household world, defined by its objects, that his mother has offered; he simultaneously wants the illuminating knowledge that might shatter this world. Like many of the other characters in these plays, he seeks an object to solve an impasse in thought. In his case, however, the object cannot possibly be given to him. This impasse cannot possibly be solved. Oswald responds to his mother's offer to "Point at anything you want;" yet what he is drawn to look at is the sun, and the illumination it promises.

Instead, the play's final action is Mrs. Alving reaching into her dress for the morphine powders that will potentially euthanize her son. Another speech gives extended dramatization to the character's inability to act, moving her through apparent extremes of both feeling and numbness:

> Mrs Alving (*jumps to her feet in despair, tears her hair with both hands and screams*). I can't bear this! (*Whispers as though numbed*) I can't bear it! No! (*Suddenly*) Where did he put them? (*Fumbles quickly across his breast*) Here! (*Shrinks a few steps backwards and screams*) No; no; no! Yes! No; no! (*She stands a few steps away from him with her hands twisted in her hair, speechless, and stares at him in horror*)
>
> —98

Mrs. Alving—like Virginius—contemplates killing her child, looking to a stage property to move her past inaction. And this play concludes before the action can take place, evoking the continued domestic life that must inevitably follow the play's conclusion. And within this life, the conditions that triggered the behavior that caused Oswald's illness seem likely to continue. These same events might occur again: if the Alving maid Regina joins her father's proposed brothel, they seem likely to. The tragedy's waste of good, then, is potentially reproducible on a society-wide scale—indeed it seems built into the structure of society itself.

CONCLUSION: THE PHANTASMAGORIA OF TRAGIC OBJECTS

In his unfinished *Arcades Project* (1927–40), Walter Benjamin notes the tendency of nineteenth-century bourgeois interiors to exhibit that cohesiveness of vision that Oswald also displays. Benjamin likens the accretion of things within bourgeois interiors to a "shell" that "bears the impression of its occupant" (38). For Benjamin, these shells present new "phantasmagorias of the interior - which, for the private man, represents the universe. In the interior, he brings together the far away and the long ago. His living room is a box in the theater of the world."[38] Knowles, Lewis, and Ibsen alike suggest a possible interruption of the hermetic, accretive world that Benjamin describes. Benjamin extends the power of domestic objects even further, eventually claiming their nineteenth-century dominion over time as well as space.

In performance, these plays offered a possible alternative to this phantasmagoria—even as their plots often demonstrate the triumph of this object-world. As a live medium, theater invites audiences to sympathize with the human performers appearing in the midst of such an enduring and determinate object-world. Re-encountering these nineteenth-century tragedies, we are struck by the particular harshness of vision these object-world tragedies present. There is a kind of horror in the relentless materialism, the lack of metaphysics, in Oswald's condition. Virginia's fate suggests that, even after such an outcome, she might be put to use. The Burgomaster's household suggests a space constituted of such dead presences and their ghostly invocation of those extremes of human experience in which tragedy traditionally dealt. As they considered these new tragedies on the nineteenth-century stage, we may imagine audiences feeling horror at the transience of human life amidst such enduring objects—and, indeed, at the ease with which bodies themselves could be converted into such objects.

CHAPTER SEVEN

Society and Family

DANA VAN KOOY

Tragedy's focus on the family is not new. As Bennett Simon has argued, tragedy and the family have been inextricably intertwined for millennia.[1] The Greek tragedies of Sophocles and Aeschylus depict murder, incest, suicide, and betrayal amongst Oedipus' family and within the mythic house of Atreus. A stranger does not commit these acts but rather one or more family member perpetrates the given offense. At every turn, the family is at risk of destroying itself, and yet, there exists an obsession with the family's ability to propagate and to perpetuate its authority. In the nineteenth century, we witness a similar degree of violence within the family. One pronounced difference is that dramatists in this era ask repeatedly what it means to exist in a modern world that was and, arguably, still is—borrowing Hannah Arendt's words—"neither private nor public."[2] A contemporary and familiar notion of society emerged out of this early modern liminal space that is neither private nor public. According to Arendt, modern society blurs political and private interests and renders the private realm of the individual and the family subject to public forms of organization; it also prompts a desire for privacy. This yearning to withdraw or escape from society, however, precipitates the conditions for social dispossession and a ubiquitous sensation of being deprived of some thing or some experience. Individuals feel alienated, anonymous, and become more easily subject to the ideological forces of public opinion and institutionalized violence. Subsequently, they lose their personal voice, and politics is transformed into the faceless bureaucracy of mass society.

The cultural production of tragedy in the nineteenth century is clearly reflective of the historical moment, which is rife with imperial incursions into every part of the world, revolutionary upheaval, slavery, and cascading world crises. Worldwide struggles for freedom spanned from the American colonies (1775–83), France (1789), Haiti (1791–1804), Ireland (1798), and South America (1817), to Greece (1821–32) and India (1857). These revolutions cast doubt on the legitimacy of Europe's social and political structures, particularly, its aristocracy, its religious institutions, and the governing monarch's "right" to rule. This uncertainty generated a pervasive experience of insecurity. Social and familial structures, C.A. Bayly notes, were subject to "overlapping forms of power and authority, rather than a close centralized control."[3] Arguably, this social and political upheaval prompted dramatists to experiment with old and new dramatic forms. They reconceived familiar tragedies and wrote new tragedies, compiling a distinctive tragic tradition that Jeffrey N. Cox describes as emerging "in response to the perceived collapse of the traditional providential and hierarchical order."[4] During the first half of the century, dramatists penned tragedies that responded both to the revolutionary politics of late eighteenth-century gothic drama and to melodrama's conservative ideology. Joanna Baillie, Lord Byron, Samuel Coleridge, Percy Shelley, and William Wordsworth reimagined and repurposed gothic performances. With other dramatists in the period, they also adopted melodrama's stage practices as a means of exposing and undermining the social and familial order popularized in melodrama. Dramatists across the European and American continents also examined alternative forms of human bonding outside the traditional family and imagined new possibilities for tolerant and more open communities. These tragedies hinged on the play between a vision of future possibilities and its catastrophic failure; however, the requisite catastrophic turn in tragedy is not attributed to some tragic flaw in the heroic figure. In contrast with the contemporary concern with individuality and individual psychology, these plays were rooted in the social realm of history, in the revelation of social and familial taboos, and in the unveiling of realities that sustained the bone-chilling violence that accompanied global war in its many forms.

Examining nineteenth-century tragedy more closely, we see writers like Shelley in *The Cenci* recasting classical motifs within the setting of the Italian Renaissance. In that play's terrifying banquet scene, Count Cenci welcomes his friends, kinsmen, princes, and the pillars of the Catholic Church into his home and confesses he has been too long withdrawn from society and that in his absence from "merry meetings / An evil word is gone abroad of me."[5] He appears concerned with his public reputation, but it becomes clear that he cares nothing for what society thinks of him; he is not a reformed man, and his alienation is absolute. Although the attending guests are nervous, Beatrice Cenci is terrified, and whispers to her stepmother, Lucretia, "Great God! How horrible! Some dreadful ill / Must have befallen my brothers" (1.3.33–4). A moment later, her premonition is verified when her father declares,

> My disobedient and rebellious sons
> Are dead!—Why, dead!—What means this change of cheer?
> You hear me not, I tell you they are dead;
> And they will need no food or raiment more:
> The tapers that did light them the dark way
> Are their last cost. The Pope, I think, will not
> Expect I should maintain them in their coffins.
> Rejoice with me—my heart is wondrous glad.
>
> —1.3.43–50

Prior to this moment, Count Cenci has wished and prayed for his sons' deaths, though they have neither betrayed nor plotted against him. Likening himself to God, he justifies his anger by referring to them as "disobedient and rebellious sons." In the past, when he denied them support, the Pope had intervened and forced Cenci to maintain them. Now that they are dead, he celebrates publicly that "they will need no food or raiment more." Noting the "change of cheer" amongst his guests, Count Cenci openly disregards familial and social norms. His extreme alienation from both his family and society allows him to more fully manipulate others, including Cardinal Camillo and the Pope, through bribes and threats of committing more violence. The conspiracy that forms around Count Cenci's innumerable crimes is expansive. In his mind, it stretches from God through the Pope and the cardinal to his family and neighbors who attend the banquet. This scene stages the disturbing realities that emerge within a society that is neither public nor private. Everyone knows that Count Cenci has committed innumerable crimes and yet no one will hold him accountable. This makes everyone culpable, and Cenci's realization of this fact gives him power over them.

Count Cenci is and is not a typical villain. He is a powerful aristocrat akin to the eighteenth-century rake who disregards the lives of others. Yet, his craving for stimulation and sensation equates him with the common man of the nineteenth century: someone whose life is marked by the century's mind-numbing economic changes as well as the life-threatening realities of global war. Boredom and the desire to commit unimaginable crimes drive Cenci's illicit actions. Wordsworth offered his readers poetry as a means of reflecting on and mitigating these societal influences that threatened individual lives and fragmented social and familial bonds. In contrast, Shelley and other playwrights formulated tragedies and other forms of theatrical performances to reproduce and make visible these modern realities that shaped the popular and illegitimate theater of "physical peril, visual spectacle and ideological confrontation."[6]

The innovation, the sensationalism, and the unprecedented and sometimes perplexing mixing of genres and forms within theatrical productions spurred public debates about both the viability and vitality of tragedy.[7] Largely due to the anti-theatrical thrust of these debates, the nineteenth century is still more often identified with the advent of the historical novel,[8] lyric poetry, and the revival of romance than it is with tragedy. Walter Scott, Byron, and Alfred Tennyson recreated the aesthetic registers of romance, but one need only glance over their plots to discern the conspicuous presence of tragedy there as well. Stuart Curran has argued that Scott's ingenuity was to "recognize that the period offered an unlimited field not just for the creation of romance but for its simultaneous critique."[9] Byron's Oriental tales, Scott's Border romances, Tennyson's Arthurian sagas, and the longer poems in John Keats' final published collection, *Lamia, Isabella, The Eve of St. Agnes, and other Poems* (1820), interweave tragedy with romance. None conclude as they should, with a marvelous scene or with the performance of a social union through marriage. Instead, each subjects romance to critique by unveiling its fictionalized "romantic" world as all too real. Consonant with tragedy, characters die or are paralyzed by grief or horror. The tyranny opposed by the hero remains firmly ensconced. When a character embraces a vision of hope or love, audiences remain skeptical and willing to condemn the heroic figure. In his preface to *The Cenci*, Shelley described this critical stance as "anatomizing casuistry" (142), where audiences focus less on the potential for what could have been and more on the disturbing realization that the villain and the heroic figure are more similar than they first appeared. No character can be judged innocent; everyone is condemned.

What we see in Byron's and Scott's romances, then, we also find throughout nineteenth-century tragedy: isolated and alienated men who commit acts of violence against those they are compelled by duty and affiliation to love. The strong-willed, intelligent, and capable women attempt to constrain these men, often in the midst of fighting, war, or scenes of torture. Almost inevitably, both the nuclear family and the larger community suffer catastrophically and the characters' efforts to effect change are thwarted. Characters like Baillie's Orra, Shelley's Beatrice Cenci, Byron's Marina Foscari, Dion Boucicault's George Peyton, and Ibsen's Halvard Solness repeatedly must contend against social, sexual, and familial conventions within plays that portray either the absence or the destruction of the traditional family. Almost universally, there is—as in Schiller's *The Robbers* (1781)—a struggle with codes of vengeance. The violence that saturates the battlefield seeps into the family home, and pervades social, civil, and religious institutions, where it further dissolves communal and familial bonds. Characters are alienated in their personal and collective confrontations against the faceless anonymity of prejudice, patriotism, and public opinion. Families are fragmented; children are orphaned; an orphan is betrayed by her guardian; a mother must choose between her children and her husband; a father rapes his daughter; a daughter murders her father; a father stands silently as his son is tortured in a court of law; a father allows his daughter to remain a slave during his lifetime because she is illegitimate and an octoroon; a husband builds new houses and his career on the ruins of his wife's family home. As familial bonds are dissolved by violence, society becomes more formidable as a mundane and nondescript organizational force.

In many of these tragedies, the experience of war—or what Mary Favret describes as wartime[10]—functions as a crucible pressing characters invariably toward the play's concluding catastrophe. In Kleist's *Penthesilea* (1808), the eponymous Amazon Queen, and the Greek hero, Achilles, are, as Odysseus tells Antilochus, "Locked in dread conflict like two rav'ning wolves. / And by the gods, neither can tell the cause!"[11] Their visceral hostility toward one another is as inexplicable as the riddling Sphinx in Sophocles' *Oedipus*. What madness could possibly embroil Penthesilea and Achilles, Odysseus asks, when "the war calls us urgently to Troy" (5, 185)? The answer is simple and yet absurd: love. Their internecine battle erases and reifies traditional gender roles. Both are warriors; both are driven by "impotent lust" (5, 185). Kleist's tragedy violently undermines the conventional ideals of love and family, and yet, the final catastrophe affirms their love for one another as it attests to its impossibility.

During the nineteenth century, European playwrights made a concerted effort to restore and renovate tragedy. A.W. Schlegel in his *Lectures on Dramatic Art and Literature* (1809–11) draws attention to the classical tradition, especially Aeschylus' *Prometheus Bound*. Shelley too turned to Aeschylus, penning *Prometheus Unbound*, adapting *The Persians* when composing *Hellas*, and deploying Sophocles' *Oedipus* in his burlesque tragedy, *Oedipus Tyrannus; or Swellfoot the Tyrant*. Even the plot of *The Cenci*, grounded in the Italian Renaissance, resurrects the figure of Antigone.[12] Goethe's *Iphigenia in Tauris* (1779, 1781, 1786) also breathed new life into classical source material—in this case the plays of Euripides, Sophocles' *Antigone*, and Aeschylus' *The Oresteia*.

In Goethe's tragedy, Diana/Artemis saves Iphigenia from her father, Agamemnon, who believes he sacrifices her so that Greek warships can sail to Troy. Unbeknownst to her family, Iphigenia survives and lives as a priestess in the isolated country, Tauris, ruled by Thoas. When she first arrives, strangers are mercilessly and savagely caught and sacrificed. Eventually, Iphigenia convinces Thoas to abandon this practice. As the play opens, Thoas attempts to leverage his power as king to convince Iphigenia to marry him by threatening to impose the former barbaric laws of human sacrifice if she refuses his offer. The king's desire for domestic bliss is catastrophically violent and it is similar to that which Zeus imposed on the many generations of Tantalus—from Pelops to Atreus and Agamemnon—who sacrificed, murdered, and literally consumed each other. Instead of murdering and sacrificing his children, Thoas threatens to forswear the laws of hospitality and his basic humanity, potentially plunging his country and its citizens into war. Iphigenia's position, like that of Beatrice Cenci and so many other female characters in nineteenth-century tragedy, is untenable. If she succumbs to Thoas's intimidation, she betrays herself, the people of Tauris, and the strangers who arrive in Tauris. If she refuses to marry him, she will be responsible for the subsequent savage and brutal acts she will be forced to commit. Like Count Cenci in Shelley's tragedy, Thoas will not be held accountable for the crimes he commits or for those offenses he forces others to enact; Iphigenia—despite her nobility and her goodness—will be judged as both complicit and culpable.

As the friendship between Thoas and Iphigenia becomes increasingly strained, it is clear that the first two people to be sacrificed after many years of peace will be Orestes, Iphigenia's long lost brother, and his faithful companion, Pylades. Similar to Oedipus, Iphigenia will unknowingly commit fratricide if Thoas has his way. Orestes speaks out against ritualized sacrifice and pleads with Thoas to "Let me, the stranger, fight for other strangers" (140).[13] The "new custom" for which Orestes advocates will let him fight "for [his and Pylades'] freedom." Iphigenia recognizes that Orestes' alternative of armed conflict is no better than religious sacrifice. Neither can provide a means of realizing truth nor does either act secure the rights of a person or those of a nation. Iphigenia acknowledges that the single combatant may achieve glory and become immortal in the bard's song, but, she tells them, this tale of glory will fail to staunch "the unending tears / Of his survivors, of his wife abandoned" (140). Despite the threat of more bloodshed, the play closes more as a comedy than a tragedy. Prior to the play, Agamemnon has sacrificed his daughter, Iphigenia; Clytemnestra has heard news of her husband's death on the battlefield of Troy many times, and when he returns home, she and her lover murder Agamemnon; Orestes, in revenge for his father's death, commits matricide and subsequently, he is pursued by the Furies. It seems impossible that such a family could survive, and yet, Iphigenia is saved, and she and her brother, Orestes, are reunited. All the characters, in fact, are emancipated from the "rigid bonds" (142) of marriage, revenge, and religious sacrifice. Friendship displaces banishment, and hospitality becomes "the link" that reunites family, friends, and strangers (143). The play envisions a society of "familiar strangers," where everyone can be greeted as if they were a god-in-disguise, given a bed, and seated by the fire (143). Goethe's innovative adaptation of classical tragedy combined with his revolutionary politics clearly undermines the precepts of tragedy insofar as there is no catastrophic turn. *Iphigenia in Tauris*, however, establishes an alternative cultural perspective of tragedy that will be employed by nineteenth-century writers to challenge conservative and patriotic iterations of the nuclear family and social values, which vilify and alienate strangers.

Early nineteenth-century tragedies expose social and religious mores as accountable for destruction of the family. In Britain, the late eighteenth century was marked by revolutionary hope in the immediate aftermath of the French Revolution, followed by the fearful alarm of a French invasion, and a push toward war. In the midst of these unfolding events, gothic drama dominated British theaters for a brief period because it capitalized on the popularity of the gothic novel and was associated with the newly popular German drama being translated and adapted by British playwrights. The plays of Schiller, translated by Coleridge, as well as those of August von Kotzebue, highlighted the radical and revolutionary politics of the era. The London Treason Trials of 1794 and the French invasion scare Coleridge contemplates in *Fears in Solitude* (1798) generated a culture of xenophobia and political censorship. Writing in the wake of this cultural backlash, Wordsworth capitalized on this "patriotic" anti-theatrical prejudice in his criticism of the "sickly and stupid German Tragedies" in the preface to *Lyrical Ballads* (1800).[14] This and other virulent responses to gothic drama labeled and condemned these performances as morally and politically suspect German and French "imports." The century thus opened with a fervent public debate about reviving and producing "legitimate" comedy and tragedy in British theaters.

Joanna Baillie picked up this thrown gauntlet to restore tragedy and comedy to the British stage and became one of the most influential and respected dramatists in the early nineteenth century. Baillie's tragedies unveil the passions secreted away in the depths of the individual, behind the doors of the domestic household, and within institutional and social frameworks. There, the individual's heart and mind prove to be no less mysterious than the political institutions to which they are subject.

Baillie published the first volume of her *Plays on the Passions* anonymously in 1798 and continued to write plays for this series of dramatic experiments until 1812, publishing a belated fourth volume in 1836.[15] By the time she published her third volume in 1812, the dark clouds of war had encircled the British Isles. Britain's prospects against Napoleon's forces were bleak. The political hopes that accompanied the establishment of the Regency in 1811 were dashed immediately after war was declared between the United States and Britain in 1812. The political upheaval had a significant cultural effect on the production of drama in this period, more than halving the number of new tragedies produced in the first years of the nineteenth century.[16]

Set in Germany at the end of the fourteenth century, Baillie's tragedy *Orra* revives the gothic machinery popularized in the 1790s. Like other plays written in this series, *Orra* focuses on a particular emotional state (fear) with the aim of stripping a character's life of its "decoration and ornament" to expose "one simple trait of the human heart, one expression of passion genuine and true to nature," and to let it "stand forth alone in the boldness of reality, whilst the fake and unnatural around it, fades away."[17] This radical attempt to liberate the individual from cultural prejudices presupposes the existence of an essential self: a concept promulgated by Jean-Jacques Rousseau in the eighteenth century. As Jennifer Wallace notes, Coleridge further popularized this notion of the self in his interpretation of Hamlet, which emphasized "his internal life of the mind."[18] This attention to the individual is one of the constitutive developments in nineteenth-century tragedy and it represents a formal vehicle for depicting the suffering and the conflict that defines human existence.[19]

For Baillie, the theater represented a school for moral, social, and political reform. Drama, as she wrote in her 1798 "Introductory Discourse," "improves us by the knowledge we acquire of our own minds, from the natural desire we have to look into the thoughts, and observe the behaviour of others" (90), an argument echoed by Shelley in his preface to *The Cenci*.[20] Tragedy for Baillie appeals to humanity's "inclination . . . for scenes of horror and distress, of passion and heroick exertion" (84). More significantly, she argues, it teaches individuals to "listen to the voice of reason" in the midst of life's "wild uproar"; it provides opportunities to save "ourselves from [the] destruction" (94) that would ensue if we had not witnessed others confront their "ungovernable rage" (95) against tyranny, "which it is impossible to repell" [sic] (91). Baillie's attempt to make visible those repressed passions and emotions that remain "unacceptable to the publick" (93) is reminiscent of the early gothic tragedies and melodramas. In each case, drama and its performance in the theater offer audiences a means of externalizing the often-disguised inner workings of human emotion. Baillie does not endorse dogmatic moral positions, nor does her work idealize the hearth and home as melodrama often did. To "enjoy" one's privacy in Baillie's tragedies is staged as what it is: a culturally manufactured privilege, one that constitutes an enormous cost to society because it represents—as the word privacy suggests—loss as social deprivation and alienation.[21] Baillie's tragedies, like Goethe's *Iphigenia in Tauris*, raise the all too familiar question of whose lives matter and what conditions make their lives visible and meaningful to others.

In *The Theatres of War*, Gillian Russell examines how British theaters capitalized on creating spectacles of patriotic pageantry and re-enactments of famous battles during the Napoleonic Wars.[22] Many theatrical performances mediated the war's events for public consumption, and theater management and stage actors made decisions about who and what would be socially commemorated. Theaters reconstructed the culture of war by placing the spotlight on audiences (which often included discharged soldiers or soldiers on leave), by encouraging them to identify with the patriotic actor and/or the soldier-character, and by concluding the night's performances with patriotic songs. Baillie's *Orra* is less concerned with rousing patriotic fervor than it is with staging the experience of wartime. Mary Favret has defined wartime as a lived condition rather than an event: "a melee of temporal synchronies and discontinuities that results not in the end of history but its reopening, [thus challenging] the 'settlements' of history."[23] Consonant with Anna Barbauld's *Eighteen Hundred and Eleven* (1812), Baillie's *Orra* recreates the dark war-torn landscape of the early nineteenth century, which echoes with "the loud death drum, thundering from afar."[24] Like Barbauld's poem, her drama crosses generic boundaries and depicts a shifting social and gender divide. It does so, as Julie Carlson observes, by "uncovering the strangeness of home, and woman's estrangement from the familiar."[25]

Orra centers on a young woman determined to live "without another's leave" and willing to openly scorn every man's attempt to usurp her "lands and rights."[26] Despite the fierce and contentious violence of this feudal society, Orra envisions a community where she and Falkenstein can live as "two co-burghers"—significantly, not as a married couple or a family—and where she will "keep . . . a merry house" (2.1.108). Her greatest desire is to improve "the low condition of [her] peasants" (2.1.25) and to provide sustenance in "her ample hall" to the "way-worn folks" as well as the "worn-out man of arms, (of whom too many, / Noble descended, rove like reckless vagrants . . .)" (2.1.110–14). Orra is heiress to her father's fiefdom as well as the ward of Hughobert, her dead father's friend and the current Count of Aldenberg. In the first half of the play, readers discover that Orra is haunted by her perceived complicity in the ongoing violence. She is unsure whether the bloodshed began with or was exacerbated by her ancestor's horrible deed, but her declaration—"Merciful Heaven! And in my veins there runs / A murderer's blood" (2.1.185–6)—suggests a deep historical connection between events of the past and those of the present. Orra, like Iphigenia and Beatrice Cenci, is a good and noble figure, but her fate suggests that there is little if any possibility of escaping the terrors of war in this society.

When Catherina relates the story about Orra's dead relative, a former Count Aldenberg, Orra becomes captivated by the gothic tale that gives form and substance to her underlying fear that repeatedly causes her to start and shrink from the wartime terrors that define every character's life in this tragedy. As events begin to unfold, it becomes clear that Orra's disdain for her suitors, her "wild gestures" (2.2.91), and "unruly humour" (1.3.108) are the public demeanor she employs to mask her fears. What many critics have failed to acknowledge is that Orra is extraordinary in her ability to acknowledge her fears. After making a fool of himself by falling in the Lists, Glottenbal confronts his father, Hughobert, who challenges him, "art thou afraid of me? / That thus thou shrinkest like a skulking thief / To make disgrace the more apparent on thee?" (1.3.28–30). In this war-torn feudal society men frown upon the open display and acknowledgment of fear. Glottenbal dismisses his martial failure as caused by "damned witchery" (1.1.78). Other men allow for this posturing, but Orra (and afterwards, his father) will not. After isolating Orra from her protectors and friends, the obvious villain, Rudigere, convinces Orra that he, unlike other men, can own his fear because, he claims, I "plainly feel / We are all creatures, in the wakeful hour / Of ghastly midnight, form'd to cower together, / Forgetting all distinctions of the day, / Beneath its awful and mysterious power" (3.1.49–53). In this moment Orra sympathizes with her captor. Rudigere's fear may be real, but he will use this disclosure to compromise Orra. We know this because he has manipulated and exploited Catherina's fear of being publicly exposed as less than virtuous after being physically involved with him. Even the best of men in this drama, Theobald of Falkenstein, confesses to Orra, "I should be more heroic than I am" (2.1.21). No one embodies the idealized heroic standards of fearlessness, but very few will openly acknowledge their fear as Orra does. That said, her fear will paralyze her fully in the play's final scene.

Like Shelley's *The Cenci*, Baillie's tragedy is uncompromising in its tragic trajectory. The story follows a gothic plot and provides little more than a feint toward romance. The haunted castle, the spectral hunter-knights, and the absolute power of feudal and patriarchal law are revealed as little more than ornamental masks. World-shattering violence stands behind a thin veneer of chivalric imagery. Baillie's tragedy reveals the chilling realities individuals face in this early modern world. David Simpson's description of modernity in terms of its "massive mobilizations of armies and navies and [its] appalling fatalities," and its "[d]eath-dealing economic changes . . . that damaged human bodies just as visibly as did weapons of war"[27] aptly resonates with *Orra*. Baillie's tragedy neither reassures its audiences nor gives way to nihilism; rather, it stages the discomforts of home, where so many, like Orra, are orphans and dispossessed. The tragedy exposes the misogyny that deprives women of their homes, reputations, fortunes, and even their lives. It also reveals the limits of the feudal system and its masculine code of chivalry, which cannot accommodate the various psychological and economic plights faced by former soldiers who feel they have no other choice than to be reduced to vagrancy or become outlaws.

In contrast to tragedy in this period, melodrama assured audiences that heroic acts and bravery would end in romance, and that tales of dispossession would conclude in the restoration of lost family members and the family fortune. Baillie's Orra will not discover a lost relative, and her guardian will attempt to coerce her to marry his son in order to control her fortune. Orra's refusal to adhere to social conventions—basically, to marry and spend her money as others direct her—endangers her life. For this breach, she is secluded in a distant castle, which she believes his haunted. The audience knows there is a plot afoot to save her from Rudigere, but she remains unaware of what is happening deep within and outside the castle. When Rudigere isolates her from Catherina, Orra's fear escalates far beyond what she imagined possible. Orra's fear progresses in distinct stages: initially, she experiences fear as invigorating and exciting. Her vulnerability is limited, and she feels delight as well as terror. At this juncture, she dares to imagine a community defined by the Anglicized French revolutionary motto, liberty, equality, and fraternity. When Hughobert exercises his power against her, sending her into isolation, it appears that Falkenstein and the relatively benign band of discharged soldiers will liberate her from the oppressive patriarchy represented by Hughobert and Rudigere. But the intensification of Orra's fear makes it impossible to save her or for her to realize her aspiration to create a more equitable community. Instead of awakening to the warmth of humanity, she, like Glottenbal, shrinks from what she fears, namely, the threatening specter of her own culpability. The final scene stages her full regression into madness.

The Napoleonic Wars came to an end on the fields of Waterloo in June 1815. The political, social, and economic turmoil brought on by the war, however, continued to escalate, effectively marking this period as an era of unprecedented war *and* invention. As a "new" world order emerged after Napoleon was exiled a second time, it became clear that the combination of restored monarchies and the unleashed forces of industrial capitalism and global imperialism would not be enough to suppress the agents of revolutionary change. As with Goethe and Baillie, dramatists continued to adopt and resist cultural conventions. Byron, Musset, Boucicault, amongst others transformed tragedy into a cultural vehicle for reflecting on this unprecedented scale of destruction. New forms of cultural and political life evolved out of an awareness of the scope and this underlying violence that structured everything from the family and tragedy to government policy. Nineteenth-century tragedy opened the door to the personal and collective acknowledgment of a shared vulnerability to and a responsibility for this vast landscape of death and destruction. Post-Waterloo, there emerged a vision of hope that Leigh Hunt, writing for *The Examiner* on July 2, 1815, described as eclipsing "the common feelings of hostility or of triumph" that follow war.[28] Echoing Goethe's Iphigenia and Baillie's Orra, Hunt directs attention toward war's "survivors," the broken family of humanity, who now confront what it means to be "fatherless," "childless," and "husbandless." Allowing for feelings of despair and loss, Hunt consoles his readers by creating a narrative of charitable interaction, thus providing the groundwork for a future sociability. Hunt's vignette reaffirms a belief in humanity. The anonymous stranger becomes familiar; alienation is transformed into recognition.[29]

In this essay Hunt marks the emergence of a new social consciousness. He sees this reflected in the experience of shared grief that follows in the wake of national catastrophe. Even the Duke of Wellington—the commander of the British forces and the hero of Waterloo—has been transformed. Hunt recounts the Duke's description "of the intrepidity, firmness, and heroic exertions with which [the English army] maintained themselves in their positions, – a corporate image, it is observable, being invariably in his mind" (2, 34). Hunt later cites a letter written by Wellington to his mother, Lady Mornington, wherein he acknowledges Napoleon as a man who "'did his duty – he fought the battle with infinite skill, perseverance, and bravery'" and credits the victory at Waterloo to "'the superior *physical* force and *invincible constancy* of British soldiers'" (2, 35). Before Waterloo, the Duke of Wellington was known more for his disparaging and derogatory remarks about British soldiers, but at this juncture, he humanizes the common soldier and the enemy, Napoleon. One of the most demonized figures in the British media at the time, Napoleon is recognized publicly by Wellington as a deft military leader who performed his duty. Wellington's redirection of the public limelight to the common soldier, and Hunt's emphasis on the anguish felt by the soldiers' families reflect the growing social importance of commemorating the sacrifices of soldiers and civilians during wartime.[30] Considering Waterloo as a national tragedy as Hunt and Wellington obviously did, it is significant that they both recognize the scope of destruction while they also embrace a more cohesive image of society and a new-found hope for the future.

This alternative social vision had an almost immediate impact on tragedy produced in the post-Waterloo era. Although tragedy remains focused predominantly on noble and aristocratic characters, they are more frail, more alienated, and more self-aware than their predecessors. Their increasingly complex personalities reflect the challenges to traditional social and political hierarchies. Byron's *Sardanapalus* (1821), for example, takes as its subject the last Assyrian monarch who recalls an eighteenth-century rake hero. He embodies aristocratic arrogance and he believes in the power of love and compassion to change the world. Married with two sons, Sardanapalus is in love with his Greek slave, Myrrha. He insists his "life is love" and that he has "done all [he] could to soothe them."[31] "I made no wars," he tells his brother-in-law, Salemenes: "I added no new imposts, / I interfered not with their civic lives, / I let them pass their days as best might suit them" (1.2.356–9). Like Hamlet, albeit for different reasons—citing love rather than justice—Sardanapalus refuses to play the tragic hero. Throughout the play, friends and foes, and even his ghostly ancestors, attempt to rouse him to perform his heroic part. Eventually, he does and to great acclaim, but not before he has exposed tyranny as integral to the tragic heroic narrative. Believing in this tale, everyone—including slaves, servants, religious leaders, loyal military leaders, loving wives and mistresses, and the larger public—is willing to sacrifice their lives to uphold and sustain as a cultural ideal.

Byron's *The Two Foscari* (1821) offers a similar study of the fatal interplay between a republican ethos and imperial force. Byron sets *The Two Foscari* in Renaissance Venice, a literary and historical site that figured prominently in English political and cultural debates. The Venetian state, as Susan Staves observes, "combines its republican constitution and public pageantry with regular recourse to torture and secrecy."[32] The plot, Staves notes, is "reminiscent of Jacobean tragedy" (95). It also looks back to plays like Shakespeare's *Othello* and *A Merchant of Venice*, both of which portray the changing relationship between the state and the individual, specifically, the extent to which an individual will be asked to sacrifice themselves, their livelihood, and their family to the state. Byron—similar to Kleist in *Penthesilea*—directs his audience to consider the raw *power* of love and hate. James Loredano's hatred for the Foscari family drives the plot. The two Foscari, Francis and Jacopo, his son, exemplify a patriotic fervor for the Venetian state that has no bounds. Marina Foscari's love for her husband, Jacopo, contests this blind patriotism, but to no effect. Byron's tragedies, like Baillie's *Orra*, stage the alienation and otherworldliness of modernity while making explicit the costs of war exacted on the people by the state. They also make clear the increasingly entangled complexity of modern social and political networks. Written and published during the post-Waterloo era, *The Two Foscari* is set at the dawn of a new era of peace. After "almost / Thirty-four years of nearly ceaseless warfare" (2.1.13–14), one senator tells the Doge (Frances Foscari), the "state had need of some repose" (2.1.16). But the end of the war has brought no real relief or any evidence of peace and tranquility. The constant crises of war have undermined and erased the republican concept of the people. Instead, the Doge tells the Chief of the *Ten*, there is now a *"populace* ... whose looks / May shame you; but they dare not groan nor curse you, / Save with their hearts and eyes" (5.1.259–61). The populace's silence in the face of Venice's victory is indicative of the sacrifices imposed upon them. The state has survived; it has even prospered in that its imperial borders have expanded and its realms have "doubled" (2.1.372). However, in the process of subduing its enemies and its people (2.1.408), Venice has transformed into a mysterious, faceless entity. Patriotism, the love of one's country, Marina argues, countering both her husband and his father, has become the "worst barbarity" (2.1.427–8).

Byron's tragedy reduces the extensive theaters of war to a single room, the courtroom, where the oligarchic *Ten* bear witness to the punitive ordeal imposed upon Jacopo Foscari, the Doge's sole surviving son. Jacopo Foscari's case is discussed behind closed doors. Accusation, verbal insinuation, and subtle acts of surrender in these scenes indicate where the truth might exist, but it remains impossible to locate. In a post-war imperial society where apathy, exhaustion, and despair vie against an unquestioning patriotic duty to clear away the ruinous past and rebuild the future, the male characters focus on keeping silent their remembrance of things past.[33] History remains locked behind the closed doors of a furtive legal system controlled by the *Ten* or between the covers of Loredano's business ledger. Cloaked in obscurity, the past is never brought into clear view, except in the form of a tortured or dead body. From the play's opening scene it is clear that "there must be more in this strange process than / the apparent crimes of the accused disclose" (1.1.309–10). Jacopo has returned prematurely from exile "With some faint hope, ... that time, which wears / The marble down, had worn away the hate / Of men's hearts" (3.1.7–9). For the Doge's son, there is no place like home; everywhere else is *"there,"* an "accursed isle of slaves, and captives, / And unbelievers" (3.1.132–4). Although he has been cleared of charges for the murder of Almoro Donato and has satisfied his interrogators that his letter to the Duke of Milan was not treason but merely a means of securing his journey home, albeit as a prisoner, his torture-driven interrogation continues. Readers might suspect Loredano's invisible hand moving behind these brutal machinations for the purposes of personal revenge, but "in such a state / An individual, be he richest of / Such rank as is permitted, or the meanest, / Without a name, is alike nothing" (2.1.407–11). More than revenge, what seems to drive this system of legalized terror is "policy," which irrevocably tends "To one great end" (2.1.412–13). As mysterious as this "end" is, the plot directs more attention to the dynamics between the Foscari family and Loredano. These characters dwell in their private individuality, which, in all cases, is a mental landscape of grief and despair. The persistent realities of violence—even in war's aftermath—impede any possibility for sociability. While Jacopo is being tortured, his father sits silently and watches his son submit to the ordeal. Each suffers in intransigent silence. Loredano also refrains from speaking and writes instead in his ledger.

The Foscaris are undoubtedly ambitious, maybe even noxious, as Barbarigo asserts in the first scene (1.1.11), but Loredano proves just as intractable in pursuing "hereditary hate too far" (1.1.18). Each character acts like a "prince" who works in secret and thereby makes "proofs and process ... difficult" (1.1.40–1) to trace. Additionally, Venice too has become unfathomable. The Doge tells Marina that the people no longer know her (the state), nor, he adds does "she know herself" (2.1.85). Only Marina Foscari speaks out and challenges the absurdity of this alienation, this "code" of silence, and this mysterious lack of identity, which allows people and the state to act with impunity. Marina Foscari angrily tells the Duke that her children "must live ... to serve the state, and die / As did their father" (4.1.208–10) and she wishes she and her mother had not born children to be sacrificed to a faceless nonentity. She understands fully that the nuclear family exists tenuously, united less by the bonds of love than those of patriotism and sacrifice. Challenging the patriarchal and the patriotic silence repeatedly, she intrudes into the *Ten*'s chamber early in the play to loudly protest her husband's innocence, but all she discovers is his silent, tortured body. Her action saves his life, but when she subsequently pleads with Jacopo and Francis to speak out, to act on the other's behalf, and to consider how she and her children have suffered or will survive, her words fall on deaf ears. Later, she assents to leave her children and live in exile to save Jacopo's life. After father and son have died, she attempts to retain the Doge's body and spend her dowry on his burial (5.1.344–5), but even at this moment, her efforts are thwarted by a legal system that has no place for either love or humanity. Audiences might speculate about Loredano's role in this unfolding plot, but it impossible to discover his motivation.

Goethe, Baillie, and Byron highlight resilient women who are cognizant that their lives are subject to patriarchal power. But the men prove to have very little capacity to effect any real change or to resolve their conflicted interests either. The patriarchy is formidable, but mostly as a means of structuring society and imposing a gendered hierarchy. Despite their ability to wield weapons and hold positions of power, the men are as powerless as the women when confronted by scenes of personal and social destruction. Thoas is willing to sacrifice the whole of civil society to coerce Iphigenia's consent to marriage; Orestes' response to the situation is to perpetuate the barbarity and the violence by other means. Hughobert believes he can force Orra to marry his son, Glottenbal, against her will and he will abdicate his paternal responsibility for her and abandon her to Rudigere's tyranny in his attempt to intimidate her. In the end, his son is killed and Orra is traumatized by her fear, leaving Hughobert with no heir and no future. Mind-numbing patriotism paralyzes the two Foscari men and silences the populace in Byron's tragedy. Regardless of their rank, characters in these plays are subject to larger historical and cultural forces, which isolate and alienate individuals within a complex social landscape. Although characters envision alternative possibilities, often taking form as unconventional familial bonding, these alternatives (along with any vestige of the traditional family) are destroyed in the inexorable march toward tragedy's catastrophe. The nineteenth-century concern with social and political rebellion prompted writers to experiment with tragedy, and their focus tended to be on the detrimental general retreat from the public realm into private and domestic spheres.[34] Simon Goldhill describes this trend in Hegelian terms as an attempt to "construct a universalizing view of *the* family and of *the* state as abstract and general principles."[35] Coleridge in his lectures and essays on Shakespearean drama advocated for tragedy that made the individual and their suffering paramount. Both models competed with the philhellenic impulse to revive the social vision of Greek tragedy.

Kleist, Goethe, Baillie, Byron, Shelley, and Musset in *Lorenzaccio* concentrate less on the individual's plight or their character's deaths than on what Jeffrey N. Cox describes as "the loss of a traditional cultural order."[36] In these tragedies characters do not struggle to come to terms with what, in Rowen Williams' words, has been "genuinely and irreplaceably lost."[37] Characters do not fear death nor do they have any illusions that they can control their situation. In these tragedies the actor and the action they take are secondary to the main character's social vision, which proves impossible to realize because the government has become faceless, the populace is silent, and individuals are both alienated and anonymous. Who is responsible for Orra's madness? Orra? Hughobert? Rudigere? The Patriarchy? Arguably, everyone is complicit, but it is the inescapable experience of wartime that renders everyone powerless to confront their fears. In the case of *The Two Foscari*, Loredano appears to take responsibility, but he also shares that responsibility with the more abstract entity of "Nature," and throughout the play, the state, the court, and the anonymous Ten are implicated repeatedly. Denial in *Sardanapalus*, *The Two Foscari*, and *Orra* proliferates and responsibility circulates indeterminately. Orra refuses to deny either her fear or her complicity; Jacopo breaches Venetian law to return home to Venice (not his family); Marina, acting in the name of kinship—something that both Jacopo and Francis Foscari refuse to do—transgresses normative prescriptions. Like Beatrice Cenci, Orra, and their predecessor, Antigone, Marina Foscari and Myrrha destabilize the normative dimensions of kinship and social hierarchy by adopting a defiant masculine position and, quoting Judith Butler's description of Antigone, "embodying the norms of the power she opposes."[38]

Early and mid-nineteenth-century British tragedies thus expose the limitations associated with the modern rhetoric of personal and political agency and they do so by implicating everyone and no one. This is not to say that audiences and readers do not place blame. They do, and they do so quite often by referring to an individual's or the hero's fatal flaw. We tend to associate this concept of the fatal flaw with Aristotle's remarks about classical tragedy rather than modernity. But Coleridge's popular interpretation of Shakespearean tragedy and the Manichaean idea of good and evil, which was popularized in nineteenth-century melodrama, arguably shaped nineteenth-century and even more contemporary ideas of personal responsibility more than the classics. As noted earlier, Percy Shelley in his preface to *The Cenci* was all too aware of this social proclivity for "anatomizing casuistry" or what Jeffrey N. Cox refers to as "self-anatomy," "the inward turn that alienates the self from the other."[39] Personal agency in nineteenth-century tragedy disintegrates in the ghostliness of symbolic power. As we look at tragedies composed later in the century—those written by Dion Boucicault, Henrik Ibsen, George Bernard Shaw, and August Strindberg, for example—we witness characters struggle against the unassailable authority of social norms. Paternal prerogative along with economic and political necessity are rhetorical ploys to justify manipulation, torture, rape, slavery, and war. Even in those instances where the central figure's position is held together by gossamer threads, their identity is fractured by the duplicity and plurality of characters with the same family name. Wives and daughters and fathers and sons defy the assumed singularity and the stability of an individual's identity. This undermines the "given" cultural privilege of male characters, but it also offers no advantage and very few concessions to the female characters.

Shifting to mid-century tragedy and crossing the Atlantic, the language of commodification complicates tragedy's characterization of social responsibility, family unity, and individual identity. Slavery, specifically, the trans-Atlantic slave trade had existed for centuries. According to Ned and Constance Sublette, 1619 marks the first known sale of Africans in Virginia.[40] Although Britain abolished the slave trade in 1807 and emancipated the slaves throughout its empire in 1832, slavery and the slave trade persisted in the Americas. Slavery lacks the characteristics of nobility and honor often associated with the battlefield and with tragedy, but it pits the life of one person against another, and it is a war catastrophic in its consequences. In the nineteenth century, slavery was often staged as melodrama rather than tragedy. Melodrama's basic plot is similar to that of gothic drama in that it oscillates between two or more antithetical forms of cultural production: most often, comedy and tragedy, comedy and romance, or romance and tragedy. The highly mixed forms of melodrama and the gothic generated frightening specters, disturbing scenes of abjection and horror, and as Jerrold E. Hogle writes, "contradictory hopes and fears" and "entangled contradictions" that appear alien, grotesque, and "incompatible [with] established standards of normality."[41] Jeffrey N. Cox and I have argued elsewhere that melodrama seemed at first to be created specifically for representing the terrors of slavery.[42] But, the radical potential and the political charge of melodrama and gothic drama is often diffused by the oppositional play of its many formal elements. More than the death of an individual or a heroic figure, audiences viewing a tragedy like Dion Boucicault's *The Octoroon* (1859) witness what Orlando Patterson refers to as social death, a process of social negation through which the slave and slavery are constituted.[43] The economics and the politics of slavery identify the slave as a non-being, with no claim to resources or to human rights. The sad irony of this is that although socially dead, the slave and the institution of slavery remain incorporated within society. The slave's occupation of the liminal border between life and death threatens to undermine any claim to social and moral order, and yet, society attempts repeatedly to prove how slaves and slavery are essential to the order it threatens.[44]

Boucicault's *The Octoroon; or Life in Louisiana* premiered at New York's Winter Garden City Theatre in 1859, days after the execution of John Brown and a little more than a year before the American Civil War erupted. Zoe—like Byron's Greek character,

Myrrha in *Sardanapalus*—is a slave. Both characters are beloved and both have a certain degree of what we might call freedom in that they have the necessities of food, clothing, and shelter. They do not endure the tribulations of forced labor, and generally speaking, they can do what they desire and they exert a great deal of influence over those in power. The significant difference is that Myrrha is a Greek brought into the Assyrian Court, and Zoe is an octoroon and the illegitimate daughter of her recently deceased owner/father. In contrast with Myrrha, Zoe has multiple suitors and, arguably, she can choose her father's nephew, George Peyton, because her father's will grants her freedom. But tragedy turns on irresolvable conflicts that precipitate what Raymond Williams refers to as "tragic experience."[45] The pivotal turn in Byron's and Boucicault's tragedies is the threat of revolution and disorder. These characters reify and challenge the possibilities for their performances as free and/or enslaved women who fall in love with men who remain ostensibly powerless to liberate them.[46]

This turn to slavery raises the question of whether slaves can be the subjects of tragedy. The answer in the nineteenth century is yes. Myrrha and Zoe are commodities; they are things, not people. Slaves represent the antithesis of sovereign power and entitlement. Their status as slaves renders them chattel in the eyes of the law. Myrrha and Zoe have no legal authority, no rights; they are nonentities, nonpersons, nothings, and yet, both characters are *objects* of sexual desire. Just as in Kleist's play and Goethe's *Faust*, sexual desire is the disruptive and revolutionary force. Zoe's illegitimacy, her status as the daughter of a slave owner and subject to her father's will, threatens the social and economic order, and her body represents a locus for emotional and legal disorder as well as revolutionary upheaval in a society organized around the twinned nodes of natural and civil law.

Zoe's racialized status as an octoroon locates her as the site of her father's moral and financial bankruptcy. As an octoroon slave, Zoe is a valuable object and selling her will alleviate the family's debts. But her father's nephew and heir, George Peyton, falls in love with her. Having spent much of his youth abroad in France and ignorant of Zoe's status as either an octoroon or his uncle's "natural" daughter, George is stunned by the range of responses to Zoe's presence. His neighbor, Mr. Sunnyside, ignores her; she is invisible in polite society; subsequently, she remains silent in these scenes. Scudder's outburst renders her visible as an object of sexual desire. The lustful and violent machinations of the overseer, Jacob M'Closky, make the conditions of her visibility more clear. He will do anything—he will press the "civil" law into action, he will commit murder, and spend every last dollar he has—to secure her body as either his mistress or his slave. His aunt makes excuses for George's attraction to Zoe, and she insists, "he will soon understand" (I, i; 497), but she will not talk to George. Zoe proves his instructor; she teaches him that she is "an unclean thing—forbidden by laws" (II, i; 511). This statement and Zoe's presence on the auction block later in the play reconfigure the revolutionary energy she embodies and the "unmanageable instability" she represents as a "white" mixed-race person and a "free" slave.[47]

One way to read the familial dynamics in *Sardanapalus* and *The Octoroon* is through the critical lens of she-tragedy. Like Nicholas Rowe's *The Fair Penitent*, which, according to Kathleen Wilson, was, "after Shakespeare, the sixth most frequently performed tragedy in the London theater between 1702 and 1800,"[48] *Orra*, *Sardanapalus*, and *The Octoroon* employ love triangles as a means of negotiating gender roles within and outside the familial structure. In these plays, the tragic catastrophe turns on a collision with the subaltern figure. In *The Octoroon*, Dora Sunnyside, George Peyton, and Zoe constitute a love triangle in which the neighborhood heiress, acting out of a selfless love for George Peyton, does all she can to save the Peyton plantation, buying its slaves, and attempting to purchase Zoe. Like Calista in Rowe's tragedy, Zoe sacrifices herself—committing suicide—to insure there will be no more unlawful heirs on the plantation, thus resolving the choice between familial duty and sexual desire for George Peyton.[49] The emotional and financial bonds that define this family are not maintained by acts of collective unity or kindness, but rather through Zoe's death. This act as well as the judge's (Zoe's father) seemingly untimely investment in the slave trade years earlier secures George Peyton's future and the Terrebonne plantation. In *The Octoroon*, a father's desire for his illegitimate daughter's freedom is doomed to failure. Familial legitimacy and succession are re-established on the Terrebonne plantation through multiple acts of surrogation, which manage and regulate Dora Sunnyside's financial independence while blocking George Peyton's and Zoe's sexual desires.

Reading Boucicault's tragedy as a later development of she-tragedy helps us understand how the realities and the rhetorics of slavery and racism framed the modern conception of freedom as a form of entitlement: as something that can be bought and sold. *The Octoroon* reifies and contests the practices of everyday life that ensure the continuance of racism and slavery. As Zoe attempts to make clear to George, race is a legal matter that cannot be ignored or made invisible. Zoe tells George, if he examines her closely, he will see "the ineffaceable curse of Cain," "the fatal dark mark" at the roots of her hair and the "blueish tinge" of their finger nails.[50] Led to see these "marks" by Zoe, George affirms their visibility for the audience. Zoe's complicity and George's assent further endorses and sanctions the racism that structures and destroys families in the nineteenth century. Despite the fact that Zoe's father grants her freedom, his will does not allow her to marry George Peyton nor does it guarantee her freedom. Boucicault's tragedy stages the realities of social death and the impact it has on the "natural" family that defies social norms.

Domestic space and the family are politicized for a variety of motives in nineteenth-century tragedy. As Kathleen Wilson notes in her remarks about Nicholas Rowe's eighteenth-century tragedy, *The Fair Penitent*, this reflects "a larger [and, arguably, earlier] epistemic shift ... as the family went from a model to the instrument of 'governance,' a term applied not only to political organization but also to problems of self-control, household management, and spiritual guidance."[51] Throughout this discussion, I have directed attention to how tragedies in the period disrupted society's romance with the nuclear family. Byron's Cain, for example, discovers that his love for his sister, Adah, will eventually become taboo and labeled as incestuous. The orphans, Orra and Iphigenia, attempt to reconfigure the family by extending its boundaries to include strangers, war veterans, and the homeless. Marina Foscari will abandon her children to live with her husband in exile, and Cenci reenacts two classical motifs of familial destruction—incest and parricide—that mark the nuclear family as a site of social ruin. Tragedies throughout this century stage the social consequences of privacy as personal and social deprivation. Caught in the liminal space between the public and the private, characters confront the systemic power of the Church and the State, and tragic plots expose the underlying taboos that destroy the family. Significantly, melodrama preserves and idealizes the family as the symbolic core of the nation and the European Christian community.

At the end of the century, Henrik Ibsen portrayed, in *The Master Builder* (1892), the family unit as fragmented, childless, and undermined by infidelity, personal ambition, and empty illusions about the past and the future. His two main characters, Halvard and Aline

Solness, live together as strangers. Halvard, the master builder, has literally built his reputation as a builder on the ruins of his wife's family home; the fire that destroyed Aline's former family residence, a castle, was catastrophic in its destruction. As in earlier gothic dramas, the castle marks the site of aristocratic power, but here society and Solness's family suffer irreversible losses in the accident. Symbolically, the fire destroys the aristocratic apex that structures society. There is no possibility of rebuilding the past and no viable potential for the future, especially since the two Solness boys die in the fire's aftermath. Nonetheless, the bourgeois middle class is born out of the ashes of aristocratic ruin. Solness builds and sells many homes where, formerly, only one existed. With his new-found personal wealth, he establishes a successful business, employing his former employer, an architect. Despite his financial success and his self-affirming symbolic status as a builder solely of family homes, Halvard Solness has an affair with his secretary. He does not love this woman; he is using her to control his younger, equally ambitious employee. Like Count Cenci, he believes events like the fire happen because he wishes them to, that his sons' lives had to be sacrificed, and that like Faust, he has "helpers and servers" who obey his will.[52] Although he is prosperous, he is haunted by the past: particularly by the fire's impact on his wife's happiness. When a young woman arrives at the Solness household, she has the potential to become their "daughter" and thus to inhabit one of the three empty nurseries. In contrast with Aline Solness who struggles with questions of duty and loyalty to her husband, Hilde Wagnel is motivated by the promise made by Halvard Solness to her ten years earlier, when she was just a child watching him dedicate a newly constructed church. Solness has long abandoned building churches and his sole focus is building family homes, but Hilde Wagnel insists that Solness bring her fantasy to life: to build her a castle and to make her a princess. This unmarried young woman subdues Solness and subverts his vision of the emerging middle class. Solness—who refuses to acknowledge the claims of time (represented by the death of Knut Brovik, the former architect) or those of the younger generation (Ragnar Brovik and Kaja Fosli)[53]—will be attracted to Hilde Wagnel's refusal to accept anything other than her imaginary kingdom. Seduced by Hilde's childhood fantasy—the ghostly afterimage of Aline Solness's life—Solness will climb the tower of his new home and fall to his death, and Hilde, in some ways similar to Orra, will be captivated not by fear but rather by the specter of virile masculinity that comes to life in the moment of its destruction.

As the century draws to a close, Ibsen's tragedies throw into relief an intersecting nexus of social concerns. As in the works of Goethe, Kleist, Byron, and Shelley, characters explore the potential for social, political, and personal transformation. As in Baillie's *Orra*, there is a bourgeois preoccupation with social responsibility and capitalism and the fact that events—like war or a house burning down—can throw these interests into disarray. The Romantic anxieties about alienation and remorse—the latter marked by Coleridge's 1813 smash hit, *Remorse*—and its attempts to embody different forms of desire prove to be as relevant to Ibsen as is the recognition that many of the long-lived social and cultural institutions are limited, if not obsolete. In nineteenth-century tragedy, we do not witness the evolution of an ongoing struggle so much as its continuation. The ideologies that promote a vision of familial and social coherence are exposed repeatedly as both false and destructive of the very things they proclaim to protect.

Solness, like Orra, Sardanapalus, Iphigenia, and Zoe, comprehends the world in which he lives. Characters are trapped by the compromises they feel they must make to live in the world, but their struggle ultimately turns self-destructive. It is not because the hero or heroine is burdened by some tragic flaw; rather, there exists something unnamable and mysterious about modern society. Humanity is subject to history and to its institutions that reconfigure and distort human relationships and humanity's connection with nature. As each character in these tragedies attempts repeatedly to find a way to defer or alter tragedy's inevitable catastrophe, they encounter a haunting specter or ghost. Sardanapalus has a dream about his ghostly ancestors and is constantly reminded of them by Myrrha and his brother-in-law, Salamenes. Orra's encounter paralyzes her to the point of madness. Zoe creates for George and the audience the ghostly and haunting image of her inescapable status as a slave. In Ibsen's *Ghosts*, Mrs. Alving tells Pastor Manders,

> I almost believe we are all ghosts, Pastor Manders. It is not only what we have inherited from our fathers and mothers that walks in us. It is every kind of dead idea, lifeless old beliefs and so on. They are not alive, but they cling to us for all that, and we can never rid ourselves of them. Whenever I read a newspaper I seem to see ghosts stealing between the lines. There must be ghosts the whole country over, as thick as the sands of the sea. And when we are all of us so wretchedly afraid of the light.[54]

History's ghosts permeate the physical landscape, the media, and politics, and they structure family norms and society. These ghosts haunt nineteenth-century tragedy, and as such, they confirm each character's isolation and their alienation from a more progressive and collective social vision they have imagined and attempted to create. Ibsen's characters are caught in the liminal spaces of modern society. Like other tragic characters in the period, Solness, his wife, Hilde Wagnel, and Ragnar Brovik look to the past in their futile attempts to reproduce its ghostly facsimile or reformulate it as the future. In every case, they tap into and become captivated with the historical and cultural tragedies that construct and reflect their tormented imaginations. Arguably, the closed world of tragedy haunted and inspired writers like Baillie, Boucicault, Byron, Goethe, Kleist, Shelley, Ibsen, and others, who were unsure how to navigate forward without looking to the past. Goethe revised tragedy into comedy in the second part of *Faust* and *Iphigenia in Tauris*; Shelley abandoned tragedy after writing *The Cenci*, reconfiguring its plots and mixing tragedy with other dramatic forms to affirm the future. Other writers perhaps felt either more pessimistic or more assured about what tragedy could and could not do as a cultural form. Regardless, nineteenth-century tragedy created a storm like that described by Walter Benjamin in his "Theses on the Philosophy of History." The many formulations of nineteenth-century tragedy remained subject to history's violent storms, and like Paul Klee's angel, these plays looked to the past while being drawn into the future as the pile of cultural debris kept growing skyward, creating a precarious effigy to progress.

CHAPTER EIGHT

Gender and Sexuality

COLE HEINOWITZ

INTRODUCTION: THE RISE OF THE BOURGEOIS FAMILY

Familial relations have constituted the foundation of tragic drama since its origins in classical Athens. From Aeschylus' *Oresteia*, Sophocles' *Oedipus Rex*, and Euripides' *Medea* to William Shakespeare's *Macbeth* and Jean Racine's *Phèdre*, tragedy consistently emerges from violations of traditionally gendered relationships between husbands and wives, fathers and daughters, and mothers and sons. Contrary to claims that the Romantic Era marked the end of tragedy by dismantling the ancient social hierarchies and religious structures on which the genre depended,[1] tragedy's fundamental basis in the family is nowhere more pronounced than on the nineteenth-century stage. In fact, as Jeffrey Cox persuasively argues in this volume, nineteenth-century theater powerfully transformed the tragic by grounding it in the *loss* of traditional providential and hierarchical worldviews, thereby shifting its focus from the individual sufferer to the social and ideological structures that produce such suffering.[2]

The most compelling evidence of this transformation is arguably found in the *class* constitution of the tragic family. Over the course of the eighteenth century, as Europe's rising middle classes came to form the greater part of the theater-going public, playwrights increasingly turned their attention to producing characters with whom—and scenarios with which—their audiences could directly identify.[3] As George Lillo wrote in his dedication to the determinedly middle-class *London Merchant: or, the History of George Barnwell* (1731), "tragedy is so far from losing its dignity by being accommodated to the circumstances of the generality of mankind that it is more truly august in proportion to the extent of its influence and the numbers that are properly affected by it."[4] Lillo was not alone in rejecting neoclassical tragedy's fidelity to Aristotle's notion that a tragic hero "must be one who is highly renowned and prosperous."[5] As the *encyclopédiste* Jean-François Marmontel argued in his *French Poetics* of 1763: "We wrong the human heart, we misread nature, if we believe that it requires titles to rouse and touch us. The sacred names of friend, father, lover, husband, son, mother . . . these are far more pathetic than aught else and retain their claims forever."[6] Quoting Marmontel with approval in his influential *Hamburg Dramaturgy* of 1767–9, Gotthold Ephraim Lessing adds: "The names of princes and heroes can lend pomp and majesty to a play, but they contribute nothing to our emotions. The misfortunes of those whose circumstances most resemble our own, must naturally penetrate most deeply into our hearts."[7] In practice as well as in theory, eighteenth-century tragedy stands out for its depiction of bourgeois families instead of aristocratic and high-ranking ones. Inspired by *The London Merchant*, works such as Lessing's *Miss Sara Sampson* (1755) and Denis Diderot's *The Natural Son* (1758) increasingly displaced the neoclassical repertoire of Dryden, Gottsched, and Corneille.[8]

These bourgeois tragedies sought to present more natural, more affectionate, ostensibly natural forms of social organization than those found in noble or high-ranking families. As Johann Gottfried Herder wrote in *Ideas on the Philosophy of the History of Mankind* (1784–5), the family was "the eternal work of nature ... the growing household in which the seeds of the humanity of mankind are planted and raised."[9] The drama, along with works of philosophy and history, as well as popular publications such as moral weeklies and conduct manuals, promoted a vision of the middle-class household as a haven of mutual respect, tender guidance, and filial devotion. "What can be more charming," Adolph Freiherr von Knigge declared in his 1788 manual *Polite Intercourse*, "than the expression of a beloved father amongst his grown-up children who, through his wise and friendly manner, are keen not to hide any thought of their hearts from him, their truthful adviser, their most considerate friend."[10] Such ideas took deep root in the hearts and minds of Europe's rising bourgeoisie. On the death of the English manufacturer Samuel Galton in 1832, for example, his adult children fondly recalled him as "their friend, their companion, their everything. ... In all troubles he was our adviser and sympathiser."[11] Drawing on such evidence, historians Leonore Davidoff and Catherine Hall conclude that, from 1780 to 1850, the bourgeois home came to be seen as "the basis for a proper moral order," a belief predicated on "the *naturalness* of the family as the primary form of social organization."[12] Such naturalized representations of the family are at the core of bourgeois tragedy and exemplify the morality it sought to codify.

In a culture still governed by patrilineal descent and the laws of primogeniture—according to which the eldest son inherited his father's name, wealth, and social standing—one might reasonably expect eighteenth-century tragedy to concentrate on the bond between the patriarch and his male heir.[13] Yet despite the socio-economic primacy of the father–son relationship, bourgeois tragedy overwhelmingly privileges the bond between doting fathers and their unmarried daughters. From Lessing's *Emilia Galotti* (1772) to Friedrich Schiller's *Intrigue and Love* (1784), the paradigmatic works of this genre follow a consistent pattern. Despite the father's vigilance, his beautiful daughter attracts the attentions of an aristocratic admirer. By contrast with the eighteenth-century novel, in which such overtures might appeal to a father eager to dispose of his daughter through an advantageous marriage, bourgeois tragedy looks askance at the prospect of upward mobility. Herr Miller's reaction on learning of his daughter's courtship by the President's son in *Intrigue and Love* is representative: "I'll say to His Excellency: 'Your Excellency's son has an eye on my daughter; my daughter is not good enough to be Your Excellency's son's wife, but to be Your Excellency's son's whore my daughter is too precious, and that's all there is to it.'"[14] The resolutions of *Emilia Galotti* and *Intrigue and Love* follow those of many bourgeois tragedies: after a hard-fought battle against the machinations of courtly corruption, the affective bond between father and daughter ultimately prevails and the daughter willingly forfeits her life to save her honor. With her death, the heroine sanctifies the father–daughter dyad as the measure of moral integrity for an entire class.

This much-rehearsed plot in which daughters are sacrificed to safeguard the honor of the family raises a troubling question for cultural historians. Given that the socio-economic perpetuation of the patriarchal family rests solely on the male heir, and given that the daughter generally inherits nothing, losing even her father's name upon marriage, why does the father–daughter relationship assume such consummate significance in bourgeois tragedy?[15] As we shall see, nineteenth-century tragedy would propose an answer to this question by reconsidering the essential nature of paternal inheritance. Although many middle-class brides did receive some form of marriage portion from their fathers and were allowed to own property in cases of a pre-nuptial legal settlement, more often than not those assets were assumed by the husband after marriage—ostensibly as compensation for the material support of his wife.[16] But if a married woman did not inherit her father's name or augment his wealth, she *did* inherit and transmit his genetic material and character (in nineteenth-century terms, his "blood"). By emphasizing the physiological and psychological dimensions of the father's legacy in the absence of socio-economic transmission, nineteenth-century tragedy foregrounds the father–daughter relationship as the central site in which prevailing ideas of paternal authority and influence are negotiated, contested, and transformed.

THEATERS OF CRUELTY: FATHERS AND DAUGHTERS ON THE ROMANTIC-ERA STAGE

If tragedies such as *Emilia Galotti* and *Intrigue and Love* affirmed the ideals of paternal devotion and daughterly renunciation that exemplified bourgeois morality, they also dramatized the extreme physical and psychic violence such father–daughter intimacy entailed. In *Intrigue and Love*, for instance, Herr Miller prevents his daughter's attempted suicide through a heart-rending avowal of love: "You were my idol. Listen, Luise, if you still have any room for a father's feelings . . . you were my all . . . my heavenly kingdom!" (5.1.82). Luise's protest, however, suggests a darker vision of paternal affection: "Stop! Stop! O my father! . . . To think that tenderness compels more barbarously than tyrant's fury!" (5.1.83). In *Emilia Galotti*, the violence of father–daughter affection is depicted in much starker terms. To spare Emilia from the depravities of Prince Gonzaga, Odoardo Galotti stabs his daughter through the heart. As she collapses in his arms, Emilia gratefully kisses the hand that "save[d] her from disgrace" and "brought her thus to life a second time," dying peacefully with the words "Ah—my father" on her lips.[17]

In eighteenth-century bourgeois tragedy, such displays of intra-familial violence are directly offset by reference to an extra-familial threat, namely the sexual rapacity of decadent aristocrats. Yet, notwithstanding the real sexual vulnerability of unmarried young women at the time, one of the main ideological functions of the licentious aristocrat on the eighteenth-century stage was to justify the subjugation of women in the middle-class home by deflecting domestic violence onto an extrinsic force. Such, at least, is the critique suggested by many nineteenth-century tragedies in which paternal figures are identical with corrupt, predatory aristocrats—from Joanna Baillie's *Orra* (1812), in which the eponymous heroine is driven to madness through the machinations of her guardian Count Hughobert, to Victor Hugo's *Hernani* (1830), in which Doña Sol and her lover commit suicide to escape the wrath of her lustful uncle Don Ruy Gomez de Silva.

Significantly, however, neither Hughobert nor Don Ruy is his victim's *biological* father.[18] Nowhere in nineteenth-century tragedy is the bourgeois myth of the loving father more ruthlessly unmasked than in Percy Bysshe Shelley's *The Cenci* (1819), whose malevolent *pater familias* lives solely for the pleasure of exercising his ancient prerogative to destroy his family members.[19] The tragedy opens with a regal banquet held, as the assembled kinsmen soon learn, to celebrate the deaths of Count Cenci's two eldest sons. As the guests fall into confusion and begin to leave, Cenci's daughter Beatrice entreats them to protect herself and her family from her father's wrath:

> What although tyranny, and impious hate
> Stand sheltered by a father's hoary hair?
> What, if 'tis he who clothed us in these limbs
> Who tortures them, and triumphs? What, if we,
> The desolate and the dead, were his own flesh,
> His children and his wife, whom he is bound
> To love and shelter? Shall we therefore find
> No refuge in this merciless wide world?[20]

But Beatrice's pleas are no match for Cenci's threats:

> I hope my good friends here
> Will think of their own daughters—or perhaps
> Of their own throats—before they lend an ear
> To this wild girl.
>
> —1.3.129–32

After the guests depart, leaving father and daughter alone, the Count vows to punish Beatrice's insolence: "I know a charm that shall make thee meek and tame" (1.3.165–7).

Although the actualization of Cenci's threat is never shown onstage or even named, Beatrice's evasions and circumlocutions when questioned leave little doubt as to its nature:

> Of all words,
> That minister to mortal intercourse,
> Which wouldst thou hear? For there is none to tell
> My misery: if another ever knew
> Aught like it, she died as I will die,
> And left it, as I must, without a name.
>
> —3.1.111–16

Despairing of legal redress because, as Beatrice's stepmother Lucretia laments, such "unnatural, strange and monstrous" wrongs "[e]xceed all measure of belief," the family determines to murder the Count (3.1.188–9). Their hired assassins are quickly discovered and Beatrice is tried, found guilty of parricide, and executed, but not before she delivers a damning critique of the Roman justice system which winks at Cenci's crimes and punishes his victims, "hold[ing] it of most dangerous example / In aught to weaken the paternal power, / Being, as 'twere, the shadow of [its] own" (2.2.54–6). Lacking the gold, land, and influence by which the Count purchases immunity for his crimes, Beatrice can only call on God to avenge what human law permits. "What!" she expostulates,

> will human laws . . .
> Bar all access to retribution first,
> And then, when heaven doth interpose to do
> What ye neglect . . .
> Make ye the victims who demanded it
> Culprits? 'Tis ye are culprits!
>
> —4.4.117, 119–21, 123–4

"Wherefore should I have wielded [the sword]," she continues, "Unless / The crimes which mortal tongue dare never name / God therefore scruples to avenge" (4.4.128–30)?

With these words, Beatrice not only exposes the hypocrisy of her accusers, but also indicts their charges as an impious disavowal of divine—and by extension, paternal—law. Her defiant ultimatum, according to which the imputation of her guilt impugns the law of God the Father, harks back to the fundamental question posed by all tragic suffering, from *Oedipus* to *Hamlet*: How can divine justice permit such human suffering?

Due ostensibly to its treatment of incest, *The Cenci* was not staged in Shelley's lifetime. Nonetheless, the published play sold remarkably well[21]—not least thanks to the spectacular hostility it elicited from critics. The opinion expressed by the *Literary Gazette* is representative: "Of all the abominations which intellectual perversion, and poetical atheism, have produced in our times, this tragedy appears to us the most abominable... the whole design, and every part of it, is a libel upon humanity."[22] While expressing unanimous horror at Cenci's deeds, however, early nineteenth-century critics reserved their most vicious opprobrium for his daughter. Even worse than the crime of parricide, they insisted, was Beatrice's denial of guilt before the court. "Instead of avowing the deed, and asserting its justice, as would be strictly natural for one who had committed such a crime from such a cause," the *New Monthly Magazine* opined, Beatrice "tries to avoid death by the meanest arts of falsehood, and encourages her accomplices to endure the extremities of torture rather than implicate her by confession."[23] Similar censure greeted the unlicensed "private" premiere of *The Cenci* at London's Islington Grand Theatre, organized by the Shelley Society in 1886. *The Times* complained that any sympathy Beatrice might have commanded was undermined by "making her ... cling with such tenacity to life as to foreswear herself in the judge's presence."[24] *The Echo* found the "injured heroine" so "disingenuous" as to "excite horror" rather than sympathy, while the *Saturday Review* condemned her character as "terrible," arguing that "she should have avowed the act, but denied its criminal character. As it is, she falls below herself, and no reason is given for the fall."[25]

What such nineteenth-century assessments of Beatrice's moral turpitude failed to recognize—and what continues to generate heated scholarly debate[26]—is that Beatrice's actions are specifically calculated to strain audiences' sympathy by reinforcing the model of daughterly virtue on which that sympathy depended. Despite her noble rank, Beatrice is portrayed in ways that firmly establish her place in the eighteenth-century lineage of tragic bourgeois daughters. Like Emilia Galotti and Luise Miller, Beatrice is "an amiable being ... formed to adorn and be admired," a "gentle daughter" whose "sweet looks" make all things "[b]eauteous and glad" (1.1.43–5). From her childhood, she has borne the Count's abuse with "reverence" and even "kissed the sacred hand / Which crushed us to the earth, and thought its stroke / Was perhaps some paternal chastisement" (1.3.109, 111–13). And when she could no longer interpret Cenci's cruelty as benign fatherly discipline, still Beatrice "sought by patience, love and tears / To soften him" (1.3.115–16). In her tenderness and docility as much as in her tenacious faith in paternal authority, the aristocratic Beatrice appears the embodiment of middle-class feminine virtue.

Indeed, Beatrice's relationship with the Count reveals that the intimate father–daughter bond, even in its most perverted form, was not exclusive to the bourgeois home. From the beginning of the play, it is clear that Beatrice has deeply internalized her father's lessons. "I have no remorse and little fear, / Which are, I think, the checks of other men," Cenci boasts; nor does Beatrice, as her role in his assassination and her subsequent assertions of innocence at the trial show (1.1.84–5). The Count's greatest delight, he tells Cardinal Camillo, is to read the inner torment of his victims on their features. Having lost his youthful appetite for murder and sex, Cenci states:

> I the rather
> Look on such pangs as terror ill conceals,
> The dry fixed eye ball; the pale quivering lip,
> Which tell me that the spirit weeps within.
>
> —1.2.109–12

Though the command of such psychological penetration affords her no pleasure, Beatrice inherits and substantially refines her father's skill. Her aspiring suitor Orsino thus complains:

> I fear
> Her subtle mind, her awe-inspiring gaze
> Whose beams anatomize me nerve by nerve
> And lay me bare, and make me blush to see
> My hidden thoughts.
>
> —1.2.83–7

Even the Count himself admits to being struck "dumb" by the force of Beatrice's "fearless eye" when at the banquet

> you dared to look
> With disobedient insolence on me,
> Bending a stern and inquiring brow
> On what I meant; whilst I then sought to hide
> That which I came to tell you—but in vain.
>
> —2.1.119, 116, 106–10

In fact, it is precisely Beatrice's masterful adaptation of her father's power to "anatomize" that steels his resolve to defile her body and crush her spirit.

Beatrice's method of retaliation only underscores the adversaries' affinity. "[S]omething must be done," she announces, "something which shall make / The thing that I have suffered but a shadow / In the dread lightning which avenges it" (3.1.86–9). By equaling—and exceeding—the assault that prompted it, Beatrice's act of parricide subsumes her rape and becomes its substitute. Indeed, such parallels between daughter and father have led many twentieth-century commentators to conclude, as Beatrice herself does in Antonin Artaud's 1935 adaptation of the play, "that I have ended by resembling [my father]."[27] Read from this perspective, the bond of intimate violence that links Shelley's Beatrice and Count Cenci darkly mirrors the affectionate father–daughter dyad at the heart of bourgeois tragedy, pointedly recalling its foundation in female sacrifice and subjecting the morality it expounds to its anatomizing gaze.

While *The Cenci* was popularly condemned, at least one astute commentator understood the powerful implications Beatrice's fate would have for later nineteenth-century tragedy. As George Bernard Shaw observed in his review of the play's 1886 premiere:

> Those who have witnessed the agony and death of any innocent creature upon whom Nature has wantonly fastened a dreadful malady, will recognize here a tragedy truer and deeper than that of any conventional heroine whose lover dies in the fifth act. Shelley and Shakspere [sic] are the only dramatists who have dealt in despair of this quality; and Shelley alone has shown it driven into the heart of a girl.[28]

As Shaw recognized, by driving suffering of this magnitude "into the heart of a girl," Shelley had exploited the figure of the sacrificial daughter to impugn the patriarchal family's moral authority. In doing so, *The Cenci* anticipated the work of later nineteenth-century dramatists such as Henrik Ibsen, August Strindberg, and Oscar Wilde, whose tragedies present a world in which traditional family structures inevitably bring about their own destruction. Moreover, by creating a heroine with whom audiences could not comfortably sympathize, Shelley had undermined the affective response on which the bourgeois stage (and the families it represented) depended for its status as a "school of virtue." As such, *The Cenci* not only exposed the deadly force concealed behind the mask of paternal love, it revealed the trope of the caring father and his dutiful daughter as an ideological tool in the perpetuation of patriarchal tyranny—irrespective of social class.

THE ENEMY WITHIN: PATHOLOGIZING THE PATRIARCHAL FAMILY

By translating domestic drama from the middle-class household to the aristocratic castle, nineteenth-century tragedies such as Baillie's *Orra*, Hugo's *Hernani*, and Shelley's *The Cenci* revealed patriarchal authority in its most naked form as the principal threat to the family.[29] Such interrogations of paternal prerogative were powerfully supported by the writings of nineteenth-century philosophers, scholars, reformers, and feminists. As early as 1792, in her *Vindication of the Rights of Woman*, Mary Wollstonecraft had asserted that the neglect of women's education, coupled with their lack of social and political rights, had reduced them to the status of "convenient slaves," treated by their husbands as "subordinate beings, and not as part of the human species."[30] John Stuart Mill's *The Subjection of Women* (1869), widely adopted by the women's suffrage movement, built on Wollstonecraft's argument by comparing women's legal subordination to chattel slavery in order to refute the prevailing assumption that masculine domination was "natural":

> Did not the slaveowners of the Southern United States maintain the same doctrine, with all the fanaticism with which men cling to the theories that justify their passions and legitimate their personal interests? Did they not call heaven and earth to witness that the domination of the white man over the black is natural, that the black race is by nature incapable of freedom, and marked out for slavery?[31]

Wollstonecraft and Mill's arguments against the natural legitimacy of patriarchy was given substantial ballast by the work of social scientists such as Lewis Morgan, whose *Ancient Society, or Researches in the Lines of Human Progress from Savagery through Barbarism to Civilization* (1877) posited that, contrary to Roman and Biblical law, the origins of the family structure were matriarchal. Extending the implications of Morgan's study, Friedrich Engels contended that the emergence of the modern patriarchal family marked "the *world-historic defeat of the female sex*" by which "woman was degraded, enthralled, the slave of the man's lust, a mere instrument for breeding children," differing only from the common prostitute in that "she does not hire out her body, like a wage-worker, on piecework, but sells it into slavery once for all."[32] In his notes to *A Doll's House* (1879), Henrik Ibsen underscored this point in yet more vivid terms, comparing the mother in nineteenth-century Europe to "certain insects who go away and die when she has done her duty in the propagation of the race."[33]

As a result of these developments both on and off the stage, when the *pater familias* was restored to his seat of command over the bourgeois household in later nineteenth-century tragedy—complete with his affective mantle of tenderness and decency—he could be seen for what he truly was. Ibsen's *A Doll's House* is perhaps the most famous of such indictments, and has justly been the subject of more than a century of criticism and scholarship.[34] Ibsen's contemporary George Bernard Shaw immediately grasped the significance of the play for traditional gender identities and the institution of marriage: "Nora's revolt is the end of a chapter of human history. The slam of the door behind her is more momentous than the cannons of Waterloo or Sedan."[35] More recent critics tend to concur. As Gail Finney, for one, asserts in *Women and Modern Drama*: "Few moments in the history of theater are so famous as Nora Helmer's defiant slamming of the door of her home at the end of *A Doll's House*, a gesture widely credited with announcing the sexual revolution."[36]

On the surface, the home of Nora and Torvald Helmer is the epitome of conjugal middle-class bliss. They are an apparently loving couple with three healthy children, comfortable and tasteful furnishings, reliable servants, loyal friends, and a solid reputation. The one visible strain on their relationship—money—is about to be alleviated by Helmer's appointment as manager of the bank. Yet, beneath this placid surface lies a deception, the revelation of which will drive the tragedy to its climax. After their marriage, as Nora confesses to her friend Christine, Helmer resigned from a position that offered no prospect of promotion and, in the ensuing struggle to make ends meet, fell gravely ill. In his doctor's opinion, Helmer's only chance for survival was to spend a year in the warmer climate of Italy, a luxury the young family could not afford. After pleading ineffectually with her husband to solicit a loan, Nora takes matters into her own hands and secretly borrows the money. As a nineteenth-century wife could not legally obtain a loan without her husband's consent, Nora forges her dying father's signature on the bond, accidentally dating the forgery for several days after his death. Although she does not notice the error, her creditor Krogstad does, and plans to make good use of his knowledge. When he learns that Helmer, in his new capacity at the bank, intends to dismiss him from his position there, Krogstad has a powerful weapon at his disposal: he writes to Helmer, informing him of the illegal loan, and threatens to destroy his reputation by exposing Nora's crime.

Here, well into the play's final act, the tension appears to have reached its breaking point. Terrified, more for himself than for his wife and children, Helmer turns on Nora with unprecedented wrath, declaring that from thenceforth their marriage exists "only in the eyes of the world."[37] Since she has proven herself a "[m]iserable creature" with "[n]o religion, no morality, [and] no sense of duty," she is thereby unfit to raise their children and must be separated from them (3, 242–3). The anticipated denouement, and the one which Nora herself has repeatedly alluded to, is of course her suicide. Moments after reading Krosgard's letter, however, Helmer receives a second envelope, including the returned bond and a note from Krosgard explaining that fortune has smiled on him and he has forgiven the loan. Realizing that his reputation is saved, Helmer blithely dismisses his earlier recriminations and reaffirms Nora's place in his heart and home:

> I know that what you did, you did out of love for me. . . . You have loved me as a wife ought to love her husband. Only you had not sufficient knowledge to judge the means you used. But do you suppose you are any the less dear to me, because you don't understand how to act on your own responsibility? No, no . . . I should not

be a man if this womanly helplessness did not just give you a double attractiveness in my eyes.

—3, 244

It is at this point of absurd reversal that the tragedy's real climax occurs. In this instant, Nora understands that their idyllic marriage has been a farce in which Helmer, like her father before him, merely acted the part of the loving patriarch. "I have been greatly wronged," she begins:

> When I was at home with papa, he told me his opinion about everything, and so I had the same opinions; and if I differed from him I concealed the fact, because he would not have liked it. He called me his doll-child, and he played with me just as I used to play with my dolls. . . . I was simply transferred from papa's hands into yours. . . . You arranged everything according to your taste, and so I got the same tastes as you—or else pretended to . . . I have been your doll-wife, just as at home I was papa's doll-child.

—3, 246–7

As Nora realizes, there is only one way to break the cycle of patriarchal oppression: she must betray what Helmer calls her "most sacred duties" as wife and mother, abandon her family, and "stand quite alone" (3, 247–8).[38] Helmer desperately begs her to stay: "I have it in me to become a different man." "Perhaps," Nora icily responds, "if your doll is taken away from you," turning her back on her husband and slamming the door of the doll's house behind her forever (3, 251). As over a century of commentators have maintained, it is hard to imagine a more fateful refutation of patriarchal prerogative than the slam of that door.

By contrast with Ibsen's subsequent play, however, *A Doll's House* seems almost tame. The home of Captain and Mrs. Alving in *Ghosts* (1882) lacks even the illusion of affection and regularity found in the Helmer household. The drama unfolds on the tenth anniversary of the Captain's death. The Alvings' son Oswald, now in his twenties, has returned home after his education abroad, preparations are being made to celebrate the opening of the orphanage Mrs. Alving has founded in her husband's name, and it is only now that the "hidden abyss of misery" she endured during her nineteen years of marriage comes to light.[39] In his capacity as legal adviser, Pastor Manders has come to the house to discuss the question of insuring the orphanage. During his visit, however, Manders takes the opportunity to reproach Mrs. Alving for her lack of "principles" (1, 28). His charges are twofold. First, as he reminds her, "after barely a year of married life you . . . ran away from your husband" when "your duty was to cleave to the man you had chosen and to whom you were bound by a sacred bond" (1, 28–9). Even worse, he continues, she sought refuge at the home of the Alvings' friend and priest, Pastor Manders himself. "You should thank God," he sanctimoniously argues, "that I was able to turn you from your outrageous intention, and that it was vouchsafed to me to succeed in leading you back into the path of duty" (1, 29). But Manders' account conveniently omits one crucial detail, namely that he and Mrs. Alving were carrying on an affair and that he drove her back to her "unspeakably unhappy" home solely to protect his reputation (1, 28). Manders' hypocrisy in condemning Mrs. Alving's imprudence and eliding his own complicity foregrounds the systemic nature of patriarchal oppression according to which the exploitative priest functions as a double of the abusive husband.

Manders' second accusation is that after forsaking her "duty as a wife," Mrs. Alving betrayed her "duty as a mother" by sending her young son abroad, thus depriving him of any knowledge of "what a well-regulated home means" (1, 30, 25). What Manders conveniently forgets is that the Captain's habitual drunken exploits and sexual infidelities took place inside, as well as outside, the family home. As Mrs. Alving reminds him:

> To keep him home in the evening—and at night—I have had to play the part of boon companion in his secret drinking bouts in his room. I have had to sit there alone with him, have had to hobnob and drink with him, have had to listen to his ribald senseless talk, have had to fight with brute force to get him to bed.
>
> —1, 33

The "crowning insult," however, came when the Captain seduced and impregnated their maid Joanna. It was at this point, fearing that their son "would be poisoned if he breathed the air of this polluted house," that Oswald was sent to school abroad (1, 33). Joanna was dismissed, given "a tolerably liberal sum to hold her tongue," and married off "in a great hurry" to the carpenter Jacob Engstrand (1, 37). Here again, Ibsen emphasizes Pastor Manders' complicity in the events he condemns. After all, Mrs. Alving points out, it was Manders who performed the marriage ceremony and who, after the birth of Joanna's illegitimate daughter, signed the certificate declaring her to be Engstrand's lawful child.

Manders claims to be "shocked" by what he calls "the immorality" of Mrs. Alving's disclosure: "Just think of it—for a paltry seventy pounds to let yourself be bound in marriage to a fallen woman!" (2, 39, 37). Mrs. Alving's response strikes at the heart of the gender double standard governing Manders' concept of morality: "What about myself, then—I let myself be bound in marriage to a fallen man" (2, 37). "Heaven forgive you! what are you saying?" Manders exclaims. "A fallen man? . . . The two cases are as different as day from night." "Not so very different, after all," Mrs. Alving coolly observes (2, 37–8). Pastor Manders' blind chauvinism pointedly recalls Helmer's indignant protest to Nora: "But no man would sacrifice his honor for the one he loves," just as Mrs. Alving's retort echoes Nora's reply: "It is a thing hundreds of women have done" (*Doll's House* 3, 250). In both plays, Ibsen constructs an inverse relationship in which men's belief in the sanctity of masculine privilege is directly counterbalanced by women's factual grasp of gender inequality. And in both plays, Ibsen's heroines are the ones who underscore the fallacy of men's presumption. As Mrs. Alving tells Manders, "when you condemn my conduct as a wife you have nothing more to go upon than ordinary public opinion . . . . you never once came out here to see us in my husband's lifetime" (1, 31). Or as Nora says when Helmer charges her with abandoning her "most sacred duties": "I know quite well, Torvald, that most people would think you right, and that views of this kind are to be found in books; but I can no longer content myself with what people say, or with what is found in books" (*Doll's House* 3, 248). Whereas Nora and Mrs. Alving have learned to judge their conduct for themselves, Helmer and Manders remain the unquestioning instruments of patriarchal discourse.

His masculine prerogative exposed as a deception, the nineteenth-century tragic patriarch has only one way to reassert his authority on the stage. He must become what the defiant Beatrice Cenci became for her father: a pathogenic agent.[40] In both *A Doll's House* and *Ghosts*, Ibsen strategically couples masculine hypocrisy with the psychic and physical threat of paternal infection. Nora's alleged financial irresponsibility is thus attributed to hereditary disease. "Very like your father," Helmer tells her. "You always find some way of wheedling money out of me, and, as soon as you have got it, it seems to melt in your hands . . . It is in the blood; for indeed it is true that you can inherit these things, Nora" (1, 179). In *Ghosts*, the pathologized curse of the father is more virulent.

In an attempt to stave off the infection, Mrs. Alving has not only sent her son Oswald away to school, she has invested all of her "purchase money" in the orphanage so that he cannot inherit even "a penny that belonged to his father" (1, 34).[41] But even such scrupulous precautions prove inadequate. After attempting to seduce Mrs. Alving's maid Regina in the very room where his father once seduced her mother Joanna, Oswald succumbs to "the canker of disease," the "softening of the brain" by which, as his doctor explains, "[t]he sins of the fathers are visited on the children" (2, 52; 3, 72). "What I am suffering from is hereditary," Oswald tells his mother; "it—(*touches his forehead, and speaks very quietly*)—it lies here. . . . If only it had been an ordinary mortal disease" (3, 71).[42] As the curtain falls, Oswald devolves into a state of infantile, inarticulate prostration, leaving his mother to fulfill her promise to administer a lethal dose of morphine.

"*MATER SEMPER CERTA EST*": CONTESTED PATERNITY AND MATERNAL REVENGE

As George Bernard Shaw rightly observed, Ibsen had revolutionized the representation of traditional gender roles onstage, not only by vindicating the so-called "lost" or "ruined" woman but by reapplying the terms by which she was judged to the men that judged her.[43] In doing so, Ibsen also exposed another essential fissure in the edifice of patriarchal authority, namely the uncertainty of fatherhood. Whereas in *Ghosts*, Regina's knowledge that Engstrand is not her biological father grants her some degree of leverage in resisting his claims on her service, in Strindberg's *The Father* (1887), the issue of dubious paternity becomes the woman's consummate tool in combating paternal prerogative. At the level of plot, the battle of wills between Adolf and his wife Laura is concentrated on the future of their adolescent daughter Bertha; Laura wants Bertha to remain at home while Adolf wants her to be educated in town. In symbolic terms, however, Laura wields her maternal authority as a weapon while Adolf mounts an ineffectual resistance by invoking the patriarchal rights Ibsen's Mrs. Alving had already dispelled as mere "[g]hosts of beliefs" (3, 69). By contrast with eighteenth-century bourgeois tragedies, in which the fate of the family and the morality it purports to defend are concentrated in the body of the unmarried daughter, in *The Father* Bertha is little more than a pawn in her parents' struggle for dominance. Even before their daughter's birth, we learn, Laura spread rumors casting doubt on Adolf's sanity and, as the Captain confesses to his brother-in-law, during their twenty years of marriage, "she has treated me as if I were about to die."[44] Adolf accuses his wife of wielding "a satanic power to get your way," complaining that if he did not succumb to her will in handling the household affairs, "I'd either be in an insane asylum or in the family grave" (1, 32, 22).

Like *Ghosts*, *The Father* begins with what appears an innocuous discussion of paternity in reference to the play's secondary, working-class characters. As Captain Adolf converses with his brother-in-law, he overhears Nöjd, a young member of his regiment, consorting with the kitchen maid. Adolf summons the soldier in and calls him to account: "Out with it: are you the child's father, or aren't you?" Nöjd's guileless reply: "How can I know?" sets the terms for the entire tragedy (1, 16). After angrily dismissing the youth, Adolf reflects on the situation: "The boy most likely isn't innocent; we can't know that, but we know one thing: the girl is guilty if there is any guilt"—a casual but pointed paraphrase of the Roman juridical tenet "*pater semper incertus est; mater semper certa est*" [the father is always uncertain; the mother is always certain] (1, 18). Although she may not recommend herself as an heir who can inherit property and continue the family name, the unmarried daughter holds a negative power the son does not. Her body can provide incontestable visible evidence of sexual transgression. Unfortunately for Adolf, he relates these reflections to Laura, who instantly grasps the strategic advantage such precedent offers her. If, as Adolf informs her, "[w]ise people insist one can never know . . . the father of a child," then how, she inquires, "can the father have such rights over her child?" (1, 23). Laura's use of the exclusive female pronoun "her" to signal the mother's ownership of her child is as adroit as her subsequent intimations that Adolf is not in fact the father of their child:

> Surely you don't know if you're Bertha's father! . . . I'm only using what you've taught me. Besides, how do you know I haven't been unfaithful? . . . Assume I'd rather do anything, be driven out, be despised, do anything to keep control of my child, and that I'd tell the truth when I'd say: Bertha is *my* child but not yours! . . . then your power would be at an end!
>
> —1, 33

Rather than threatening the wife and mother with dishonor, the suggestion of her infidelity makes Laura, as Adolf frankly concedes, "a superior enemy" (1, 33).

Strindberg's most radical innovation in *The Father* was to transform the daughter's sexual vulnerability into the mother's biological power. Even Sigmund Freud, who approvingly identified the transition from a matriarchal to a patriarchal form of social organization as "a step forward in culture," noted that "[t]his turning from the mother to the father" required that logical abstraction supplant empirical evidence "since maternity is proved by the senses whereas paternity is a surmise based on a deduction and a premiss [sic]."[45] Laura's fatal advantage derives from this crucial discrepancy between the materiality of the female body and the ideality of patriarchal law. Adolf, for his part, lamely attempts to substantiate his prerogative by asserting that Laura "sold her birthright" the day she was married "and gave up her rights in return for her husband's assuming responsibility for her and her children" (1, 22). Although, as we have seen, Adolf is simply restating the terms governing most nineteenth-century marriages, his protestations fail before the sovereign fact of biology and he throws himself on Laura's mercy: "Don't you see I'm as helpless as a child? Don't you hear I'm asking for pity as from a mother? . . . I ask only sympathy as a sick human being" (2, 45). But Laura is unrelenting. Having "fulfilled your function as an unfortunately necessary father and breadwinner," she informs him, "[y]ou're not needed any more" (2, 48). With that, Adolf submits entirely: "Do with me what you wish. I no longer exist . . . Brute strength has fallen before treacherous weakness" (3, 55, 60). He is declared legally insane, deprived of his civil and family rights, coaxed into a straitjacket by his childhood nurse, and dies of a stroke in her arms.

Although the emasculation of the *pater familias* is nowhere as excruciatingly detailed as in *The Father*, Adolf's defeat is paradigmatic. Helmer's rebuke that Nora violated her "most sacred duties" by abandoning her family is met with the slam of a door. Pastor Manders' pious interdiction, "Have you forgotten that a child should love and honour his father?" is effortlessly overborne by Mrs. Alving's rebuttal, "Don't let us talk in such general terms" (*Ghosts* 2, 39). In these instances and many others, the patriarch of late nineteenth-century tragedy can produce sententious rhetoric and vague truisms, but cannot defend his authority on moral or biological grounds. Adolf's descent into madness thus comes to emblemize the collapse of patriarchal reason. Laura's denial of guilt ("I've never reflected about my actions, but they have glided along on rails you yourself have laid down") applies the exquisite finishing touch: woman is but the instrument by which masculine privilege enacts its own destruction (3, 59).

DAUGHTERS OF THE *FIN-DE-SIÈCLE*

With Strindberg, the issue of sexual reproduction assumes center stage in redefining the gender roles that underpin nineteenth-century tragedy. But if *The Father* presents the victory of female reproductive power over masculine reason, it does so on the condition that the victorious woman be both a mother and a wife. In Strindberg's next play, *Miss Julie* (1888), the sexually appetitive, unmarried daughter does not fare so well, ultimately choosing suicide as the only option after her one night stand with her father's valet Jean. Even the appearance of the university-educated, fatherless "New Woman" in plays such as Shaw's *Mrs. Warren's Profession* (1893), does little to shift the entrenched logic according to which an unmarried young woman's survival depends on renouncing erotic love. As Mrs. Warren explains to her daughter Vivie, she was driven to prostitution at an early age and, through careful management and what she refers to as "self-respect," eventually saved enough money to become a madam and then co-owner of a lucrative chain of European brothels: "Why am I independent and able to give my daughter a first-rate education, when other women that had just as good opportunities are in the gutter? Because I always knew how to respect and control myself."[46] Though initially sympathetic to her mother's early adversity and impressed by her work ethic, Vivie condemns Mrs. Warren for continuing in her profession after achieving financial independence. Marshaling all her "strength and self-possession," Vivie spurns her mother, returns to her job as a legal clerk in London, and vows thenceforth to live solely as "a woman of business, permanently single and permanently unromantic" (1, 92; 4, 149). Mrs. Warren is crushed by her daughter's rejection, yet as Vivie crucially points out, her motivations are consistent with her mother's: "I am my mother's daughter. I am like you: I must have work" (4, 160). And although she adds, "my work is not your work, and my way not your way," mother and daughter are driven by a similar impulse. The "New Woman" thus appears as a desexualized version of the prostitute and madam (4, 159).

By contrast with *Miss Julie* and *Mrs. Warren's Profession*, Ibsen's late play *The Master Builder* (1892) offers the foretaste of an alternative narrative—one in which an amorous, unmarried young woman emerges triumphant over patriarchal authority. As we learn, Ibsen's "master builder" Halvard Solness established his career by constructing modern houses on the site of his wife's family home (which burned to the ground under mysterious circumstances, killing their two infant children in the process). Plagued with guilt for his children's death and his wife's ensuing mental collapse, Solness is reinvigorated by the attentions of the young "New Woman," Hilda Wangel. Hilda, for her part, goads Solness to renew his aspirations as an architect, ultimately convincing him to erect a towering steeple where his wife's ruined home once stood. Dismissing his morbid phobia of heights, Hilda urges him to ascend the scaffold and assert his mastery once again before the town. As Solness swoons and plummets to his death, she ecstatically cries, "he mounted right to the top . . . . My—my master builder!"[47] Yet if the eroticized young woman seems to finally conquer the reigning patriarch in Ibsen's play, she conquers a "master" laden with the weight of Torvald Helmer's self-deception, Oswald Alving's degeneracy, and Adolf Alving's emasculation—a man, in short, who has already been broken.

As many scholars have suggested, the eponymous heroine of Oscar Wilde's controversial tragedy *Salome* (published in French in 1893, translated into English in 1894, and adapted as the German libretto for Richard Strauss' opera in 1905[48]) represents the culmination of "Ibsen's transgressive women," from Nora Helmer to Hilda Wangel, and "takes their rebellion to outrageous heights."[49] And it is in *Salome*, as in Shelley's *The Cenci*, that the rebellious daughter asserts herself against the seemingly immutable, totalizing law of the father by strategically matching and exceeding it. When the tragedy opens, Salome's uncle, King Herod, has recently married his half-brother's widow and Salome's mother, Herodias. Their "marriage of incest" is loudly condemned by Iokanaan (John the Baptist), who utters ominous prophecies from the cistern where Herod has imprisoned him.[50] The action is divided between two sites, the banquet hall in Herod's palace and the outdoor terrace above. Inside, as Herod indulges the pleasures of the table, his lust for his stepdaughter-niece intensifies. Salome, meanwhile, is drawn to the terrace by Iokanaan's voice. She demands to speak with the prophet and, on seeing him, is overcome with desire. When her advances are rebuffed, she returns to the hall, where Herod entreats her to dance for him, promising to grant any favor she asks in exchange. After she dances, Salome demands her prize: Iokanaan's head, served "in a silver charger" (55). Herod reluctantly fulfills his promise and, gnawed with foreboding, anxiously retires. As he exits, he catches a glimpse of Salome kissing Iokanaan's severed head. "Kill that woman!" Herod screams in revulsion and, as the final stage direction reads: *"The soldiers rush forward and crush beneath their shields Salome, daughter of Herodias, Princess of Judaea"* (67).

Due in large part to its graphic rendering of Salome's passion for Iokanaan, Wilde's tragedy continues to raise unsettling questions about the relationship between female sexuality and the patriarchal social order.[51] Critics draw particular attention to Salome's assumption of the fetishistic, masculine gaze in her insistent demand to "look on" and then to "look closer at" the body of the quintessential patriarch, John the Baptist, enclosed, as it were, in the same cistern where her father was imprisoned years before (15, 19).[52] "I am amorous of thy body, Iokanaan!" Salome exclaims on first seeing the prophet, "[t]here is nothing in the world so white as thy body. Suffer me to touch thy body" (21–2). Iokanaan, in contrast, is cast in the role of the idealized virgin daughter. "He is like a thin ivory statue," Salome muses, "I am sure he is chaste, as the moon is" (19). "Who is this woman looking at me? I will not have her look at me," the modest Iokanaan retorts (20). When the prophet spurns Salome's advances, she repudiates his body as "hideous," turning her gaze to a more specific part of his anatomy: "It is of thy hair that I am enamoured, Iokanaan. . . . There is nothing in the world that is so black as thy hair. . . . Suffer me to touch thy hair" (22–3). Again, Iokanaan rebuffs her, "Back, daughter of Sodom! Touch me not. Profane not the temple of the Lord," and again, Salome transfers her gaze to different part of his body:

> I love not thy hair. . . . It is thy mouth that I desire, Iokanaan. Thy mouth is like a band of scarlet on a tower of ivory. It is like a pomegranate cut in twain with a knife of ivory. . . . There is nothing in the world so red as thy mouth. . . . Suffer me to kiss thy mouth.
>
> —23

Salome will repeat this exact phrase ("Suffer me to kiss thy mouth") eight times before her exit. When Iokanaan's severed head is finally delivered, her refrain changes to "I *will* kiss thy mouth," followed by the triumphant chant, "I have kissed thy mouth" (italics added) (64, 66). One need not have read Freud's writing on the repetition compulsion to understand the meaning of this inexorable echo. It is explicit in the original French text, "*Laisse-moi baiser ta bouche*"—the word *baiser* meaning both "to kiss" and, in its colloquial usage, "to have sex with."

As was the case with Beatrice Cenci, however, one must question the autonomy with which the rebellious daughter acts. As Gail Finney argues, Salome's "behavior is clearly learned" and conditioned, her "foremost model" being none other than "her uncle and stepfather, Herod."[53] The play's emphasis on the possessive, objectifying act of looking and the incantatory, repetitive style of Wilde's dialogue accentuate the parity between stepfather and daughter. Just as Salome insistently rehearses her demand to look upon Iokanaan's body, so Herod confesses to Salome, "I have looked at thee and ceased not. . . . Thy beauty has grievously troubled me, and I have looked at thee overmuch" (58). And just as Salome is repeatedly warned not to look upon the prophet, so Herodias repeatedly warns her husband, "You must not look at her! "You are always looking at her!" (27). Salome's hypnotic refrain "I will kiss thy mouth" is the echo of Herod's fervent entreaties, "Dance for me, Salome. . . . I beseech thee. . . . Wilt thou not dance for me, Salome?" (46, 49, 51). The intimate link between father and stepdaughter is further instantiated by the shared imagery in which they clothe their obsessive desires. As Herod enjoins Salome: "come drink a little wine with me. . . . Dip into it thy little red lips, that I may drain the cup . . . Salome, come and eat fruits with me. I love to see in a fruit the mark of thy little teeth. Bite but a little of this fruit, that I may eat what is left," so Salome addresses the decapitated head of her beloved: "Ah! thou wouldst not suffer me to kiss thy mouth, Iokanaan. Well! I will kiss it now. I will bite with my teeth as one bites a ripe fruit . . . I am athirst for thy beauty; I am hungry for thy body; and neither wine nor apples can appease my desire" (32, 64–5). Salome, like Beatrice before her, has learned the father's lesson all too well, and their mythic bond is ratified through sexual violence.

CONCLUSION: "WHAT A WORLD WE MAKE, / THE OPPRESSOR AND THE OPPRESSED"[54]

At this point, with the emergence of the castrating, sexually liberated *femme fatale* who would come to dominate early twentieth-century theater and film, we may well seem far removed from the rigidly gendered familial relations that structure eighteenth-century bourgeois tragedy. But how far are we really? In Lessing's *Emilia Galotti* and Schiller's *Intrigue and Love*, the affective father–daughter bond prevails over courtly corruption and the daughter forfeits her life to preserve her family's virtue. In Baillie's *Orra*, the heroine is driven to madness by the sexual advances of her guardian Count Hughobert. In Shelley's *The Cenci*, God the Father (as embodied by the Pope) decapitates the avenging victim of incestuous rape. In Hugo's *Hernani*, Doña Sol and her lover commit suicide to escape the lascivious wrath of her uncle Don Ruy Gomez de Silva. In Strindberg's *Miss Julie*, the daughter assumes the role of the vigilant father by punishing her own sexual transgression with suicide. In Ibsen's *A Doll's House* and *Ghosts*, as well as Strindberg's *The Father*, patriarchal power is unmasked as a hypocritical deception. In Ibsen's *The Master Builder*, the emasculated patriarch is destroyed by the wiles of an independent "New Woman." And in Wilde's *Salome*, the heroine orders the murder of a biblical prophet and is killed, in turn, by her lustful stepfather. Despite being distributed across five countries and over more than a century, these tragedies are linked by a shared impulse to expose the domestic cruelty, deception, and sexual violence that enable and sustain patriarchal power.

In the century that saw unprecedented debates over women's rights, the institution of marriage, and the function of heredity (financial as well as physical and mental), it is no wonder that gender should emerge as a dominant force in reconceiving the tragic. As we have seen in the transition from the late eighteenth- to the late nineteenth-century stage, the tragic fatality or curse is first domesticated, then pathologized, and finally eroticized. But the questions nineteenth-century tragedy raises about the politics and psychology of domination extend well beyond national boundaries and specific legal, philosophical, or theological positions. Even when traditional domestic gender roles would seem perilously destabilized or utterly inverted, the expanded agency thus afforded to women on the tragic stage underscores the deep and troubling bond between oppressor and oppressed—however that relationship may be expressed by the reigning ideology of a given nation, epoch, or political regime.

NOTES

Introduction

1. H. Mackenzie, "Account of the German Theatre," *Transactions of the Royal Society of Edinburgh* 2 (1790), 2:156.
2. Mackenzie, "Account of the German Theatre," 2:156.
3. See G. Steiner, *The Death of Tragedy* (New York: Knopf, 1961; new edition Yale University Press, 1996), especially 9–10.
4. H. White, *Metahistory: The Historical Imagination in Nineteenth-Century Literature* (Baltimore: Johns Hopkins University Press, 1973), 12.
5. See Steiner, *The Death of Tragedy*, 10; and G. Steiner, "'Tragedy,' Reconsidered," in *Rethinking Tragedy*, ed. R. Felski (Baltimore: Johns Hopkins University Press, 2008), 29–44, which partly revises the original thesis of *The Death of Tragedy* by replacing the narrative of tragedy's death with its dispersal across forms, media, and genres: "As our literatures evolve, the concept of tragedy extends far beyond the dramatic genre. It serves for poetry and prose fiction—for d'Aubigné's *Tragiques* as for Dreiser's *An American Tragedy*. In turn, by osmosis as it were, it permeates the descriptions of ballet, of film. Composers such as Beethoven, Berlioz, Brahms incorporate the marking 'tragic' in their compositions. Throughout this seemingly unbounded and mobile spectrum, 'tragedy' and 'tragic' can lose their sometime specificity." (29)
6. R. Williams, *Modern Tragedy* (Stanford, CA: Stanford University Press, 1966), 60–1.
7. J. Wallace, *The Cambridge Introduction to Tragedy* (Cambridge: Cambridge University Press, 2007), 5.
8. S. Goldhill, *Sophocles and the Language of Tragedy* (Oxford and New York: Oxford University Press, 2012), 140.
9. See F. Moretti, "Serious Century," in *The Novel. Volume I: History, Geography and Culture*, ed. F. Moretti (Princeton and Oxford: Princeton University Press, 2006), 375–6.
10. M.S. Buckley, *Tragedy Walks the Streets: The French Revolution in the Making of Modern Drama* (Baltimore: The Johns Hopkins University Press, 2006).
11. E. Bulwer Lytton, *England and the English*, 2 vols (London: Richard Bentley, 1833), 2:150.
12. W. Hazlitt, *The Selected Writings of William Hazlitt*, ed. D. Wu, 9 vols., vol. 5: *Lectures on the English Comic Writers, Lectures on the Dramatic Literature of the Age of Elizabeth, A Letter to William Gifford, Esq.* (London: Pickering and Chatto, 1998), 324. Further references will be to this edition and cited parenthetically in the text.
13. J.N. Cox, *In the Shadows of Romance: Romantic Tragic Drama in Germany, England and France* (Athens: Ohio University Press, 1987), 15–16.
14. See M. Meisel, *Realizations: Narrative, Pictorial, and Theatrical Arts in Nineteenth-Century England* (Princeton: Princeton University Press, 1983), 52–68.
15. See A. González-Rivas Fernández, "Aeschylus and *Frankenstein, or The Modern Prometheus* by Mary Shelley," in *Brill's Companion to the Reception of Aeschylus*, ed. R. Futo Kennedy (Leiden, Boston: Brill, 2017), 292–322.

16. J. King, *Tragedy in the Victorian Novel: Theory and Practice in the Novels of George Eliot, Thomas Hardy and Henry James* (Cambridge: Cambridge University Press, 1978), 1.
17. F. Moretti, *The Way of the World: The Bildungsroman in European Culture*, trans. Albert Sbragia (London, New York: Verso, 2000), 11–13.
18. W. Hazlitt, *Lectures on the English Poets* (London: Taylor and Hessey, 1818), 13. In this passage Hazlitt refers to Edmund Burke's *A Philosophical Enquiry into the Origins of Our Ideas of the Sublime and the Beautiful* (London: Dodsley, 1757), 26.
19. M. Leonard, *Tragic Modernities* (Cambridge MA, London: Harvard University Press, 2015), 3. Further references will be to this edition and cited parenthetically in the text.

Chapter One

1. B. Musser, *Diary of a Twelve-Year-Old: Transcribed from the Early Hieroglyphic of Benjamin Musser* (Caldwell, ID: Caxton, 1932), 48–9.
2. T. Eagleton, *Sweet Violence: The Idea of the Tragic* (Malden, MA: Blackwell Publishing, 2003), 14.
3. A. Poole, *Tragedy: A Very Short Introduction* (Oxford: Oxford University Press, 2005), 7.
4. Poole, *Tragedy*, 15.
5. R. Bushnell, "Introduction," in *A Companion to Tragedy*, ed. R. Bushnell (Malden, MA and Oxford: Blackwell, 2005), 1–4.
6. R. Felski, "Introduction," in *Rethinking Tragedy*, ed. R. Felski (Baltimore: Johns Hopkins University Press, 2008), 1–25.
7. S.D. Dowden, "Introduction: The Pursuit of Unhappiness," in *Tragedy and the Tragic in German Literature, Art, and Thought*, ed. S.D. Dowden and T.P. Quinn (Rochester: Camden House, 2014), 5.
8. G. Steiner, *The Death of Tragedy* (New Haven and London: Yale University Press, 1961), 11.
9. R. Williams, *Modern Tragedy* (Stanford, CA: Stanford University Press, 1966), 62–3.
10. M. Buckley, *Tragedy Walks the Streets: The French Revolution in the Making of Modern Drama* (Baltimore: Johns Hopkins University Press, 2006), 149.
11. E. Burke, *Reflections on the Revolution in France*, ed. L.G. Mitchell (Oxford and New York: Oxford University Press, 1993), 10; and T. Paine, *The Rights of Man*, ed. M. Philp (Oxford and New York: Oxford University Press, 1998), 100.
12. Buckley, *Tragedy Walks the Streets*, 75.
13. D. Duff, *Romanticism and the Uses of Genre* (Oxford: Oxford University Press, 2009), 19.
14. V. Brombert, *Victor Hugo and the Visionary Novel* (Cambridge and London: Harvard University Press, 1984), 10.
15. D. Saglia, "The Gothic Stage: Visions of Instability, Performances of Anxiety," in *Romantic Gothic: An Edinburgh Companion*, ed. A. Wright and D. Townshend (Edinburgh: Edinburgh University Press, 2016), 78.
16. E. Hadley, *Melodramatic Tactics: Theatricalized Dissent in the English Marketplace, 1800–1885* (Stanford: Stanford University Press, 1995), 3–4.
17. Duff, *Romanticism and the Uses of Genre*, 20.
18. G. Bortolotti and L. Hutcheon, "On the Origin of Adaptations: Rethinking Fidelity Discourse and 'Success'—Biologically," *New Literary History* 38 (2007): 450–1.
19. D. Saglia, "Introduction: the Survival of Tragedy in European Romanticisms," *European Romantic Review* 20 (2009): 570.
20. Saglia, "Introduction," 569.

21. A.W. Halsall, *Victor Hugo and the Romantic Drama* (Toronto, Buffalo, and London: University of Toronto Press, 1998), 65.
22. B.T. Cooper, "French Romantic Tragedy," in *A Companion to Tragedy*, 459.
23. Williams, *Modern Tragedy*, 90–1.
24. J.N. Cox, "Romantic Redefinitions of the Tragic," in *Romantic Drama*, ed. G. Gillespie (Amsterdam and Philadelphia: John Benjamins Publishing, 1994), 155.
25. J.N. Cox, "Romantic Tragic Drama and its Eighteenth-Century Precursors," in *A Companion to Tragedy*, 411–34. Lillo's play is itself an adaptation of a seventeenth-century ballad about a murder in Shropshire.
26. See S. Forry's description of the controversy leading up to the premiere of Richard Brinsley Peake's melodrama *Presumption; or, The Fate of Frankenstein* in the summer of 1823, in *Hideous Progenies: Dramatizations of* Frankenstein *from Mary Shelley to the Present* (Philadelphia: University of Pennsylvania Press, 1990).
27. The legislation follows social changes such as the Reform Act of 1832 and enfranchisement movements such as Chartism because the binary established by notions of "legitimacy" were also fraught with divisive class connotations.
28. By the height of the gothic novel's popularity at the turn of the nineteenth century, London's legitimate and illegitimate theaters were staging adaptations of Anne Radcliffe, Matthew Lewis, and others. See F. Saggini, *The Gothic Novel and the Stage: Romantic Appropriations* (London and New York: Routledge, 2015), 137–213.
29. R.J. Goldstein, "Introduction," *The Frightful Stage: Political Censorship of the Theater in Nineteenth-Century Europe*, ed. R.J. Goldstein (New York and Oxford: Berghahn Books, 2009), 6, 18.
30. L.W. Conolly, *The Censorship of English Drama, 1737–1824* (San Marino, CA: The Huntington Library, 1976), 2.
31. Bushnell, "Introduction," 2.
32. Poole, *Tragedy*, 16.
33. I. Kliger, "Tragic Nationalism in Nietzsche and Dostoevsky," in *Nietzsche and Dostoevsky: Philosophy, Morality, Tragedy* (Evanston: Northwestern University Press, 2016), 143–72.
34. Cox, "Romantic Tragic Drama," 420.
35. See Part I of N. Moore, ed., *Censorship and the Limits of the Literary: A Global View* (New York: Bloomsbury, 2015), 13–80.
36. F. Burwick, "Staging the Byronic Hero," *European Romantic Review* 29 (2018): 3–11.
37. Scholars familiar with nineteenth-century *Frankenstein* adaptations will notice an immediate reversal of novel's tragic interiority, the gothic melodramas of the 1820s, and the Victorian comic forms that followed.
38. Poole, *Tragedy*, 79.
39. J. King, *Tragedy in the Victorian Novel: Theory and Practice in the Novels of George Eliot, Thomas Hardy, and Henry James* (Cambridge: Cambridge University Press, 1980), 39.
40. Brombert, *Victor Hugo and the Visionary Novel*, 50.
41. V. Brombert, "Madame Bovary: The Tragedy of Dreams," in *Novels of Flaubert: A Study of Themes and Techniques* (Princeton: Princeton University Press, 1966), 90.
42. L. Layton, "Flaubert's *L'Éducation sentimentale*: A Tragedy of Mind," *French Forum* 11.3 (1986): 347.
43. M. Levitt, "*Evgenii Onegin*," in *The Cambridge Companion to Pushkin*, ed. A. Kahn (Cambridge: Cambridge University Press, 2006), 54.
44. C. Emerson, "Pushkin's Drama," in *The Cambridge Companion to Pushkin*, ed. A. Kahn (Cambridge: Cambridge University Press, 2006), 58.

45. I. Kliger, "Dostoevsky and the Novel-Tragedy: Genre and Modernity in Ivanov, Pumpyansky, and Bakhtin," *PMLA* 126 (2011): 78.
46. Kliger, "Dostoevsky and the Novel-Tragedy," 75–6.
47. We see early examples even in politically ambiguous works such as Aphra Behn's *Oroonoko; or, The Royal Slave* (1688) and Thomas Southerne's popular dramatic adaptation *Oroonoko: A Tragedy* (1695), the more popular version of the story throughout the eighteenth century.
48. These included Ann Cromartie Yearsley's *Poem on the Inhumanity of the Slave Trade* (1788); Anna Barbauld's "Epistle to William Wilberforce, Esq. On the Rejection of the Bill for Abolishing the Slave Trade" (1791); Hannah More and Eaglesfield Smith's, "The Sorrows of Yamba; or, The Negro Woman's Complaint" (1797), and Robert Southey's multi-form poetry sequence *Poems Concerning the Slave Trade* (1797).
49. M. Fries, "What Tennyson Really Did to Malory's Women," *Quondam et Futurus* 1 (1991): 53. See also F.J. Sypher, "Politics in the Poetry of Tennyson," *Victorian Poetry* 14 (1976): 101–12; and S.C. Dillon, "Milton and Tennyson's 'Guinevere,'" *English Literary History* 54 (1987): 129–55.
50. E. Hall, "Tragedy Personified," in *Visualizing the Tragic: Drama, Myth, and Ritual in Greek Art and Literature*, ed. C. Kraus, S. Goldhill, H.P. Foley, and J. Elsner (Oxford: Oxford University Press, 2007), 221.
51. H. Jenkins, *Convergence Culture: Where Old and New Media Collide* (New York: New York University Press, 2008), 2–3.
52. International copyright did not exist until the 1886 Berne Convention for the Protection of Literary and Artistic works, which covered adaptation for the first time.
53. Although "Lancelot and Elaine" and "The Lady of Shalott" draw on different medieval sources, both stories are based on the figure of Elaine of Astolat and are often conflated in Victorian Arthuriana. See G.S. Layard, *Tennyson and His Pre-Raphaelite Illustrators* (London: Elliot Stock, 1894), 9; and T.R. Rodgers, *Ladies of Shalott: A Victorian Masterpiece and Its Contexts*, ed. G.P. Landow (Providence: Brown University Press, 1985).
54. For specific examples and discussions of translations and their impact across Europe, see the essays in L. Ormond, ed., *The Reception of Alfred Tennyson in Europe* (London and New York: Bloomsbury Academic, 2017).
55. W. Shakespeare, *The Oxford Shakespeare: Hamlet*, ed. G.R. Hibbard (Oxford and New York: Oxford University Press, 2008), 4.7.187–210.
56. M. Meisel, *Realizations: Narrative, Pictorial, and Theatrical Arts in Nineteenth-Century England* (Princeton: Princeton University Press, 1983), 30.
57. A.R. Young, "Sarah Bernhardt's Ophelia," *Borrowers and Lenders: The Journal of Shakespeare and Appropriation* 8 (2013), n.p. Available online: http://www.borrowers.uga.edu/662/show [accessed 01 October 2018].
58. Meisel, *Realizations*, 4, 3.
59. R. Rosenblum and H.W. Janson, *19th Century Art* (Upper Saddle River, NJ: Pearson/Prentice Hall, 2005), 128.
60. A.J. Cross, "'What a World We Make the Oppressor and the Oppressed': George Cruikshank, Percy Shelley, and the Gendering of Revolution in 1819," *ELH* 71 (2004): 167–207.
61. Kraus, Goldhill, Foley, and Elsner, "Introduction," in *Visualizing the Tragic*, 12.

Chapter Two

1. G. Steiner, *The Death of Tragedy* (London: Faber and Faber, 1961), 3.

2. R. Heilman, *Tragedy and Melodrama: Versions of Experience* (Seattle and London: University of Washington Press, 1968), 7.
3. T. Eagleton, *Sweet Violence: The Idea of the Tragic* (Oxford: Blackwell, 2003), 46.
4. *Report from the Select Committee on Dramatic Literature: With the Minutes of Evidence* (London: House of Commons, August 2, 1832), accessed at *House of Commons Parliamentary Papers Online* (ProQuest, 2006), http://parlipapers.chadwyck.co.uk, 158 [last accessed October 1, 2018].
5. See E. Fischer-Lichte, *History of European Drama and Theatre*, trans. Jo Riley (London and New York: Routledge, 2002), and M. Carlson, *The German Stage in the Nineteenth Century* (Metuchen: Scarecrow Press, 1972).
6. C.D. Grabbe, *Das Theater zu Düsseldorf mit Rückblicken auf die übrige deutsche Schaubühne* [The Düsseldorf Theater with a Look Back at Other German Theaters], 1835, repr. in *German and Dutch Theatre, 1600–1848. Theatre in Europe: A Documentary History*, ed. G.W. Brandt and W. Hogendoorn (Cambridge: Cambridge University Press, 1993), 323.
7. Grabbe, *Das Theater zu Düsseldorf*, 322.
8. M. Carlson, "The Realistic Theatre and Bourgeois Values, 1750–1900," in *A History of German Theatre*, ed. S. Williams and M. Hamburger (Cambridge: Cambridge University Press, 2008), 100.
9. M. Patterson, *The First German Theatre: Schiller, Goethe, Kleist and Büchner in Performance* (London and New York: Routledge, 1990), 9.
10. W. Macready, *Macready's Reminiscences, and Selections from his Diaries and Letters*, ed. F. Pollock (London: Macmillan, 1876), 506.
11. Macready, *Macready's Reminiscences*, 528.
12. J.N. Cox, "The Death of Tragedy; or, the Birth of Melodrama," in *The Performing Century: Nineteenth-Century Theatre's History*, ed. T.C. Davis and P. Holland (Basingstoke: Palgrave, 2007), 161.
13. A. Heinrich, "Performance for Imagined Communities: Gladstone, the National Theatre and Contested Didactics of the Stage," in *Politics, Performance and Popular Culture: Theatre and Society in Nineteenth-Century Britain*, ed. P. Yeandle, K. Newey, and J. Richards (Manchester: Manchester University Press, 2016), 97.
14. F. Schiller, "Über den Grund des Vergnügens an tragischen Gegenständen" [On the Causes of Delight in Tragic Subjects], repr. in *German and Dutch Theatre*, 223.
15. E. Hall and F. Macintosh, *Greek Tragedy and the British Theatre, 1660–1914* (Oxford: Oxford University Press, 2005), 285–7.
16. "Music and the Drama," *The Athenaeum*, June 17, 1843, 573–4.
17. "Music and the Drama," *The Athenaeum*, February 18, 1843, 166.
18. "Theatres," *John Bull*, February 18, 1843, 108–9.
19. "Drury-Lane Theatre," *The Times*, February 13, 1843, 5.
20. "Drury-Lane Theatre. A Blot in the 'Scutcheon," *The Morning Post*, February 13, 1843, 3.
21. M. Carlson, *Places of Performance: The Semiotics of Theatre Architecture* (Ithaca and London: Cornell University Press, 1989), 81.
22. S. Bennett and J. Sanders, "Rehearsing Across Space and Place: Rethinking *A Masque Presented at Ludlow Castle*," in *Performing Site-Specific Theatre: Politics, Place, Practice*, ed. A. Birch and J. Tompkins (Basingstoke: Palgrave, 2012), 37, 51.
23. M. Pearson, *Site-Specific Performance* (Basingstoke: Palgrave Macmillan, 2010), 1.
24. F.W.J. Hemmings, *Theatre and State in France, 1760–1905* (Cambridge: Cambridge University Press, 1994), 177.

25. J. McCormick, *Popular Theatres of Nineteenth-Century France* (London and New York: Routledge, 1993), 99.
26. Hemmings, *Theatre and State in France*, 190–1.
27. A. Heinrich, "Institutional Frameworks," in *A Cultural History of Theatre, Vol. 5, In the Age of Empire*, ed. P. Marx (London: Bloomsbury, 2017), 36.
28. Heinrich, "Institutional Frameworks," 47–8.
29. "The Berlin Stage," *Illustrated Sporting and Dramatic News*, January 2, 1875, 334.
30. Carlson, *Places of Performance*, 74.
31. "The Berlin Stage," 334.
32. As W.E.H. notes admiringly in "The Comedie-Francaise," *The Cornhill Magazine* (July 1879), 68.
33. J. Bratton, *The Making of the West End Stage: Marriage, Management and the Mapping of Gender in London, 1830–1870* (Cambridge: Cambridge University Press, 2011), 1–2.
34. J. Davis and V. Emeljanow, *Reflecting the Audience: London Theatregoing, 1840–1880* (Iowa City: University of Iowa Press, 2001), 167.
35. J. Donohue, "The Theatre from 1800 to 1895," in *The Cambridge History of British Theatre*, Vol. 2, ed. J. Donohue (Cambridge: Cambridge University Press, 2004), 251.
36. T.C. Davis, "Nineteenth-Century Repertoire," *Nineteenth Century Theatre and Film*, 36 (2009): 9.
37. J. Bratton, *New Readings in Theatre History* (Cambridge: Cambridge University Press, 2001), 37–8.
38. J.N. Cox, "British Romantic Drama in a European Context," in *British and European Romanticisms: Selected Papers from the Munich Conference of the German Society for English Romanticism*, ed. C. Bode and S. Domsch (Trier: Wissenschaftlicher Verlag Trier, 2007), 128.
39. R. Hogan, *Dion Boucicault* (New York: Twayne Publishers, 1969), 21; and R. Fawkes, *Dion Boucicault: A Biography* (London: Quartet Books, 1979), 59.
40. P. Thomson, "Introduction," in *Plays by Dion Boucicault*, ed. P. Thomson (Cambridge: Cambridge University Press, 1984), 6.
41. A. Parkin, "Introduction," in *Selected Plays of Dion Boucicault* (Gerrard Cross, UK: Colin Smythe, 1985), 11.
42. J.L. Smith, "Introduction," in Dion Boucicault, *London Assurance*, ed. J. L. Smith (London: Adam and Charles Black, 1984), xi.
43. R.W. Schoch, *Shakespeare's Victorian Stage: Performing History in the Theatre of Charles Kean* (Cambridge: Cambridge University Press, 1998).
44. R.W. Schoch, "Theatre and Mid-Victorian Society, 1851–1870," in *The Cambridge History of British Theatre*, Vol. 2, ed. J. Donohue (Cambridge: Cambridge University Press, 2004), 333–4.
45. "The Theatrical Examiner," *The Examiner*, January 20, 1855.
46. Thomson, "Introduction," in *Plays by Dion Boucicault*, 6.
47. Schoch, *Shakespeare's Victorian Stage*, 164.
48. Bratton, *New Readings*, 37–8.
49. See T.C. Davis on repertoire as "multiple circulating recombinative discourses of intelligibility" ("Nineteenth-Century Repertoire," 7).
50. "Princess's Theatre," *The Times*, January 15, 1855, 4.
51. "Princess's Theatre," *The Morning Post*, January 15, 1855, 5.
52. C. Scott, "Louis XI," in *From "The Bells" to "King Arthur:" A Critical Record of the First-Night Productions at the Lyceum Theatre from 1871 to 1895* (London: John Macqueen, 1897), 123.

53. Scott, "*Louis XI*," 123.
54. M. Meisel, *Realizations: Narrative, Pictorial, and Theatrical Arts in Nineteenth-Century England* (Princeton: Princeton University Press, 1983), 402–5.
55. G.A.S. [George Augustus Sala], "Echoes of the Week," *The Illustrated London News*, March 23, 1878, 267.
56. "Mr. Henry Irving in 'Louis XI,'" *Evening Telegraph*, March 19, 1878, 4.
57. Scott, "*Louis XI*," 127.
58. S. Sen, "Shakespeare Reception in France: The Case of Ambroise Thomas's *Hamlet*," in *Shakespeare and the Culture of Romanticism*, ed. Joseph M. Ortiz (London and New York: Routledge, 2016), 183.
59. Steiner, *Death of Tragedy*, 284.
60. R.R. Brettell, *Modern Art 1851–1929: Capitalism and Representation* (Oxford: Oxford University Press, 1999), 52.
61. P.G. Davis, "In Defense of the Singing Hamlet," *The New York Times*, March 12, 2010.
62. "Hamlet ein Seelenkrimi" [Hamlet, a Metaphysical Thriller], *Rheinische Post*, November 27, 2017.
63. See Sen, "Shakespeare Reception," 183–4 for a summary of adaptations and translations of *Hamlet* from English to French.
64. E. Showalter, "Representing Ophelia: Women, Madness and the Responsibilities of Feminist Criticism," in *Shakespeare and the Question of Theory*, ed. P. Parker and G. Hartman (London: Methuen, 1985), 83, and D.G. de Lafond, "Ophélie in Nineteenth-Century French Painting," in *The Afterlife of Ophelia*, ed. K.L. Peterson and D. Williams (New York: Palgrave Macmillan, 2012), 171. See also K. Rhodes, *Ophelia and Victorian Visual Culture: Representing Body Politics in the Nineteenth Century* (London and New York: Routledge, 2017).
65. Lafond, "Ophélie," 176.
66. Cited in Showalter, "Representing Ophelia," 78.
67. E. Zola, "Naturalism in the Theatre," in *The Theory of the Modern Stage*, ed. E. Bentley (Harmondsworth: Penguin, 1968), 161.

Chapter Three

1. They were first performed in 1606, approximately 429 BCE, and 1852 respectively. Giuseppe Verdi's *Rigoletto*, with libretto by Francesco Maria Piave, was adapted from Victor Hugo's banned tragedy *Le Roi s'amuse* (1832).
2. D. Gerould, "Larger than Life: Reflections on Melodrama and *Sweeney Todd*," *New York Literary Forum*, 7 (1980): 3.
3. K. Newey, *Women's Theatre Writing in Victorian Britain* (Basingstoke: Palgrave Macmillan, 2005), 105–6, 170–80.
4. K. Powell, *Women and Victorian Theatre* (Cambridge: Cambridge University Press, 1997), 81.
5. Newey, *Women's Theatre Writing*, 73. Examples are Fanny Kemble and Elizabeth St. George Planché.
6. A. Finch, *Women's Writing in Nineteenth-Century France* (Cambridge: Cambridge University Press, 2000), 68.
7. A.H. Miles, "Thomas Wade," in *The Poets and the Poetry of the Century*, Vol. 3: *John Keats to Lord Lytton*, ed. A.H. Miles (London: Hutchinson & Company, 1898), 599.

8. H. Holder, "'The 'lady playwrights' and the 'wild tribes of the East': Female Dramatists in the East End Theaters, 1860-1880," in *Women and Playwriting in Nineteenth-Century Britain*, ed. T.C. Davis and E. Donkin (Cambridge: Cambridge University Press, 1999), 175.
9. Focusing explicitly on communities of production and consumption, I exclude unproduced plays such as closet dramas. My thanks go to my excellent research assistants Ethan Gilberti and Jordan Lahaye for their invaluable help.
10. J.R. Stephens, "Playwright *In Extremis*: George Dibdin Pitt Revisited," *Theatre Notebook* 53 (1999): 47.
11. B. Lindfors, *Ira Aldridge: The Vagabond Years, 1833–1852* (Rochester: University of Rochester Press, 2011), 155.
12. "Covent-Garden Theatre," *The Standard*, April 11, 1833. For more on the melodramatic *Othello*, see V.M. Vaughan, *Othello: A Contextual History* (Cambridge: Cambridge University Press, 1994), 135. My thanks to Sarah Meer for these references.
13. J. Cox, "The Death of Tragedy; or, The Birth of the Melodrama," in *The Performing Century: Nineteenth-Century Theatre's History*, ed. T.C. Davis and P. Holland (London: Palgrave Macmillan, 2007), 161–81.
14. M. Booth, *English Plays of the Nineteenth Century*, 5 vols (Oxford: Oxford University Press, 1969), 1: 8.
15. G.H. Lewes, *Dramatic Essays* (London: Walter Scott, 1896), 104.
16. Booth, *English Plays*, 1: 21.
17. Booth, *English Plays*, 1: 24.
18. Booth, *English Plays*, 1: 239.
19. Booth, *English Plays*, 1: 238.
20. D. Mayer, "Encountering Melodrama," in *The Cambridge Companion to Victorian and Edwardian Theatre*, ed. K. Powell (Cambridge: Cambridge University Press, 2004), 146.
21. H. Birdoff, *The World's Greatest Hit* (S.F. Vanni, 1947), *passim*.
22. Booth, *English Plays*, 1: 155.
23. In 1855 Dibdin Pitt's obituary in *The Era* claimed he had written more than "700 melodramas, farces, and extravaganzas" in his career. See S. Aronofsky Weltman "Introduction: George Dibdin Pitt's 1847 *Sweeney Todd*," *Nineteenth Century Theatre and Film* 38 (2011): 4, 1.
24. Booth, *English Plays*, 1: 21.
25. C. Williams, "Melodrama," in *The Cambridge History of Victorian Literature*, ed. K. Flint (Cambridge: Cambridge University Press, 2012), 195.
26. J.N. Cox and M. Gamer, "Introduction," in *The Broadview Anthology of Romantic Drama* (Peterborough, ON: Broadview Press, 2003), xii.
27. J.L. Smith, *Melodrama* (New York: Routledge, 1973), 3.
28. Booth, *English Plays*, 1: 24.
29. R. McWilliam, "Melodrama," in *A Companion to Sensation Fiction*, ed. P.K. Gilbert (Malden, MA and Oxford: Wiley-Blackwell, 2011), 56.
30. Booth, *English Plays*, 1: 27.
31. Williams, "Melodrama," 195.
32. F.W.J. Hemmings, *Theatre and State in France, 1760–1905* (Cambridge: Cambridge University Press, 1994), 122.
33. B.V. Daniels, "Victor Hugo on the Boulevard: 'Lucrèce Borgia' at the Porte-Saint-Martin Theatre in 1833," *Theatre Journal* 32 (1980): 18.
34. A.W. Halsall, *Victor Hugo and the Romantic Drama* (Toronto: University of Toronto Press, 1998), 77.
35. Daniels, "Victor Hugo on the Boulevard," 17.

36. V. Hugo, "Preface to *Cromwell*," in *Prefaces and Prologues: To Famous Books*, ed. C.W. Eliot, The Harvard Classics Vol. 39 (New York: P.F. Collier & Son, 1909–14), www.bartleby.com/39/ [last accessed: January 14, 2018].
37. J.W. von Goethe, "Shakespeare: A Tribute" (1771), in *The Essential Goethe*, ed. M. Bell (Princeton: Princeton University Press, 2016), 873.
38. Halsall, *Victor Hugo and the Romantic Drama*, 77.
39. M. Carlson, "Hernani's Revolt from the Tradition of French Stage Composition," *Theatre Survey* 13 (1973): 7.
40. Halsall, *Victor Hugo and the Romantic Drama*, 82.
41. E. Fischer-Lichte, *History of European Drama and Theatre*, trans. Jo Riley (London and New York: Routledge, 2008), 222.
42. C. Dickens, *Oliver Twist*, ed. F. Kaplan (New York: W.W. Norton, 1993), 117–18.
43. G.H. Lewes, *On Actors and the Art of Acting* (London: Smith, Elder, & Company, 1875), 23.
44. Other great nineteenth-century actresses to play Hamlet include Sara Siddons and Charlotte Cushman.
45. J. Ruskin, *Complete Works of John Ruskin*, Vol. 22, ed. E.T. Cook and Alexander Wedderburn (London: George Allen. New York: Longmans, Green, and Co., 1903–12), 173–4.
46. H. Meilhac and L. Halévy, *FrouFrou: Comédie en Cinq Actes* (Paris: Michel Lévy Frères, 1870). The Augustin Daly translation, *"Frou": A Comedy of Powerful Human Interest, in Five Acts* (Samuel French, 1870), has no attribution to Meilhac and Halévy. The term "frou" as the rustling sound a frilly skirt makes appears to enter the English language through the appearance of this play; the earliest usage in the OED is 1870.
47. E. Ledger, "New Pieces Produced at the London Theatres, from December 1869 to November 1870," *The Era Almanack* (London, 1871), 47.
48. J. Davis, "Sarah Lane: Questions of Authorship," in *Women and Playwriting in Nineteenth-Century Britain*, 125–48.
49. C. Peters, *The King of Inventors: A Life of Wilkie Collins* (Princeton: Princeton University Press, 2014), 83.
50. Gaetano Donizetti and librettist Salvadore Cammarano's opera *Maria di Rohan* (1843) is also based on this play (its London premiere was May 8, 1847 at Covent Garden). Although Robert Hanna contends that Lockroy and Badon's French original was not performed in London until 1835 at the Olympic, a July 14, 1832 review of Boaden's play in the *Literary Gazette* states that her translation follows a production of the French original "acted at this theatre [the Haymarket] in the spring." See "Haymarket," *The Literary Gazette: A Weekly Journal of Literature, Science, and the Fine Arts*, 80 (July 14, 1832): 445. Wilkie Collins adapted it again as *A Court Duel* (1850). See R.C. Hanna, "*A Court Duel* as Performed by Wilkie Collins, with an Analysis of the Manuscript, Playbill, and Advertisement," *Dickens Studies Annual* 47 (2016): 225.
51. Theatre Royal, Haymarket. A collection of playbills from Haymarket Theatre, 1831–1833. TS British Playbills, 1754-1882, British Library, *Nineteenth Century Collections Online* (http://tinyurl.galegroup.com/tinyurl/5rAHA1 [last accessed January 28, 2018]).
52. W. Godwin, *William Godwin's Diary*, http://godwindiary.bodleian.ox.ac.uk/diary/1832-07-26.html (last accessed January 26, 2018).
53. Theatre Royal, Haymarket. A collection of playbills from Haymarket Theatre, 1831–1833. TS British Playbills, 1754–1882. British Library.
54. Halsall, *Victor Hugo and the Romantic Drama*, 73.
55. V. Hugo, *Four Plays: Marion de Lorme, Hernani, Lucretia Borgia, Ruy Blas*, ed. Claude Schumacher (London: Methuen, 2004), 108.

56. Lord Chamberlain's Plays. Vol. LIII. June-Aug. 1832. Jun. 1832-Aug. 1832. MS Lord Chamberlain's Plays, 1852–1858 Add MS 42917. British Library. *Nineteenth Century Collections Online*, http://tinyurl.galegroup.com/tinyurl/5ocMg7 (accessed January 28, 2018).
57. "Theatricals," *The Athenaeum* 246 (July 14, 1832): 460.
58. "The Drama," *The Court Magazine and Belle Assemblée*, 1 (August 1832): 108.
59. "Haymarket," *The Literary Gazette* (July 14, 1832): 445.
60. "The Drama," *The New Monthly Magazine* (August 1832): 348. See also Newey, *Women's Theatre Writing*, 73.
61. Newey, *Women's Theatre Writing*, 72–3.
62. H. Kaufman, "England's Jewish Renaissance: Maria Polack's Fiction with Romance (1830) in Context," in *Romanticism/Judaica: A Convergence of Cultures*, ed. S. Spector (Farnham and Burlington, VT: Ashgate, 2011), 77.
63. J. Franceschina, *Gore on Stage: The Plays of Catherine Gore* (New York and London: Routledge, 2004), 232.
64. Holder, "'The 'lady playwrights' and the 'wild tribes of the East,'" 174.
65. H.E. Smither, *A History of the Oratorio*, Vol. 3: *The Oratorio in the Classical Era* (Chapel Hill: University of North Carolina Press, 2012), 201.
66. For one example, see "Oratorios," *The Examiner* 1052 (March 30, 1828): 215.
67. See S.A. Weltman, "Melodrama, *Purimspiel*, and Jewish Emancipation," *Victorian Literature and Culture* 47.2 (2019): 1–41.
68. E. Polack, *Esther, The Royal Jewess, or the Death of Haman!* (London: Duncombe, 1835), 30.
69. J. Davis and V. Emeljanow, *Reflecting the Audience: London Theatregoing, 1840–1880* (Iowa City: University of Iowa Press, 2001), 92.
70. Polack, *Esther, The Royal Jewess*, 30.
71. F. Jameson, "Third-World Literature in the Era of Multinational Capitalism," *Social Text* 15 (1986): 69.
72. D. Katz, *The Jews in the History of England, 1485–1850* (Oxford: Oxford University Press, 1994), 386.
73. J. Racine, *Esther*, in *Racine's Esther*, ed. G. Saintsbury (Oxford: Clarendon Press, 1886), 2.1.383-91, 81.
74. Polack, *Esther, The Royal Jewess,* 18.
75. J. Moody, *Illegitimate Theatre in London, 1770–1840* (Cambridge: Cambridge University Press, 2000), 38, 166.
76. G.B. Shaw, "The Drama in Hoxton," in *Victorian Dramatic Criticism*, ed. G. Rowell (London: Methuen, 1971), 333–4.
77. C. Dickens, "Amusements of the People," *Household Words* 1 (April 13, 1850), 57.
78. S.A. Weltman "Introduction: George Dibdin Pitt's 1847 *Sweeney Todd*," 1.
79. She co-managed with her husband Samuel Lane until his death in 1872, then managed the theatre by herself until her own death, becoming a beloved philanthropist and "the Queen of Hoxton." A. Nicoll, *A History of English Drama, 1660–1900*, vol. 4 (Cambridge: Cambridge University Press, 1955), 223.
80. Moreover, Dibdin Pitt knew his greatest prior success involved heroines in service. His *Susan Hopley, the Vicissitudes of a Serving Girl* (1841) was performed over 100 times the first season and fifty the next. Young women in service flocked to every performance.
81. Weltman, "Introduction," 4–5.
82. For Sondheim's acknowledged debt to Christopher Bond in adding the revenge motive, see C. Bond, "Introduction," in *Sweeney Todd: The Demon Barber of Fleet Street* by S. Sondheim and H. Wheeler (New York: Applause Theatre Book Publishers, 1991).

83. Gerould explains that Sondheim visited the Grand Guignol in the 1960s, not long before it closed, citing its influence on *Sweeney Todd*. Gerould, "Larger than Life," 4–5.
84. M. Gordon, *The Grand Guignol: Theatre of Fear and Terror* (Port Townsend, WA: Amok Press, 1988), 27.
85. G.D. Pitt, "The String of Pearls, or The Fiend of Fleet Street," ed. S.A. Weltman, *Nineteenth Century Theatre and Film* 38 (2011): 81.
86. G.D. Pitt, Pett MSS B.26 SPEC COLL.
87. Davis and Emeljanow, *Reflecting the Audience*, 88.

Chapter Four

1. T. McCarthy, *Satin Island* (London: Jonathan Cape, 2015), 7.
2. McCarthy, *Satin Island*, 12.
3. Aristotle, *Poetics*, trans. R. Janko (Indianapolis, IN: Hackett, 1987), 7–8.
4. McCarthy, *Satin Island*, 12–13.
5. This latter point is the argument made by J.P. Vernant and P. Vidal-Naquet in *Myth and Tragedy in Ancient Greece*, trans. J. Lloyd (New York: Zone Books, 1988).
6. R. Williams, *Modern Tragedy* (1966; London: The Hogarth Press: 1992), 45.
7. Williams, *Modern Tragedy*, 14.
8. Williams, *Modern Tragedy*, 45–6.
9. See T. Eagleton, *Sweet Violence: The Idea of the Tragic* (Oxford: Blackwell, 2003).
10. Williams, *Modern Tragedy*, 62–3.
11. P. Szondi, *An Essay on the Tragic*, trans. P. Fleming (Stanford, CA: Stanford University Press, 2002), 1.
12. F.W.J. Schelling, *The Unconditional in Human Knowledge: Four Early Essays, 1794–1796*, trans. F. Marti (Lewisburg, PA: Bucknell University Press, 1980), 192.
13. Quoted by Szondi, *Essay on the Tragic*, 8.
14. Schelling, *Four Early Essays*, 192.
15. Schelling, *Four Early Essays*, 192–3.
16. M. Leonard, *Tragic Modernities* (Cambridge, MA: Harvard University Press, 2015), 54.
17. F.W.J. Schelling, *The Philosophy of Art*, trans. D. Stott (Minneapolis: University of Minnesota Press, 1989), 251.
18. Szondi, *Essay on the Tragic*, 10.
19. Szondi, *Essay on the Tragic*, 16.
20. G.W.F. Hegel, *Natural Law: The Scientific Ways of Treating Natural Law, Its Place in Moral Philosophy, and Its Relation to the Positive Sciences of Law*, trans. T.M. Knox (Philadelphia: University of Pennsylvania Press, 1975), 105.
21. Szondi, *Essay on the Tragic*, 15.
22. Szondi, *Essay on the Tragic*, 16.
23. G.W.F. Hegel, *Aesthetics: Lectures on Fine Art*, trans. T.M. Knox (Oxford: Clarendon Press, 1975), 1196.
24. Szondi, *Essay on the Tragic*, 19.
25. Quoted by Szondi, *Essay on the Tragic*, 20.
26. Szondi, *Essay on the Tragic*, 20.
27. Szondi, *Essay on the Tragic*, 21.
28. A. Schopenhauer, *The World as Will and Representation*, 2 vols, trans. E.F.J. Payne (New York: Dover Publications, 1966), 1: 275.
29. Schopenhauer, *World as Will and Representation*, 1: 253.

30. Schopenhauer, *World as Will and Representation*, 1: 152.
31. Schopenhauer, *World as Will and Representation*, 2:433–4.
32. F. Nietzsche, *The Birth of Tragedy and Other Writings*, trans. R. Speirs (Cambridge: Cambridge University Press, 1999), 14.
33. On this point see D.J. Schmidt, *On Germans and Other Greeks: Tragedy and the Ethical Life* (Bloomington: Indiana University Press, 2001), 191.
34. Nietzsche, *Birth of Tragedy*, 14.
35. Leonard, *Tragic Modernities*, 63.
36. Nietzsche, *Birth of Tragedy*, 70.
37. Nietzsche, *Birth of Tragedy*, 14.
38. Szondi, *Essay on the Tragic*, 42–3.
39. Nietzsche, *Birth of Tragedy*, 52–3.
40. Nietzsche, *Birth of Tragedy*, 13.
41. P.B. Shelley, *Shelley's Poetry and Prose: A Norton Critical Edition*, second edn, ed. D.H. Reiman and N. Fraistat (New York: W.W. Norton and Company, 2002), 519–20.
42. Shelley, *Poetry and Prose*, 520.
43. Shelley, *Poetry and Prose*, 520.
44. Shelley, *Poetry and Prose*, 520.
45. Shelley, *Poetry and Prose*, 521.
46. On the links between Shelley and Marx, see R. Kaufman "Intervention and Commitment Forever! Shelley in 1819, Shelley in Brecht, Shelley in Adorno, Shelley in Benjamin," *Romantic Circles Praxis* Series (May 2001); and P. Foot, *Red Shelley* (London: Sidgwick & Jackson, 1981).
47. K. Marx, *The Eighteenth Brumaire of Louis Bonaparte* (New York: International Publishers, 1963), 15.
48. Marx, *Eighteenth Brumaire*, 15.
49. Marx, *Eighteenth Brumaire*, 16–17.
50. Marx, *Eighteenth Brumaire*, 17.
51. H. Arendt, *On Revolution* (Harmondsworth: Penguin, 2006), 19.
52. For more on this point, see R. Comay, *Mourning Sickness: Hegel and the French Revolution* (Stanford: Stanford University Press 2011).

Chapter Five

1. A. Strindberg, *To Damascus* Part I, in *The Plays of Strindberg*, Vol. 2, trans. M. Meyer (New York: Vintage Books, 1976), 1.1, 34.
2. J.D. Mikalson, *Honor Thy Gods: Popular Religion in Greek Tragedy* (Chapel Hill: University of North Carolina Press, 1991); C. Sourvinou-Inwood, *Tragedy and Athenian Religion* (New York: Lexington Books, 2003).
3. Quoted in S. Fix, "Johnson and the 'Duty' of Reading *Paradise Lost*," *ELH* 52 (1985): 657. Thanks to Katherine Eggert for help on this point.
4. J. Barish, *The Antitheatrical Prejudice* (Berkeley: University of California Press, 1981).
5. Censorship of the French stage came and went with various governments. For example, the Revolution abolished it and Napoleon reinstated it. See the pioneering archival work of O. Krakovitch, *Les pièces de théâtre soumises à la censure (1800–1830)* (Paris: Archives Nationales, 1982) and *Censure des répertoires des grands théâtres parisiens (1835–1906)* (Paris: Centre Historique des Archives Nationales, 2003). In less centralized countries such as Germany and Italy, the situations were more complex. See overviews of these and other

national censorship regimes in *The Frightful Stage: Political Censorship of the Theater in Nineteenth-Century Europe*, ed. R.J. Goldstein (New York: Berghahn Books, 2009).
6. M. Lewis, *The Castle Spectre*, in *Seven Gothic Dramas 1789–1825*, ed. J.N. Cox (Athens: Ohio University Press, 1992), 4.2, 206 and 206n.
7. M. Kelly, *Reminiscences*, ed. R. Fiske (Oxford: Oxford University Press, 1975), 252; and J. Boaden, *Memoirs of the Life of John Philip Kemble*, 2 vols (1824; rpt. New York: Benjamin Blom, 1969), 2: 230. Both comments are quoted by S. Cohen, "Introduction," *The Plays of James Boaden* (New York: Garland, 1980), xxxix.
8. M. Gamer, *Romanticism and the Gothic: Genre, Reception, and Canon Formation* (Cambridge: Cambridge University Press, 2000), 132.
9. Review of *The Castle Spectre*, *The Monthly Mirror* 4 (1797), 356.
10. *The Anti-Jacobin*, June 4, 1798 (rpt. New York: AMS Press, 1968), 236.
11. W. Wordsworth, *The Borderers*, ed. R. Osborn (Ithaca: Cornell University Press, 1982), 3.1438–9, 3:1496, and 4.1817–18.
12. S.T. Coleridge, *Remorse*, in *The Collected Works of Samuel Taylor, Poetical Works, Vol III: Plays, (Part II)*, ed. J.C.C. Mays (Princeton: Princeton University Press, 2001), 4.1.105, 108–9, 113–14.
13. G.B. Shaw, *Saint Joan* (Baltimore: Penguin Books, 1951), 98–9.
14. See S. Curran, *"The Cenci": Scorpions Ringed with Fire* (Princeton: Princeton University Press, 1970).
15. For Blake's image of a patriarchal god who is not our father but a "Father of Jealousy" see "To Nobodaddy," in *The Complete Poetry and Prose of William Blake*, ed. D.V. Erdman (rev. edn; Berkeley: University of California Press, 1982), 471–2.
16. P.B. Shelley, *The Cenci*, in *Shelley's Poetry and Prose: A Norton Critical Edition*, second edn, ed. D.H. Reiman and N. Fraistat (New York: W.W. Norton and Company, 2002), 1.1.74. Further references to this play will be cited parenthetically in the text by act, scene, and line number.
17. A. de Musset, *Lorenzaccio*, 1.2.268–70, 273–6, 9–10. Act, scene, and line numbers from *La Génese de "Lorenzaccio,"* ed. P. Dimoff (Paris: Droz, 1936); page numbers from R. Bruce's lively but partial translation in *The Modern Theater*, Vol. 6, ed. E. Bentley (New York: Doubleday, 1960). Further references to this play will be cited parenthetically in the text by act, scene, line number, and page number.
18. H. Ibsen, *Brand*, trans. M. Meyer (Garden City, NY: Anchor Books, 1960), 1, 58. Further references to this play will be cited parenthetically in the text by act and page number.
19. *Byron's Letters and Journals*, ed. L.A. Marchand, 13 vols (Cambridge: Harvard University Press, 1973–82), 5: 195; "Manfred.—By Lord Byron," *The Literary Gazette* 22 (June 21, 1817): 337.
20. Lord Byron, *Manfred*, gen. eds. J. Black et al. (Peterborough, ON: Broadview 2017), 3.4.141.
21. Review of *Manfred*, *The Critical Review* 5 (June 1817), 622.
22. L. Brown, "Trauma, Radicalism, and Dramatic Form in *Till Damaskus I*," *Scandinavian Studies* 84 (2012), 401.
23. A. Strindberg, *A Dream Play*, in *Six Plays of Strindberg*, trans. E. Sprigge (Garden City, NY: Anchor Books, 1955), 257.
24. A. Strindberg, *The Ghost Sonata*, in *Six Plays of Strindberg*, 295–6.
25. F. Schiller, *The Bride of Messina, William Tell, Demetrius*, trans. C.E. Passage (New York: Frederick Ungar, 1967), 13. Further references to this play will be cited parenthetically in the text by act, scene, and line number.
26. P.B. Shelley, "Preface" to *Hellas*, in *Shelley's Poetry and Prose*, 430–1.

27. P.B. Shelley, title page for *Oedipus Tyrannus, or Swellfoot the Tyrant: A Tragedy in Two Acts*, in *The Complete Works of Percy Bysshe Shelley*, ed. R. Igpen and W.E. Peck (rpt. New York: Gordian Press, 1965), 2: 219.
28. J. Goethe, *Iphigenia in Tauris*, trans. C.E. Passage (New York: Frederick Ungar, 1963), 4.1726–66. Further references to this play will be cited parenthetically in the text by act and line number.
29. J. Goethe, letter to Schiller, January 19, 1802, in *Correspondence Between Schiller and Goethe*, trans. L.D. Schmitz (London: G. Bell, 1898), 2: 393. Schmitz gives "human" for the German *human*; the phrase is *"ganz teufelt human,"* meaning "quite devilishly [or damnably] humane."
30. Quoted in T. L. Meyers, "Shelley's Influence on 'Atalanta in Calydon,'" *Victorian Poetry* 14 (1976): 150.
31. See also, K. Paterson, "'Much Regrafted Pain': Schopenhauerian Love and the Fecundity of Pain in *Atalanta in Calydon*," *Victorian Poetry* 47 (2009): 715–31.
32. P.B. Shelley, *Prometheus Unbound*, in *Shelley's Poetry and Prose*, 2.4.119–20. Further references to this play will be cited parenthetically in the text by act, scene, and line number.
33. A. Swinburne, *Atalanta in Calydon*, in *The Pre-Raphaelites and Their Circle*, second edn, ed. C.B. Lang (Chicago: The University of Chicago Press, 1975), 308–9. Further references to this play will be cited parenthetically in the text by line number.
34. R.A. Greenberg, "Swinburne and the Redefinition of Classical Myth," *Victorian Poetry* 14 (1976): 175–95.
35. J.N. Cox, *In the Shadows of Romance: Romantic Tragic Drama in Germany, England, and France* (Athens: Ohio University Press, 1987), esp. 1–25.
36. Cox, *In the Shadows of Romance*, 199.
37. Lord Byron, *Heaven and Earth*, in Byron, *The Complete Poetical Works*, ed. Jerome J. McGann, 7 vols (Oxford: Clarendon Press, 1980–93), 6: 346. Further references to this play will be cited parenthetically in the text by scene and line number.
38. Lord Byron, *Cain*, in Byron, *The Complete Poetical Works*, 6: 232. Further references to this play will be cited parenthetically in the text by act, scene, and line number.

Chapter Six

1. B. Anderson, *Imagined Communities* (London: Verso, 2006).
2. T. Hardy, *Tess of the D'Urbervilles* (Oxford: Oxford University Press, 2008), 205.
3. Hardy, *Tess*, 419.
4. A.C. Bradley, *Shakespearean Tragedy : Lectures on Hamlet, Othello, King Lear, Macbeth* (Harmondsworth: Penguin, 1991), 50. John Orr, similarly, notes that in tragedy "The essential human experience is that of irreparable human loss" in his *Tragic Drama and Modern Society: A Sociology of Dramatic Form from 1880 to the Present*, 2nd edn. (Basingstoke: Macmillan, 1989), xii.
5. For theater syndicates in the English case, see T. Davis, *The Economics of the British Stage, 1800–1914* (Cambridge: Cambridge University Press, 2000), 41, 310. In the case of Italy, Carlotta Sorba traces the development of a series of "impresario circuits" dating from the Restoration, which "were very effective in diffusing the same operas throughout the national territory, using the dense network of urban theaters covering the entire peninsula," linking "those cities that were by tradition the cultural capitals (Milan, Rome, Naples, Venice), but also the medium-sized and small centers of urban Italy, and similarly the theaters elsewhere in continental Europe, so as to form a polycentric framework that was national and

international in scale." See "National Theater and the Age of Revolution in Italy," *Journal of Modern Italian Studies* 17.4 (2012): 410.
6. Whether old reprinted translations or new ones, it became easier to obtain classical texts throughout Europe throughout the nineteenth century. Although printing in general became cheaper throughout the century, the process of reader access to classics changed country to country and year by year, as the expanded readership made possible by lending libraries expanded still into the yet more extensive readership made possible by mass book ownership. Famed for expanding the reach of the triple-decker novel to hitherto unreachable classes in Britain, *Mudie's Select Library* included a twenty-volume series of "Ancient Classics for English Readers." (*Catalogue of books of the best authors . . . on sale at Mudie's Select Library*, London: Mudie's Select Library, [1878?].) German book historians, in contrast, mark 1867 as a decisive year when a combination of changes in the law and earlier developments in print technology made classic texts, among them the Roman and Greek classics, available to a wide audience. See C. Woodford, "Introduction," in *The German Bestseller in the Late Nineteenth Century*, ed. C. Woodford and B. Schofield (Rochester, NY: Camden House, 2012), 6. It is easy to overstate how quickly, and how early, general access to such books occurred; nevertheless, access to classical texts in translation saw a sustained expansion throughout the century.
7. So, for example, the *Communist Manifesto's* contrast of different stages of pre-bourgeois development—"here independent urban republic (as in Italy and Germany); there taxable 'third estate' of the monarchy (as in France)"—to the present situation, in which "The executive of the modern state," regardless of nation, "is but a committee for managing the common affairs of the whole bourgeoisie." See K. Marx and F. Engels, "The Communist Manifesto," Marx Engels Archive, https://www.marxists.org/archive/marx/works/1848/communist-manifesto/ch01.htm (accessed September 25, 2018).
8. I. Hodder, "The Entanglements of Humans and Things: A Long-Term View," *New Literary History* 45:1 (2014): 21.
9. Hodder, "Entanglements," 19.
10. M. Buckley, *Tragedy Walks the Streets: The French Revolution in the Making of Modern Drama* (Baltimore: Johns Hopkins University Press, 2006), 93.
11. G. Deleuze and F. Guattari, *Anti-Oedipus: Capitalism and Schizophrenia*, trans. R. Hurley, M. Seem, and H.R. Lane (London: Continuum, 2004), 125.
12. P.K. Gilbert, *Mapping the Victorian Social Body* (Albany: State University of New York Press, 2004), 106.
13. A. Schopenhauer, "The World as Will and Idea," in *Theatre/Theory/Theatre*, ed. D. Gerould (New York: Applause Books, 2003), 293.
14. Hegel's suggestion that drama involves "*collisions* of circumstances" within "a completely developed and organized national life" is similarly based on cohesiveness. G.W.F. Hegel, *Aesthetics: Lectures on Fine Art*, trans. T.M. Knox, 2 vols., vol. 2 (Oxford: Clarendon, 1998), 1159. In particular, Hegel suggests that the tragic world is essentially reconciliative: the "positive elements" advocated for by the tragic protagonist are "retained, without discord but affirmatively harmonized" (1199).
15. F. Moretti, *Distant Reading* (London: Verso, 2013), 11.
16. M. Patterson and M. Huxley, "German Drama, Theatre, and Dance," in *The Cambridge Companion to Modern German Culture*, ed. E. Kolinsky (Cambridge: Cambridge University Press, 1999), 214.
17. G. Büchner, *Woyzeck*, trans. G. Motton (London: Nick Hern Books, 1996), scene 3, *Drama Online*, http://www.dramaonlinelibrary.com (accessed September 25, 2018). Subsequent references, by scene, are cited parenthetically in the text.

18. A. Strindberg, *Plays: 1*, trans. M. Meyer (London: Bloomsbury Methuen, 2014), 186. Subsequent references are cited parenthetically in the text.
19. T. Eagleton, *Culture and the Death of God* (New Haven: Yale University Press, 2015), 180.
20. M. Meeuwis, "Representative Government: The 'Problem Play,' Quotidian Culture, and the Making of Social Liberalism," *ELH* 80.4 (2013): 1092 and *passim*.
21. M.R. Booth, "Introduction," in *English Plays of the Nineteenth Century* (Oxford: Clarendon Press, 1976), 21–2.
22. E. Hall and F. Macintosh, *Greek Tragedy and the British Theatre, 1660–1914* (Oxford: Oxford University Press, 2005), 330.
23. Davis, *Economics*, 310.
24. The Larpent Catalogue, for example, shows many new plays calling themselves tragedies, but these are not given repeat performances with the same frequency as other genres. See D. Macmillan, *Catalogue of the Larpent Plays in the Huntington Library* (San Marino: Huntington Library, 1939).
25. "The Opera and Theatres," *The Ladies' Monthly Magazine* 689 (1881): 11.
26. H. Ritchie, "Kean Versus Macready: Sheridan Knowles' *Virginius*," *Theatre Survey* 17.1 (1976): 28.
27. Ritchie, "Kean Versus Macready," 32.
28. Hall and Macintosh, *Greek Tragedy*, 273.
29. Quoted in Ritchie, "Kean Versus Macready," 32.
30. Buckley notes that melodrama "contain[ed]" the "threat" presented by the revolution "in the exercise of passion and the reassuring confinement of action to the bounds of the stage" (*Tragedy Walks the Streets*, 150).
31. J.S. Knowles, *Virginius* (London: James Ridgway, 1820), 17–18. Subsequent references are given parenthetically by page number.
32. "Mr. Knowles' Dramas: Virginius—Caius Gracchus," *The Scots Magazine* 13 (1823): 722.
33. J. Plotz, *Portable Property: Victorian Culture on the Move* (Princeton: Princeton University Press, 2008), 8.
34. L. Lewis and Erckmann-Chatrian, *The Bells* (London: Harrap, 1978), 10. All subsequent citations are given parenthetically by page number.
35. H. Ibsen, *Ghosts*, trans. M. Meyer (London: Eyre Methuen, 1973), 38. All subsequent citations are given parenthetically by page number.
36. T. Moi, *Henrik Ibsen and the Birth of Modernism: Art, Theater, Philosophy* (Oxford: Oxford University Press, 2006), 8.
37. Moi, *Henrik Ibsen*, 8.
38. Moi, *Henrik Ibsen*, 8.

Chapter Seven

1. B. Simon, *Tragic Drama and the Family: Psychoanalytic Studies from Aeschylus to Beckett* (New Haven: Yale University Press, 1988), 1–12.
2. H. Arendt, *The Human Condition* (Chicago: University of Chicago Press, 1958), 28.
3. C.A. Bayly, *The Birth of the Modern World, 1780-1914* (London: Blackwell, 2004), 64.
4. J.N. Cox, *In the Shadows of Romance: Romantic Tragic Drama in Germany, England, and France* (Athens: Ohio University Press, 1987), 16.
5. P.B. Shelley, *Shelley's Poetry and Prose: A Norton Critical Edition*, second edn, ed. D.H. Reiman and N. Fraistat (New York: W.W. Norton and Company, 2002), 1.3.4–5. Further citations will be quoted parenthetically in the text by act, scene, and line number.

NOTES 171

6. J. Moody, *Illegitimate Theatre in London, 1770-1840* (Cambridge: Cambridge University Press, 2000), 10.
7. This opinion is grounded in the continued influence of G. Steiner's *The Death of Tragedy* (1961) and T. Otten's *The Deserted Stage* (1972). In spite of transformative work done by, among others, J.N. Cox, J. Carlson, and M. Gamer, many accounts of nineteenth-century theater and its tragedy still begin with tragedy's decline and even demise.
8. G. Lukács, *The Historical Novel*, trans. H. and S. Mitchell (1962; Lincoln: University of Nebraska Press, 1983), 19.
9. S. Curran, *Poetic Form and British Romanticism* (Oxford: Oxford University Press, 1986), 140.
10. M. Favret, *War at a Distance: Romanticism and the Making of Modern Wartime* (Princeton: Princeton University Press, 2010).
11. H. Kleist, *Penthesilea*, in *Plays*, ed. W. Hinderer (New York: Continuum Publishing, 1996), 1, 167. Subsequent references are cited parenthetically by scene and page number.
12. I discuss Shelley's dramas as reformulations of cultural and historical tragedies in *Shelley's Radical Stages: Performance and Cultural Memory in the Post-Napoleonic Era* (New York: Routledge, 2016).
13. J. Goethe, *Iphigenia in Tauris*, in *Plays: Egmont, Iphigenia in Tauris, Torquato Tasso*, ed. F. Ryder (New York: Continuum, 1992). Subsequent references are cited parenthetically by scene and page number.
14. W. Wordsworth, *Lyrical Ballads*, 2 vols (London: Longman, 1800), xix.
15. The full title highlights the significance of individual passions: *A Series of Plays: in which it is attempted to delineate the stronger passions of the mind. Each passion being the subject of a tragedy and a comedy.*
16. My thanks to Michael Gamer for this information, compiled from D. Macmillan, *Catalogue of the Larpent Plays in the Huntington Library* (San Marino, CA: Huntington Library Press, 1939). According to his tabulation, only 1.6 percent of new plays produced between 1803 and 1813 were tragedies, half of what was customary in the final quarter of the eighteenth century.
17. J. Baillie, "Introductory Discourse," in *Plays on the Passions (1798 edition)*, ed. P. Duthie (Peterborough, ON: Broadview Press, 2001), 80.
18. J. Wallace, *The Cambridge Introduction to Tragedy* (Cambridge: Cambridge University Press, 2007), 64. See also S. Valladares' discussion of Coleridge in *Staging the Peninsular War: English Theatres, 1807–1815* (New York: Routledge, 2015).
19. See S. Goldhill's essay, "Generalizing About Tragedy," in *Rethinking Tragedy*, ed. R. Felski (Baltimore: Johns Hopkins University Press, 2008), 53.
20. See *Shelley's Poetry and Prose*, where Shelley claims that the "highest moral purpose aimed at in the highest species of the drama, is the teaching the human heart, though its sympathies and antipathies, the knowledge of itself; in proportion to the possession of which knowledge, every human being is wise, just, sincere, tolerant and kind" (142).
21. Arendt, *The Human Condition*, 38.
22. G. Russell, *The Theatres of War: Performance, Politics, and Society, 1793–1815* (Oxford: Clarendon Press, 1995), 65.
23. Favret, *War at a Distance*, 39, 33.
24. A.L. Barbauld, *The Works of Anna Laetitia Barbauld*, 2 vols (London: Longman, 1825), 232.
25. J. Carlson, "Baillie's *Orra*: Shrinking in Fear," in *Joanna Baillie, Romantic Dramatist: Critical Essays*, ed. T. Crochunis (New York: Routledge, 2004), 208.
26. J. Baillie, *Orra*, in *The Broadview Anthology of Romantic Drama*, ed. J.N. Cox and M. Gamer (Peterborough: Broadview Press, 2003), 2.1.24 and 2.1.4. Subsequent references to this play are cited parenthetically in the text by act, scene, and line number.

27. D. Simpson, *Wordsworth, Commodification and Social Concern: The Poetics of Modernity* (Cambridge: Cambridge University Press, 2009), 1.
28. L. Hunt, "Victory of Waterloo – Bonaparte's Abdication." First published in *The Examiner*, 8 (July 2, 1815): 417–18. Reprinted in *The Selected Works of Leigh Hunt*, ed. R. Morrison, M. Eberle-Sinatra, J.N. Cox, G. Kucich, C. Mahoney, and J. Strachan, 6 vols (London: Pickering & Chatto, 2003), 2, 33. Subsequent references are cited parenthetically by volume and page number.
29. D. Simpson touches on these ideas in *Wordsworth, Commodification and Social Concern* and further develops his study of the stranger in this period in *Romanticism and the Question of the Stranger* (Chicago: University of Chicago Press, 2013).
30. D. Simpson discusses this transformation more at length in *9/11: The Culture of Commemoration* (Chicago: University of Chicago Press, 2006), 25–9.
31. Lord Byron, *Sardanapalus; The Two Foscari; Cain* (London: John Murray, 1821), 1.2.406 and 1.2.356. Subsequent references to these plays are cited parenthetically by act, scene, and line number.
32. S. Staves, "Tragedy," in *The Cambridge Companion to British Theatre, 1730-1830*, ed. J. Moody and D. O'Quinn (Cambridge: Cambridge University Press, 2007), 95.
33. W.G. Sebald discusses this dynamic in a different context in his *On the Natural History of Destruction*, trans. A. Bell (1999; New York: The Modern Library, 2004), 3–9.
34. Wallace, *The Cambridge Introduction to Tragedy*, 63.
35. Goldhill, "Generalizing About Tragedy," 51.
36. Cox, *In the Shadows of Romance*, 141.
37. R. Williams, *The Tragic Imagination* (Oxford: Oxford University Press, 2016), 101
38. J. Butler, *Antigone's Claim: Kinship between Life and Death* (New York: Columbia University Press, 2002), 10.
39. Cox, *In the Shadows of Romance*, 152.
40. N. and C. Sublette, *The American Slave Coast: A History of the Slave-Breeding Industry* (Chicago: Chicago Review Press, 2015).
41. J. Hogle, "Introduction," in *The Cambridge Companion to Gothic Fiction*, ed. J. Hogle (Cambridge: Cambridge University Press, 2002), 6–7.
42. D. Van Kooy and J.N. Cox make this point in "Melodramatic Slaves," *Modern Drama*, 55.4 (Winter 2012): 459.
43. O. Patterson, *Slavery and Social Death: A Comparative Study* (Cambridge, MA: Harvard University Press, 1982), 39.
44. Patterson, *Slavery and Social Death*, 46.
45. R. Williams, *Modern Tragedy* (1966; London: Verso, 1979).
46. J. Butler, "Performative Acts and Gender Constitution: An Essay in Phenomenology and Feminist Theory," *Theatre Journal* 40.4 (December 1988): 522.
47. J. Roach, "Slave Spectacles and Tragic Octoroons: A Cultural Genealogy of Antebellum Performance," *Theatre Survey* 33 (November 1992): 176–7.
48. K. Wilson, "Rowe's *Fair Penitent* as Global History: Or, A Diversionary Voyage to New South Wales," *Eighteenth-Century Studies* 41.2 (2008): 233.
49. Wilson discusses this aspect of Rowe's tragedy in "Rowe's *Fair Penitent*," 236.
50. D. Boucicault, *The Octoroon; or, Life in Louisiana*, in *Major Voices: The Drama of Slavery*, ed. E. Gardner (New Milford, CN: Toby, 2005), 2.1.510.
51. Wilson, "Rowe's *Fair Penitent*," 235.
52. H. Ibsen, *The Master Builder and Other Plays*, trans. B.J. Haveland (New York: Penguin, 2014), 2, 348. Subsequent references are cited parenthetically by act and page number.

53. Toril Moi makes this point in her Introduction to Ibsen's *The Master Builder and Other Plays* (London: Penguin, 2014), xxv.
54. H. Ibsen, *Ghosts*, in *Ghosts and Other Plays*, trans. Peter Watts (New York: Penguin, 1964), 2, 61. Subsequent references will be cited parenthetically by act and page number.

Chapter Eight

1. According to George Steiner, genuine tragedy demands the certainty that "mortal actions are encompassed by forces which transcend man." By contrast, the eighteenth- and nineteenth-century "liberation of the individual from predetermined hierarchies of social station and caste" resulted in the conviction that "[t]he misery and injustice of man's fate were not . . . the consequence of some tragic, immutable flaw in human nature" but rather "arose from the absurdities and archaic inequalities built into the social fabric by generations of tyrants and exploiters." This belief that "the quality of being could be radically altered and improved by changes in . . . the social and material circumstances of existence" meant, for Steiner, that "because the individual is not wholly responsible, he cannot be wholly damned." As such, it marked the end of "authentic tragedy." G. Steiner, *The Death of Tragedy* (London: Faber and Faber, 1961), 193, 124–5, 127–8. For similar assessments of tragedy's decline, see R. Sewall, *The Vision of Tragedy* (New Haven, CT: Yale University Press, 1959); and G. Brereton, *Principles of Tragedy: A Rational Examination of the Tragic Concept in Life and Literature* (Coral Gables, FL: University of Miami Press, 1968).
2. See also J.N. Cox, "Romantic Redefinitions of the Tragic," in *Romantic Drama*, ed. G. Gillespie (Amsterdam and Philadelphia, PA: John Benjamins Publishing Company, 1994), 154.
3. According to Steiner, "the centre of social gravity shifted toward the middle classes" during the eighteenth century, and particularly after the French Revolution, which "plunged ordinary men into the stream of history." Consequently, "theatrical managers and their playwrights were no longer catering to a literate aristocracy or *élite* drawn from the magistracy and high finance; they were trying to attract the *bourgeois* family" (115–16).
4. G. Lillo, *The London Merchant: or, the History of George Barnwell*, in *Eighteenth Century Plays*, ed. J. Hampden (London: J.M. Dent, 1958), 3. Despite Lillo's insistence that his play be considered a serious tragedy, critical appraisals from the eighteenth to the twenty-first century have questioned its generic status, emphasizing the distinction between classical or neoclassical tragedy and "bourgeois drama." For compelling analyses of the aesthetic and political stakes of this debate, see D. Wallace, "Bourgeois Tragedy or Sentimental Melodrama? The Significance of George Lillo's *The London Merchant*," *Eighteenth-Century Studies* 25.2 (1991–2): 123–43; and J.N. Cox, "The Death of Tragedy; or, the Birth of Melodrama," in *The Performing Century: Nineteenth-Century Theatre's History*, ed. T.C. Davis and P. Holland (Basingstoke: Palgrave Macmillan, 2007), 161–81.
5. *Aristotle's Poetics*, trans. S. Butcher (New York: Hill and Wang, 1961), 76.
6. J. Marmontel, "The Stage Considered as a Moral Institution," in *Essays on German Theater*, ed. M. Herzfeld-Sander (New York: Continuum, 1985), 7.
7. G. Lessing, "Excerpts from *The Hamburg Dramaturgy*, in *Essays on German Theater*," 7.
8. This is not to suggest that all late eighteenth-century tragedies were focused on middle-class families. Notable exceptions include Vittorio Alfieri's *Mirra* (1784–6), Joanna Baillie's *Count Basil* and *De Monfort* (both 1798), Samuel Taylor Coleridge's *Remorse* (1797), Johann Wolfgang von Goethe's *Egmont* (1773) and *Iphigenia in Tauris* (1779), and Friedrich Schiller's *Don Carlos* (1787). Important early nineteenth-century tragedies focused on nobles

and people of rank include Joanna Baillie's *Ethwald* (1802) and *Orra* (1812), Lord Byron's *Marino Faliero* and *Sardanapalus* (both 1821), Victor Hugo's *Marion de Lorme* (1829) and *Hernani* (1830), Heinrich von Kleist's *The Prince of Homburg* (1809–10), Alfred de Musset's *Lorenzaccio* (1834), Friedrich Schiller's *Maria Stuart* (1800), and Percy Bysshe Shelley's *The Cenci* (1819).

9. Quoted in E. Fischer-Lichte, *History of European Drama and Theatre*, trans. J. Riley (London: Routledge, 2002), 154.
10. Quoted in Fischer-Lichte, *History of European Drama and Theatre*, 155.
11. Quoted in L. Davidoff and C. Hall, *Family Fortunes: Men and Women of the English Middle Class 1780-1850*, revised edition (London: Routledge, 2002), 333.
12. Davidoff and Hall, *Family Fortunes*, 74, 109.
13. In his account of the rise of the bourgeois family in England, Lawrence Stone notes: "Younger sons, and particularly daughters, were often unwanted and might be regarded as no more than a tiresome drain on the economic resources of the family." See L. Stone, *The Family, Sex, and Marriage in England 1500-1800*, abridged edition (New York: Harper and Row, 1979), 87.
14. F. Schiller, *Intrigue and Love*, trans. C.E. Passage, in *Intrigue and Love* and *Don Carlos* (New York: Continuum, 1994), 1.1.5–6. Further references to this play will be cited parenthetically by act, scene, and page number(s).
15. In an effort to interpret the well-documented bond between eighteenth-century fathers and daughters offstage, Davidoff and Hall suggest: "As young single women, daughters were more available than the busy wife and mother. Their role as attentive listener made them a welcome audience and they could be counted on as a loving aide in illness or old age. Early training in docility and their potentially weaker economic position," they add, "meant that daughters did not arouse as much anxiety as sons." Interestingly, in the cases they study in which "the mother was dead, incapacitated or absent" (a circumstance particularly common in bourgeois tragedy), Davidoff and Hall deduce: "It is not difficult to understand why . . . erotic overtones sometimes seep into these father–daughter relationships" (*Family Fortunes*, 332, 346–7).
16. See Stone, *Family, Sex and Marriage*, 222; S. Staves, *Married Women's Separate Property in England, 1660-1833* (Cambridge: Harvard University Press, 1990), 4; and E.K. Sedgwick, *Between Men: English Literature and Male Homosocial Desire* (New York: Columbia University Press, 1985), 16.
17. G.E. Lessing. *Emilia Galotti*, in *Nathan the Wise, Minna von Barthelm, and Other Plays and Writings*, ed. P. Demetz (New York: Continuum, 1991), 5.7.134–5. Further references to this play will be cited parenthetically by act, scene, and page number(s).
18. On the significance of father–daughter incest in nineteenth-century literature and drama, see P. Thorslev, "Incest as Romantic Symbol," *Comparative Literature Studies* 2.1 (1965): 41–58; B. Groseclose, "The Incest Motif in Shelley's 'The Cenci,'" *Comparative Drama* 19.3 (Fall 1985): 222–39; R. Cronin, "Shelleyan Incest and the Romantic Legacy," *Keats-Shelley Journal* 45 (1996): 61–76; and F. Burwick, "Incest on the Romantic Stage: Baillie, Byron, and the Shelleys," in *Decadent Romanticism, 1780–1914*, ed. K. Boyiopoulos and M. Sandy (London: Routledge, 2016), 38–9.
19. According to the earliest extant juridical texts, the father is the head of the household, invested with the absolute power to dispose of his property (including the lives of his wife and children) at will. Such laws were still in place as the nineteenth century turned. As the *German Encyclopedia* of 1784 states, "the patriarch may employ a certain domestic violence where needed." Quoted in Fischer-Lichte, *History of European Drama and Theatre*, 216.

And, as Lawrence Stone observes, the rise of the affectionate family model in the eighteenth century was in fact "accompanied by a positive reinforcement of the despotic authority of husband and father." See *The Family, Sex, and Marriage*, 109.

20. P.B. Shelley, *The Cenci*, in *Shelley's Poetry and Prose: A Norton Critical Edition*, second edition, eds. D.H. Reiman and N. Fraistat (New York: W.W. Norton and Company, 2002), 1.3.100–7. Further references to this play will be cited parenthetically by act, scene, and line number(s).
21. *The Cenci* was published in an edition of 250 copies in 1820 and went into a second edition the following year. It was the only volume of Shelley's work to go into an authorized second printing during his lifetime. For comparative sales figures, see the Introduction to *Percy Bysshe Shelley: The Critical Heritage*, ed. J. Barcus (London: Routledge, 1975).
22. Quoted in *Shelley: The Critical Heritage*, 164.
23. Quoted in *Shelley: The Critical Heritage*, 183–4.
24. *Notebook of the Shelley Society*. Series 1, number 2, part 1 (London, 1886), 54.
25. *Notebook of the Shelley Society*, 63, 66.
26. For key twentieth-century arguments that Beatrice forfeits any moral claim to sympathy, see R. Whitman, "Beatrice's 'Pernicious Mistake' in *The Cenci*," *PMLA* 74 (1959): 249–53; J. Rees, "Shelley's Orsino: Evil in *The Cenci*," *Keats-Shelley Memorial Bulletin* 12 (1966): 3–6; J. Donohue, *Dramatic Character in the English Romantic Age* (Princeton: Princeton University Press, 1970), 177; J. Wilson, "Beatrice Cenci and Shelley's Vision of Moral Responsibility," *Ariel* 9 (1978): 75–89; L. Lockridge, "Justice in *The Cenci*," *The Wordsworth Circle* 19.2 (1988): 95–8; and W. Ulmer, *Shelleyan Eros: The Rhetoric of Romantic Love* (Princeton: Princeton University Press, 1990), 109–30. For compelling counterarguments that Beatrice is a victim of social circumstance, see S. Curran, *"The Cenci": Scorpions Ringed with Fire* (Princeton: Princeton University Press, 1970), 129–54; P. Cantor, "'A Distorting Mirror': Shelley's *The Cenci* and Shakespearean Tragedy," in *Shakespeare: Aspects of Influence*, ed. G.B. Evans (Cambridge: Harvard University Press, 1976), 91–108; R. Blood, "Allegory and Dramatic Representation in *The Cenci*," *Studies in Romanticism* 33.3 (1994): 364; and M. Harrison, "No Way for a Victim to Act?: Beatrice Cenci and the Dilemma of Romantic Performance," *Studies in Romanticism* 39.2 (2000): 187–211.
27. A. Artaud, *The Cenci*, trans. S. Taylor (New York: Grove Press, 1970), 4.3.52. On the problem of Beatrice's identification with her father, see R. Paulson, *Representations of Revolution* (New Haven: Yale University Press, 1959); R. Lemoncelli, "Cenci as a Corrupt Dramatic Poet," *English Language Notes*, 16.2 (1978): 112–15; J.E. Hogle, *Shelley's Process: Radical Transference and the Development of his Major Works* (Oxford: Oxford University Press, 1988), 153–6; and A. Richardson, *A Mental Theater: Poetic Drama and Consciousness in the Romantic Age* (University Park: Pennsylvania State University Press, 1988), 118.
28. G.B. Shaw, "Review of *The Cenci*," *Our Corner* 7 (1886): 372.
29. By locating the central organizing tropes of bourgeois tragedy in the aristocracy, such plays also worked to consolidate the status of bourgeois tragedy as "authentic tragedy."
30. M. Wollstonecraft, *A Vindication of the Rights of Woman*, ed. D.S. Lynch (New York: W.W. Norton, 2009), 7, 10.
31. J.S. Mill, *The Subjection of Women* (London: Longmans, Green, Reader, and Dyer, 1869), 21.
32. F. Engels, *The Origins of the Family, Private Property, and the State*, in *The Marx-Engels Reader* (New York: W.W. Norton, 1978), 738.
33. Quoted in *Playwrights on Playwriting: The Meaning and the Making of Modern Drama from Ibsen to Ionesco*, ed. T. Cole (New York: Hill and Wang, 1960), 152.

34. For an overview of seminal critical discussions of *A Doll's House*, see Y. Shafer, ed., *Approaches to Teaching Ibsen's "A Doll House"* (New York: Modern Language Association of America, 1985); E. Durbach, *A Doll's House: Ibsen's Myth of Transformation* (Boston: Twayne, 1991); and G. Finney, "Ibsen and Feminism," in *The Cambridge Companion to Ibsen*, ed. J. McFarlane (Cambridge: Cambridge University Press, 1994), 89–105.
35. G.B. Shaw, "A Doll's House," in *Our Theatres in the Nineties* (London: Constable, 1948), 131.
36. G. Finney, *Women in Modern Drama: Freud, Feminism, and European Theater at the Turn of the Century* (Ithaca: Cornell University Press, 1989), 149.
37. H. Ibsen, *A Doll's House*, in *Eleven Plays of Henrik Ibsen* (New York: The Modern Library, 1935), 3, 242. Further references to this play will be cited parenthetically by act and page number(s).
38. As several critics have noted, this decision is foreshadowed by Nora's frenzied dancing of the tarantella, a dance originally performed in southern Italy, described by Declan Kiberd as "a dance of androgynes, after which women behave like men." D. Kiberd, *Men and Feminism in Modern Literature* (London: Macmillan, 1985), 69.
39. H. Ibsen, *Ghosts*, in *Eleven Plays of Henrik Ibsen* (New York: The Modern Library, 1935), 1, 32. Further references to this play will be cited parenthetically by act and page number(s).
40. In Count Cenci's famous curse, he refers to his daughter as "this my blood, / This particle of my divided being; / Or rather, this my bane and my disease, / Whose sight infects and poisons me" (4.1.116–19).
41. Although this measure fails to save Mrs. Alving's son, it does succeed in interrupting the system of homosocial exchange whereby women serve to transmit wealth from one generation of men to another.
42. As Elaine Showalter, among other critics, has pointed out, Oswald Alving "goes mad in the final stages of cerebral syphilis inherited from his promiscuous father." As Showalter goes on to argue, however, "Ibsen's ghosts are not the invisible spirochetes of syphilis but the virulent prohibitions of religion and bourgeois morality. Mistaken ideas about sexuality constitute the true hereditary taint." Showalter cites the outpouring of hostile articles published in England following the play's 1891 London production as evidence of "how threatened conventional readers felt by Ibsen's intimations that the principles of conjugal obligation, feminine purity, and religious inhibition were not the forces of spiritual evolution but of aesthetic and sexual degeneration." E. Showalter, *Sexual Anarchy: Gender and Culture at the Fin de Siècle* (New York: Penguin, 1990), 199–200.
43. G.B. Shaw, *The Quintessence of Ibsenism* (Boston: Benjamin R. Tucker, 1891), 145.
44. A. Strindberg, *The Father*, in *Pre-Inferno Plays*, trans. W. Johnson (New York: Norton, 1976), 1, 21. Further references to this play will be cited parenthetically by act and page number(s).
45. S. Freud, *Moses and Monotheism*, trans. K. Jones (London: The Hogarth Press, 1939), 180.
46. G.B. Shaw, *Mrs. Warren's Profession* (Peterborough, ON: Broadview Press, 2005), 2, 125. Further references to this play will be from this edition and cited parenthetically by act and page number(s).
47. H. Ibsen, *The Master Builder*, in *Eleven Plays of Henrik Ibsen*, 3, 94.
48. *Salome* premiered in Berlin in 1901 and, as Mario Praz notes, "since then—thanks also to the music of Richard Strauss—it has continued to figure in the repertories of European theaters. In Germany it has held the boards for a longer period than any other English play, including the plays of Shakespeare." M. Praz, *The Romantic Agony*, trans. A.S. Davidson (New York: Meridian Books, 1956), 302–3.

49. P. Dierkes-Thrun, *Salomé's Modernity: Oscar Wilde and the Aesthetics of Transgression* (Ann Arbor: University of Michigan Press, 2011), 134. See also K. Powell, "Wilde and Ibsen," *English Literature in Transition, 1880–1920*, 28.3 (1985): 224–42, and *Oscar Wilde and the Theatre of the 1890s* (Cambridge: Cambridge University Press, 1990).
50. O. Wilde, *Salome*, trans. Lord A. Douglas (New York: Dover, 1967), 48. Further references to this play will be cited parenthetically by page number(s).
51. For a discussion of Salome as the quintessential *fin-de-siècle* femme fatale, see M. Praz, *The Romantic Agony*; C. Schorske, *Fin de Siècle Vienna* (New York: Knopf, 1980); and B. Dijkstra, *Idols of Perversity: Fantasies of Feminine Evil in Fin-de-Siècle Culture* (Oxford: Oxford University Press, 1986). For treatments of Salome as a figure of political and/or ideological resistance, see R. Gagnier, *Idylls of the Marketplace: Oscar Wilde and the Victorian Reading Public* (Stanford: Stanford University Press, 1986); T. Finney, *Women in Modern Drama*; A. Fernbach, "Wilde's 'Salomé' and the Ambiguous Fetish," *Victorian Literature and Culture*, 29.1 (2001): 195–218; and T. Bentley, *Sisters of Salome* (New Haven: Yale University Press, 2002), 30.
52. Finney, *Women in Modern Drama*, 59.
53. Finney, *Women in Modern Drama*, 61.
54. Shelley, 5.3.74–5.

BIBLIOGRAPHY

PERIODICALS

The Anti-Jacobin
The Athenaeum
The Cornhill Magazine
The Critical Review
The Court Magazine and Belle Assemblée
The Era Almanack
Evening Telegraph
The Examiner
Household Words
The Illustrated London News
Illustrated Sporting and Dramatic News
John Bull
The Ladies' Monthly Magazine
The Literary Gazette
The Monthly Mirror
The Morning Post
The New Monthly Magazine
The New York Times
Notebook of the Shelley Society
Our Corner
Rheinische Post
The Scots Magazine
The Standard
The Times

PRIMARY AND SECONDARY SOURCES

Anderson, B. *Imagined Communities*. London: Verso, 2006.
Arendt, H. *The Human Condition*. Chicago: University of Chicago Press, 1958.
Arendt, H. *On Revolution*. Harmondsworth: Penguin, 2006.
Aristotle. *Aristotle's Poetics*. Trans. S. Butcher. New York: Hill & Wang, 1961.
Aristotle. *Poetics*. Trans. R. Janko. Indianapolis, IN: Hackett, 1987.
Artaud, A. *The Cenci*. Trans. S. Taylor. New York: Grove Press, 1970.
Baillie, J. *Plays on the Passions (1798 edition)*. Ed. P. Duthie. Peterborough, ON: Broadview Press, 2001.
Barbauld, A.L. *The Works of Anna Laetitia Barbauld*. 2 vols. London: Longman, 1825.
Barcus, J. ed. *Percy Bysshe Shelley: The Critical Heritage*. London: Routledge, 1975.
Barish, J. *The Antitheatrical Prejudice*. Berkeley: University of California Press, 1981.

Bayly, C.A. *The Birth of the Modern World, 1780–1914*. London: Blackwell, 2004.
Bennett, S. and Sanders, J. "Rehearsing Across Space and Place: Rethinking *A Masque Presented at Ludlow Castle*." In *Performing Site-Specific Theatre: Politics, Place, Practice*, edited by A. Birch and J. Tompkins, 37–53. Basingstoke: Palgrave, 2012.
Bentley, T. *Sisters of Salome*. New Haven: Yale University Press, 2002.
Birdoff, H. *The World's Greatest Hit: Uncle Tom's Cabin*. S.F. Vanni, 1947.
Blake, W. *The Complete Poetry and Prose of William Blake*. Ed. D.V. Erdman. Berkeley: University of California Press, 1982.
Blood, R. "Allegory and Dramatic Representation in *The Cenci*." *Studies in Romanticism* 33.3 (1994): 355–89.
Boaden, J. *Memoirs of the Life of John Philip Kemble* (1824). 2 vols. New York: Benjamin Blom, 1969.
Boaden, J. *The Plays of James Boaden*. Ed. S. Cohen. New York: Garland, 1980.
Booth, M.R. *English Plays of the Nineteenth Century*. 5 vols. Oxford: Oxford University Press, 1969.
Booth, M.R. *English Plays of the Nineteenth Century*. Oxford: Clarendon Press, 1976.
Bortolotti, G.R. and Hutcheon, L. "On the Origin of Adaptations: Rethinking Fidelity Discourse and 'Success'—Biologically." *New Literary History* 38 (2007): 443–58.
Boucicault, D. *London Assurance*. Ed. J.L. Smith. London: Adam and Charles Black, 1984.
Boucicault, D. *Plays by Dion Boucicault*. Ed. P. Thomson. Cambridge: Cambridge University Press, 1984.
Boucicault, D. *Selected Plays of Dion Boucicault*. Introd. A. Parkin. Gerrard Cross, UK: Colin Smythe, 1985.
Boucicault, D. *The Octoroon; or, Life in Louisiana*. In *Major Voices: The Drama of Slavery*, edited by E. Gardner. New Milford, CN: Toby, 2005.
Bradley, A.C. *Shakespearean Tragedy: Lectures on Hamlet, Othello, King Lear, Macbeth*. Harmondsworth: Penguin, 1991.
Brandt, G.W. and Hogendoorn, W. eds. *German and Dutch Theatre, 1600–1848. Theatre in Europe: A Documentary History*. Cambridge: Cambridge University Press, 1993.
Bratton, J. *The Making of the West End Stage: Marriage, Management and the Mapping of Gender in London, 1830–1870*. Cambridge: Cambridge University Press, 2011.
Bratton, J. *New Readings in Theatre History*. Cambridge: Cambridge University Press, 2001.
Brereton, G. *Principles of Tragedy: A Rational Examination of the Tragic Concept in Life and Literature*. Coral Gables, FL: University of Miami Press, 1968.
Brettell, R.R. *Modern Art 1851–1929: Capitalism and Representation*. Oxford: Oxford University Press, 1999.
Brombert, V. *Novels of Flaubert: A Study of Themes and Techniques*. Princeton: Princeton University Press, 1966.
Brombert, V. *Victor Hugo and the Visionary Novel*. Cambridge and London: Harvard University Press, 1984.
Brown, L. "Trauma, Radicalism, and Dramatic Form in *Till Damaskus I*." *Scandinavian Studies* 84 (2012): 395–412.
Büchner, G. *Woyzeck*. Trans. G. Motton. London: Nick Hern Books, 1996.
Buckley, M.S. *Tragedy Walks the Streets: The French Revolution in the Making of Modern Drama*. Baltimore: Johns Hopkins University Press, 2006.
Bulwer Lytton, E. *England and the English*. 2 vols. London: Richard Bentley, 1833.
Burke, E. *A Philosophical Enquiry into the Origins of Our Ideas of the Sublime and the Beautiful*. London: Dodsley, 1757.

Burke, E. *Reflections on the Revolution in France*. Ed. L.G. Mitchell. Oxford and New York: Oxford University Press, 1993.

Burwick, F. "Incest on the Romantic Stage: Baillie, Byron, and the Shelleys." In *Decadent Romanticism, 1780–1914*, edited by K. Boyiopoulos and M. Sandy, 27–42. London: Routledge, 2016.

Burwick, F. "Staging the Byronic Hero." *European Romantic Review* 29 (2018): 3–11.

Bushnell, R. ed. *A Companion to Tragedy*. Malden, MA and Oxford: Blackwell, 2005.

Butler, J. *Antigone's Claim: Kinship between Life and Death*. New York: Columbia University Press, 2002.

Butler, J. "Performative Acts and Gender Constitution: An Essay in Phenomenology and Feminist Theory." *Theatre Journal* 40 (1988): 519–31.

Byron, G.G. Lord. *Byron's Letters and Journals*. Ed. L.A. Marchand, 13 vols. Cambridge: Harvard University Press, 1973–82.

Byron, G.G. Lord. *The Complete Poetical Works*. Ed. Jerome J. McGann, 7 vols. Oxford: Clarendon Press, 1980–93.

Byron, G.G. Lord. *Manfred*. Gen. eds. J. Black et al. Peterborough, ON: Broadview 2017.

Byron, G.G. Lord. *Sardanapalus; The Two Foscari; Cain*. London: John Murray, 1821.

Cantor, P. "'A Distorting Mirror': Shelley's *The Cenci* and Shakespearean Tragedy." In *Shakespeare: Aspects of Influence*, edited by G.B. Evans, 91–108. Cambridge: Harvard University Press, 1976.

Carlson, J.A. "Baillie's *Orra*: Shrinking in Fear." In *Joanna Baillie, Romantic Dramatist: Critical Essays*, ed. T. Crochunis, 206–20. New York: Routledge, 2004.

Carlson, M. *The German Stage in the Nineteenth Century*. Metuchen: Scarecrow Press, 1972.

Carlson, M. "Hernani's Revolt from the Tradition of French Stage Composition." *Theatre Survey* 13 (1973): 1–27.

Carlson, M. *Places of Performance: The Semiotics of Theatre Architecture*. Ithaca and London: Cornell University Press, 1989.

Carlson, M. "The Realistic Theatre and Bourgeois Values, 1750–1900." In *A History of German Theatre*, edited by S. Williams and M. Hamburger, 92–119. Cambridge: Cambridge University Press, 2008.

Cole, T. ed. *Playwrights on Playwriting: The Meaning and the Making of Modern Drama from Ibsen to Ionesco*. New York: Hill & Wang, 1960.

Coleridge, S.T. *Remorse*, in *The Collected Works of Samuel Taylor Coleridge. Poetical Works, Vol III: Plays, (Part II)*. Ed. J.C.C. Mays. Princeton: Princeton University Press, 2001.

Comay, R. *Mourning Sickness: Hegel and the French Revolution*. Stanford: Stanford University Press, 2011.

Conolly, L.W. *The Censorship of English Drama, 1737–1824*. San Marino, CA: The Huntington Library, 1976.

Cooper, B.T. "French Romantic Tragedy." In *A Companion to Tragedy*, edited by R. Bushnell, 452–68. Malden, MA and Oxford: Blackwell, 2005.

Cox, J.N. "British Romantic Drama in a European Context." In *British and European Romanticisms: Selected Papers from the Munich Conference of the German Society for English Romanticism*, edited by C. Bode and S. Domsch, 115–30. Trier: Wissenschaftlicher Verlag Trier, 2007.

Cox, J.N. "The Death of Tragedy; or, the Birth of Melodrama." In *The Performing Century: Nineteenth-Century Theatre's History*, edited by T.C. Davis and P. Holland, 161–81. Basingstoke: Palgrave, 2007.

Cox, J.N. *In the Shadows of Romance: Romantic Tragic Drama in Germany, England and France*. Athens: Ohio University Press, 1987.
Cox, J.N. "Romantic Redefinitions of the Tragic." In *Romantic Drama*, edited by G. Gillespie, 153–65. Amsterdam and Philadelphia: John Benjamins, 1994.
Cox, J.N. "Romantic Tragic Drama and its Eighteenth-Century Precursors." In *A Companion to Tragedy*, edited by R. Bushnell, 411–34. Malden, MA and Oxford: Blackwell, 2005.
Cox, J.N. ed. *Seven Gothic Dramas 1789–1825*. Athens: Ohio University Press, 1992.
Cox, J.N. and Gamer, M. eds. *The Broadview Anthology of Romantic Drama*. Peterborough, ON: Broadview Press, 2003.
Cronin, R. "Shelleyan Incest and the Romantic Legacy." *Keats-Shelley Journal* 45 (1996): 61–76.
Cross, A.J. "'What a World We Make the Oppressor and the Oppressed': George Cruikshank, Percy Shelley, and the Gendering of Revolution in 1819." *ELH* 71 (2004): 167–207.
Curran, S. *"The Cenci": Scorpions Ringed with Fire*. Princeton: Princeton University Press, 1970.
Curran, S. *Poetic Form and British Romanticism*. Oxford: Oxford University Press, 1986.
Daniels, B.V. "Victor Hugo on the Boulevard: 'Lucrèce Borgia' at the Porte-Saint-Martin Theatre in 1833." *Theatre Journal* 32. 1980): 17–42.
Davidoff, L. and Hall, C. *Family Fortunes: Men and Women of the English Middle Class 1780–1850*. London: Routledge, 2002.
Davis, J. "Sarah Lane: Questions of Authorship." In *Women and Playwriting in Nineteenth-Century Britain*, edited by T.C. Davis and E. Donkin, 125–48. Cambridge: Cambridge University Press, 1999.
Davis, J. and Emeljanow, V. *Reflecting the Audience: London Theatregoing, 1840–1880*. Iowa City: University of Iowa Press, 2001.
Davis, T.C. *The Economics of the British Stage, 1800–1914*. Cambridge: Cambridge University Press, 2000.
Davis, T.C. "Nineteenth-Century Repertoire." *Nineteenth Century Theatre and Film* 36 (2009): 6–28.
Deleuze, G. and Guattari, F. *Anti-Oedipus: Capitalism and Schizophrenia*. Trans. R. Hurley, M. Seem, and H.R. Lane. London: Continuum, 2004.
Dickens, C. *Oliver Twist*. Ed. F. Kaplan. New York: W.W. Norton, 1993.
Dierkes-Thrun, P. *Salomé's Modernity: Oscar Wilde and the Aesthetics of Transgression*. Ann Arbor: University of Michigan Press, 2011.
Dijkstra, B. *Idols of Perversity: Fantasies of Feminine Evil in Fin-de-Siècle Culture*. Oxford: Oxford University Press, 1986.
Dillon, S.C. "Milton and Tennyson's 'Guinevere.'" *English Literary History* 54 (1987): 129–55.
Dimoff, P. ed. *La Génese de "Lorenzaccio."* Paris: Droz, 1936.
Donohue, J. *Dramatic Character in the English Romantic Age*. Princeton: Princeton University Press, 1970.
Donohue, J. "The Theatre from 1800 to 1895." In *The Cambridge History of British Theatre, Vol. 2: 1660 to 1895*, edited by J. Donohue, 219–71. Cambridge: Cambridge University Press, 2004.
Dowden, S.D. and Quinn, T.P. eds. *Tragedy and the Tragic in German Literature, Art, and Thought*. Rochester: Camden House, 2014.
Duff, D. *Romanticism and the Uses of Genre*. Oxford: Oxford University Press, 2009.
Durbach, E. *A Doll's House: Ibsen's Myth of Transformation*. Boston: Twayne, 1991.
Eagleton, T. *Sweet Violence: The Idea of the Tragic*. Malden, MA: Blackwell Publishing, 2003.
Eagleton, T. *Culture and the Death of God*. New Haven: Yale University Press, 2015.

Eliot, C.W. ed. *Prefaces and Prologues: To Famous Books*, The Harvard Classics Vol. 39. New York: P.F. Collier & Son, 1909–14.

Emerson, C. "Pushkin's Drama." In *The Cambridge Companion to Pushkin*, edited by A. Kahn, 57–64. Cambridge: Cambridge University Press, 2006.

Engels, F. *The Origins of the Family, Private Property, and the State*. In *The Marx-Engels Reader*. New York: W.W. Norton, 1978.

Favret, M. *War at a Distance: Romanticism and the Making of Modern Wartime*. Princeton: Princeton University Press, 2010.

Fawkes, R. *Dion Boucicault: A Biography*. London: Quartet Books, 1979.

Felski, R. ed. *Rethinking Tragedy*. Baltimore: Johns Hopkins University Press, 2008.

Fernbach, A. "Wilde's 'Salomé' and the Ambiguous Fetish." *Victorian Literature and Culture* 29 (2001): 195–218.

Finch, A. *Women's Writing in Nineteenth-Century France*. Cambridge: Cambridge University Press, 2000.

Finney, G. "Ibsen and Feminism." In *The Cambridge Companion to Ibsen*, edited by J. McFarlane, 89–105. Cambridge: Cambridge University Press, 1994.

Finney, G. *Women in Modern Drama: Freud, Feminism, and European Theater at the Turn of the Century*. Ithaca: Cornell University Press, 1989.

Fischer-Lichte. E. *History of European Drama and Theatre*. Trans. Jo Riley. London and New York: Routledge, 2002.

Fix, S. "Johnson and the 'Duty' of Reading *Paradise Lost*." *ELH* 52 (1985): 649–71.

Foot, P. *Red Shelley*. London: Sidgwick & Jackson, 1981.

Forry, S.E. *Hideous Progenies: Dramatizations of* Frankenstein *from Mary Shelley to the Present*. Philadelphia: University of Pennsylvania Press, 1990.

Franceschina, J. *Gore on Stage: The Plays of Catherine Gore*. New York and London: Routledge, 2004.

Freud, S. *Moses and Monotheism*. Trans. K. Jones. London: The Hogarth Press, 1939.

Fries, M. "What Tennyson Really Did to Malory's Women." *Quondam et Futurus: A Journal of Arthurian Interpretations* 1 (1991): 44–55.

Gagnier, R. *Idylls of the Marketplace: Oscar Wilde and the Victorian Reading Public*. Stanford: Stanford University Press, 1986.

Gamer, M. *Romanticism and the Gothic: Genre, Reception, and Canon Formation*. Cambridge: Cambridge University Press, 2000.

Gardner, E. ed. *Major Voices: The Drama of Slavery*. New Milford, CN: Toby, 2005.

Gerould, D. "Larger than Life: Reflections on Melodrama and *Sweeney Todd*." *New York Literary Forum* 7 (1980): 3–14.

Gerould, D. ed. *Theatre/Theory/Theatre*. New York: Applause Books, 2003.

Gilbert, P.K. *Mapping the Victorian Social Body*. Albany: State University of New York Press, 2004.

Godwin, W. *William Godwin's Diary*. Available online: http://godwindiary.bodleian.ox.ac.uk/diary/1832-07-26.html

Goethe, J.W. von. *The Essential Goethe*. Ed. M. Bell. Princeton: Princeton University Press, 2016.

Goethe, J.W. von. *Iphigenia in Tauris*. Trans. C.E. Passage. New York: Frederick Ungar, 1963.

Goethe, J.W. von. *Plays: Egmont, Iphigenia in Tauris, Torquato Tasso*. Ed. F. Ryder. New York: Continuum, 1992.

Goethe, J.W. von and F. Schiller. *Correspondence Between Schiller and Goethe*. Trans. L.D. Schmitz. London: G. Bell, 1898.

Goldhill, S. "Generalizing About Tragedy." In *Rethinking Tragedy*, edited by R. Felski, 45–65. Baltimore: Johns Hopkins University Press, 2008.

Goldhill, S. *Sophocles and the Language of Tragedy.* Oxford and New York: Oxford University Press, 2012.

Goldstein, R.J. ed. *The Frightful Stage: Political Censorship of the Theater in Nineteenth-Century Europe.* New York and Oxford: Berghahn Books, 2009.

González-Rivas Fernández, A. "Aeschylus and *Frankenstein, or The Modern Prometheus* by Mary Shelley." In *Brill's Companion to the Reception of Aeschylus,* edited by R. Futo Kennedy, 292–322. Leiden, Boston: Brill, 2017.

Gordon, M. *The Grand Guignol: Theatre of Fear and Terror.* Port Townsend, WA: Amok Press, 1988.

Grabbe, C.D. *Das Theater zu Düsseldorf mit Rückblicken auf die übrige deutsche Schaubühne* [The Düsseldorf Theater with a Look Back at Other German Theaters], 1835. Repr. in *German and Dutch Theatre, 1600–1848. Theatre in Europe: A Documentary History,* edited by G.W. Brandt and W. Hogendoorn. Cambridge: Cambridge University Press, 1993.

Greenberg, R.A. "Swinburne and the Redefinition of Classical Myth." *Victorian Poetry* 14 (1976): 175–95.

Groseclose, B. "The Incest Motif in Shelley's 'The Cenci,'" *Comparative Drama* 19 (1985): 222–39.

Hadley, E. *Melodramatic Tactics: Theatricalized Dissent in the English Marketplace, 1800–1885.* Stanford: Stanford University Press, 1995.

Hall, E. "Tragedy Personified." In *Visualizing the Tragic: Drama, Myth, and Ritual in Greek Art and Literature,* edited by C. Kraus, S. Goldhill, H.P. Foley, and J. Elsner, 221–56. Oxford: Oxford University Press, 2007.

Hall, E. and Macintosh, F. *Greek Tragedy and the British Theatre, 1660–1914.* Oxford: Oxford University Press, 2005.

Halsall, A.W. *Victor Hugo and the Romantic Drama.* Toronto, Buffalo, and London: University of Toronto Press, 1998.

Hampden, J. ed. *Eighteenth Century Plays.* London: J.M. Dent, 1958.

Hanna, R.C. "*A Court Duel* as Performed by Wilkie Collins, with an Analysis of the Manuscript, Playbill, and Advertisement." *Dickens Studies Annual* 47 (2016): 223–88.

Hardy, T. *Tess of the D'Urbervilles.* Oxford: Oxford University Press, 2008.

Harrison, M. "No Way for a Victim to Act?: Beatrice Cenci and the Dilemma of Romantic Performance." *Studies in Romanticism* 39 (2000): 187–211.

Hazlitt, W. *Lectures on the English Poets.* London: Taylor and Hessey, 1818.

Hazlitt, W. *The Selected Writings of William Hazlitt.* Ed. D. Wu, 9 vols. London: Pickering and Chatto, 1998.

Hegel, G.W.F. *Aesthetics: Lectures on Fine Art.* Trans. T.M. Knox. 2 vols. Oxford: Clarendon Press, 1975.

Hegel, G.W.F. *Natural Law: The Scientific Ways of Treating Natural Law, Its Place in Moral Philosophy, and Its Relation to the Positive Sciences of Law.* Trans. T.M. Knox. Philadelphia: University of Pennsylvania Press, 1975.

Heilman, R. *Tragedy and Melodrama: Versions of Experience.* Seattle and London: University of Washington Press, 1968.

Heinrich, A. "Institutional Frameworks: Britain and Germany, 1800 to 1920." In *A Cultural History of Theatre,* general editors C.B. Balme and T.C. Davis, *Vol. 5: In the Age of Empire (1800–1920),* edited by P.W. Marx, 33–50. London: Bloomsbury, 2017.

Heinrich, A. "Performance for Imagined Communities: Gladstone, the National Theatre and Contested Didactics of the Stage." In *Politics, Performance and Popular Culture: Theatre and Society in Nineteenth-Century Britain,* edited by P. Yeandle, K. Newey, and J. Richards, 96–110. Manchester: Manchester University Press, 2016.

Hemmings, F.W.J. *Theatre and State in France, 1760–1905*. Cambridge: Cambridge University Press, 1994.
Herzfeld-Sander, M. ed. *Essays on German Theater*. New York: Continuum, 1985.
Hodder, I. "The Entanglements of Humans and Things: A Long-Term View." *New Literary History* 45 (2014): 19–36.
Hogan, R. *Dion Boucicault*. New York: Twayne Publishers, 1969.
Hogle, J.E. ed. *The Cambridge Companion to Gothic Fiction*. Cambridge: Cambridge University Press, 2002.
Hogle, J.E. *Shelley's Process: Radical Transference and the Development of his Major Works*. Oxford: Oxford University Press, 1988.
Holder, H. "The 'lady playwrights' and the 'wild tribes of the East': Female Dramatists in the East End Theaters, 1860–1880." In *Women and Playwriting in Nineteenth-Century Britain*, edited by T.C. Davis and E. Donkin, 174–92. Cambridge: Cambridge University Press, 1999.
Hugo, V. *Four Plays: Marion de Lorme, Hernani, Lucretia Borgia, Ruy Blas*. Ed. Claude Schumacher. London: Methuen, 2004.
Hunt, J.H. Leigh, *The Selected Works of Leigh Hunt*. Ed. R. Morrison, M. Eberle-Sinatra, J.N. Cox, G. Kucich, C. Mahoney, and J. Strachan, 6 vols. London: Pickering & Chatto, 2003.
Ibsen, H. *Brand*. Trans. M. Meyer. Garden City, NY: Anchor Books, 1960.
Ibsen, H. *Eleven Plays of Henrik Ibsen*. New York: The Modern Library, 1935.
Ibsen, H. *Ghosts*. Trans. M. Meyer. London: Eyre Methuen, 1973.
Ibsen, H. *Ghosts and Other Plays*. Trans. Peter Watts. New York: Penguin, 1964.
Ibsen, H. *The Master Builder and Other Plays*. Trans. B.J. Haveland. Introd. T. Moi. New York: Penguin, 2014.
Jameson, F. "Third-World Literature in the Era of Multinational Capitalism." *Social Text* 15 (1986): 65–88.
Jenkins, H. *Convergence Culture: Where Old and New Media Collide*. New York: New York University Press, 2008.
Katz, D. *The Jews in the History of England, 1485–1850*. Oxford: Oxford University Press, 1994.
Kaufman, H. "England's Jewish Renaissance: Maria Polack's Fiction with Romance (1830) in Context." In *Romanticism/Judaica: A Convergence of Cultures*, edited by S. Spector, 69–84. Farnham and Burlington, VT: Ashgate, 2011.
Kaufman, R. "Intervention and Commitment Forever! Shelley in 1819, Shelley in Brecht, Shelley in Adorno, Shelley in Benjamin." *Romantic Circles Praxis* Series (May 2001). Available online: http://www.rc.umd.edu/praxis/interventionist/kaufman/kaufman.html
Kelly, M. *Reminiscences*. Ed. R. Fiske. Oxford: Oxford University Press, 1975.
Kiberd, D. *Men and Feminism in Modern Literature*. London: Macmillan, 1985.
King, J. *Tragedy in the Victorian Novel: Theory and Practice in the Novels of George Eliot, Thomas Hardy and Henry James*. Cambridge: Cambridge University Press, 1978.
Kleist, H. *Plays*. Ed. W. Hinderer. New York: Continuum Publishing, 1996.
Kliger, I. "Dostoevsky and the Novel-Tragedy: Genre and Modernity in Ivanov, Pumpyansky, and Bakhtin." *PMLA* 126 (2011): 73–87.
Kliger, I. *Nietzsche and Dostoevsky: Philosophy, Morality, Tragedy*. Evanston: Northwestern University Press, 2016.
Knowles, J.S. *Virginius*. London: James Ridgway, 1820.
Krakovitch, O. *Les pièces de théâtre soumises à la censure (1800–1830)*. Paris: Archives Nationales, 1982.

Krakovitch, O. *Censure des répertoires des grands théâtres parisiens (1835–1906)*. Paris: Centre Historique des Archives Nationales, 2003.
Lafond, D.G. de. "Ophélie in Nineteenth-Century French Painting." In *The Afterlife of Ophelia*, edited by K.L. Peterson and D. Williams, 169–91. New York: Palgrave Macmillan, 2012.
Lang, C.B. ed. *The Pre-Raphaelites and Their Circle*, second edn. Chicago: The University of Chicago Press, 1975.
Layard, G.S. *Tennyson and His Pre-Raphaelite Illustrators*. London: Elliot Stock, 1894.
Layton, L. "Flaubert's *L'Éducation sentimentale*: A Tragedy of Mind." *French Forum* 11 (1986): 335–51.
Lemoncelli, R. "Cenci as a Corrupt Dramatic Poet." *English Language Notes*, 16 (1978): 112–15.
Leonard, M. *Tragic Modernities*. Cambridge MA, London: Harvard University Press, 2015.
Lessing, G.E. *Nathan the Wise, Minna von Barthelm, and Other Plays and Writings*. Ed. P. Demetz. New York: Continuum, 1991.
Levitt, M. "*Evgenii Onegin*." In *The Cambridge Companion to Pushkin*, edited by A. Kahn, 41–56. Cambridge: Cambridge University Press, 2006.
Lewes, G.H. *Dramatic Essays*. London: Walter Scott, 1896.
Lewes, G.H. *On Actors and the Art of Acting*. London: Smith, Elder, & Company, 1875.
Lewis, L. and Erckmann-Chatrian. *The Bells*. London: Harrap, 1978.
Lillo, G. *The London Merchant: or, the History of George Barnwell*. In *Eighteenth Century Plays*, edited by J. Hampden. London: J.M. Dent, 1958.
Lindfors, B. *Ira Aldridge: The Vagabond Years, 1833–1852*. Rochester: University of Rochester Press, 2011.
Lockridge, L. "Justice in *The Cenci*." *The Wordsworth Circle*, 19 (1988): 95–8.
Lord Chamberlain's Plays. Vol. LIII. June-Aug. 1832. Jun. 1832-Aug. 1832. MS Lord Chamberlain's Plays, 1852–1858 Add MS 42917. British Library. *Nineteenth Century Collections Online*, http://tinyurl.galegroup.com/tinyurl/5ocMg7
Lukács, G. *The Historical Novel*. Trans. H. and S. Mitchell. 1962; Lincoln: University of Nebraska Press, 1983.
McCarthy, T. *Satin Island*. London: Jonathan Cape, 2015.
McCormick, J. *Popular Theatres of Nineteenth-Century France*. London and New York: Routledge, 1993.
Mackenzie, H. "Account of the German Theatre." *Transactions of the Royal Society of Edinburgh* 2 (1790): 154–92.
Macmillan, D. *Catalogue of the Larpent Plays in the Huntington Library*. San Marino: Huntington Library, 1939.
Macready, W. *Macready's Reminiscences, and Selections from his Diaries and Letters*. Ed. F. Pollock. London: Macmillan, 1876.
McWilliam, R. "Melodrama." In *A Companion to Sensation Fiction*, edited by P.K. Gilbert, 54–66. Malden, MA and Oxford: Wiley-Blackwell, 2011.
Marx, K. *The Eighteenth Brumaire of Louis Bonaparte*. New York: International Publishers, 1963.
Marx, K. and Engels, F. "The Communist Manifesto." Marx Engels Archive. Available online: https://www.marxists.org/archive/marx/works/1848/communist-manifesto/ch01.htm
Mayer, D. "Encountering Melodrama." In *The Cambridge Companion to Victorian and Edwardian Theatre*, edited by K. Powell, 145–63. Cambridge: Cambridge University Press, 2004.
Meeuwis, M. "Representative Government: The 'Problem Play,' Quotidian Culture, and the Making of Social Liberalism." *ELH* 80 (2013): 1093–1120.

Meilhac, H. and Halévy, L. *FrouFrou: Comédie en Cinq Actes*. Paris: Michel Lévy Frères, 1870.
Meisel, M. *Realizations: Narrative, Pictorial, and Theatrical Arts in Nineteenth-Century England*. Princeton: Princeton University Press, 1983.
Meyers, T.L. "Shelley's Influence on 'Atalanta in Calydon.'" *Victorian Poetry* 14 (1976): 150–4.
Mikalson, J.D. *Honor Thy Gods: Popular Religion in Greek Tragedy*. Chapel Hill: University of North Carolina Press, 1991.
Miles, A.H. "Thomas Wade." In *The Poets and the Poetry of the Century*, Vol. 3: *John Keats to Lord Lytton*, edited by A.H. Miles. London: Hutchinson & Company, 1898.
Mill, J.S. *The Subjection of Women*. London: Longmans, Green, Reader, and Dyer, 1869.
Moi, T. *Henrik Ibsen and the Birth of Modernism: Art, Theater, Philosophy*. Oxford: Oxford University Press, 2006.
Moody, J. *Illegitimate Theatre in London, 1770–1840*. Cambridge: Cambridge University Press, 2000.
Moore, N. ed. *Censorship and the Limits of the Literary: A Global View*. New York: Bloomsbury, 2015.
Moretti, F. *Distant Reading*. London: Verso, 2013.
Moretti, F. "Serious Century." In *The Novel. Volume I: History, Geography and Culture*, edited by F. Moretti, 364–400. Princeton and Oxford: Princeton University Press, 2006.
Moretti, F. *The Way of the World: The Bildungsroman in European Culture*. Trans. Albert Sbragia. London, New York: Verso, 2000.
Musser, B. *Diary of a Twelve-Year-Old: Transcribed from the Early Hieroglyphic of Benjamin Musser*. Caldwell, ID: Caxton, 1932.
Newey, K. *Women's Theatre Writing in Victorian Britain*. Basingstoke: Palgrave Macmillan, 2005.
Nicoll, A. *A History of English Drama 1660–1900*, 6 vols. Cambridge University Press, 1969.
Nietzsche, F. *The Birth of Tragedy and Other Writings*. Trans. R. Speirs. Cambridge: Cambridge University Press, 1999.
Olsen, V.C. "Idylls of Real Life." *Victorian Poetry* 33 (1995): 371–89.
Ormond, L. ed. *The Reception of Alfred Tennyson in Europe*. London and New York: Bloomsbury Academic, 2017.
Orr, J. *Tragic Drama and Modern Society : A Sociology of Dramatic Form from 1880 to the Present*. Basingstoke: Macmillan, 1989.
Paine, T. *The Rights of Man*. Ed. M. Philp. Oxford and New York: Oxford University Press, 1998.
Paterson, K. "'Much Regrafted Pain': Schopenhauerian Love and the Fecundity of Pain in *Atalanta in Calydon*." *Victorian Poetry* 47 (2009): 715–31.
Patterson, M. *The First German Theatre: Schiller, Goethe, Kleist and Büchner in Performance*. London and New York: Routledge, 1990.
Patterson, M. and Huxley, M. "German Drama, Theatre, and Dance." In *The Cambridge Companion to Modern German Culture*, edited by E. Kolinsky, 213–32. Cambridge: Cambridge University Press, 1999.
Patterson, O. *Slavery and Social Death: A Comparative Study*. Cambridge, MA: Harvard University Press, 1982.
Paulson, R. *Representations of Revolution*. New Haven: Yale University Press, 1959.
Pearson, M. *Site-Specific Performance*. Basingstoke: Palgrave Macmillan, 2010.
Peters, C. *The King of Inventors: A Life of Wilkie Collins*. Princeton: Princeton University Press, 2014.
Pitt, G.D. "The String of Pearls, or The Fiend of Fleet Street." Edited by S.A. Weltman. *Nineteenth Century Theatre and Film* 38 (2011): 29–54.

Plotz, J. *Portable Property: Victorian Culture on the Move*. Princeton: Princeton University Press, 2008.
Polack, E. *Esther, The Royal Jewess, or the Death of Haman!* London: Duncombe, 1835.
Poole, A. *Tragedy: A Very Short Introduction*. Oxford: Oxford University Press, 2005.
Powell, K. *Oscar Wilde and the Theatre of the 1890s*. Cambridge: Cambridge University Press, 1990.
Powell, K. *Women and Victorian Theatre*. Cambridge: Cambridge University Press, 1997.
Powell, K. "Wilde and Ibsen." *English Literature in Transition, 1880–1920* 28 (1985): 224–42.
Praz, M. *The Romantic Agony*. Trans. A.S. Davidson. New York: Meridian Books, 1956.
Rees, J. "Shelley's Orsino: Evil in *The Cenci*." *Keats-Shelley Memorial Bulletin* 12 (1966): 3–6.
Report from the Select Committee on Dramatic Literature: With the Minutes of Evidence. London: House of Commons, August 2, 1832.
Rhodes, K. *Ophelia and Victorian Visual Culture: Representing Body Politics in the Nineteenth Century*. London and New York: Routledge, 2017.
Richardson, A. *A Mental Theater: Poetic Drama and Consciousness in the Romantic Age*. University Park: Pennsylvania State University Press, 1988.
Ritchie, H.M. "Kean Versus Macready: Sheridan Knowles' *Virginius*." *Theatre Survey* 17 (1976): 28–37.
Roach, J. "Slave Spectacles and Tragic Octoroons: A Cultural Genealogy of Antebellum Performance." *Theatre Survey* 33 (1992): 167–87.
Rodgers, T.R. *Ladies of Shalott: A Victorian Masterpiece and Its Contexts*. Ed. G.P. Landow. Providence: Brown University Press, 1985.
Rosenblum, R. and Janson, H.W. *19th Century Art*. Upper Saddle River, NJ: Pearson/Prentice Hall, 2005.
Rowell, G. ed. *Victorian Dramatic Criticism*. London: Methuen, 1971.
Racine, J. *Racine's Esther*. Ed. G. Saintsbury. Oxford: Clarendon Press, 1886.
Ruskin, J. *The Works of John Ruskin*, 39 vols. Ed. E.T. Cook and A.D.O. Wedderburn. London: George Allen, 1903–12.
Russell, G. *The Theatres of War: Performance, Politics, and Society, 1793–1815*. Oxford: Clarendon Press, 1995.
Saggini, F. *The Gothic Novel and the Stage: Romantic Appropriations*. London and New York: Routledge, 2015.
Saglia, D. "The Gothic Stage: Visions of Instability, Performances of Anxiety." In *Romantic Gothic: An Edinburgh Companion*, edited by A. Wright and D. Townshend, 73–94. Edinburgh: Edinburgh University Press, 2016.
Saglia, D. "Introduction: the Survival of Tragedy in European Romanticisms." *European Romantic Review* 20 (2009): 567–79.
Schelling, F.W.J. *The Philosophy of Art*. Trans. D. Stott. Minneapolis: University of Minnesota Press, 1989.
Schelling, F.W.J. *The Unconditional in Human Knowledge: Four Early Essays, 1794–1796*. Trans. F. Marti. Lewisburg, PA: Bucknell University Press, 1980.
Schiller, F. *The Bride of Messina, William Tell, Demetrius*. Trans. C.E. Passage. New York: Frederick Ungar, 1967.
Schiller, F. *Intrigue and Love* and *Don Carlos*. Trans. C.E. Passage. New York: Continuum, 1994.
Schiller, F. "Über den Grund des Vergnügens an tragischen Gegenständen" [On the Causes of Delight in Tragic Subjects]. Repr. in *German and Dutch Theatre, 1600–1848. Theatre in Europe: A Documentary History*, edited by G.W. Brandt and W. Hogendoorn. Cambridge: Cambridge University Press, 1993.

Schmidt, D.J. *On Germans and Other Greeks: Tragedy and the Ethical Life.* Bloomington: Indiana University Press. 2001.

Schoch, R.W. *Shakespeare's Victorian Stage: Performing History in the Theatre of Charles Kean.* Cambridge: Cambridge University Press, 1998.

Schoch, R.W. "Theatre and Mid-Victorian Society, 1851–1870." In *The Cambridge History of British Theatre, Vol. 2: 1660 to 1895*, edited by J. Donohue, 331–51. Cambridge: Cambridge University Press, 2004.

Schopenhauer, A. *The World as Will and Representation.* 2 vols. Trans. E.F.J. Payne. New York: Dover Publications, 1966.

Schorske, C. *Fin de Siècle Vienna.* New York: Knopf, 1980.

Scott, C. "*Louis XI*." From "The Bells" to "King Arthur:" *A Critical Record of the First-Night Productions at the Lyceum Theatre from 1871 to 1895.* London: John Macqueen, 1897.

Sebald, W.G. *On the Natural History of Destruction.* Trans. A. Bell. 1999; New York: The Modern Library, 2004.

Sedgwick, E.K. *Between Men: English Literature and Male Homosocial Desire.* New York: Columbia University Press, 1985.

Sen, S. "Shakespeare Reception in France: The Case of Ambroise Thomas's *Hamlet*." In *Shakespeare and the Culture of Romanticism*, edited by Joseph M. Ortiz, 183–204. London and New York: Routledge, 2016.

Sewall, R. *The Vision of Tragedy.* New Haven, CT: Yale University Press, 1959.

Shafer, Y. ed. *Approaches to Teaching Ibsen's "A Doll House".* New York: Modern Language Association of America, 1985.

Shakespeare, W. *The Oxford Shakespeare: Hamlet.* Ed. G.R. Hibbard. Oxford and New York: Oxford University Press, 2008.

Shaw, G.B. *Mrs. Warren's Profession.* Peterborough, ON: Broadview Press, 2005.

Shaw, G.B. *Our Theatres in the Nineties.* London: Constable, 1948.

Shaw, G.B. *The Quintessence of Ibsenism.* Boston: Benjamin R. Tucker, 1891.

Shaw, G.B. *Saint Joan.* Baltimore: Penguin Books, 1951.

Shelley, P.B. *Shelley's Poetry and Prose: A Norton Critical Edition*, second edn. Ed. D.H. Reiman and N. Fraistat. New York: W. W. Norton and Company, 2002.

Shelley, P.B. *The Complete Works of Percy Bysshe Shelley.* Ed. R. Igpen and W.E. Peck. New York: Gordian Press, 1965.

Showalter, E. "Representing Ophelia: Women, Madness and the Responsibilities of Feminist Criticism." In *Shakespeare and the Question of Theory*, edited by P. Parker and G. Hartman, 77–94. London: Methuen, 1985.

Showalter, E. *Sexual Anarchy: Gender and Culture at the Fin de Siècle.* New York: Penguin, 1990.

Simon, B. *Tragic Drama and the Family: Psychoanalytic Studies from Aeschylus to Beckett.* New Haven: Yale University Press, 1988.

Simpson, D. *9/11: The Culture of Commemoration.* Chicago: University of Chicago Press, 2006.

Simpson, D. *Romanticism and the Question of the Stranger.* Chicago: University of Chicago Press, 2013.

Simpson, D. *Wordsworth, Commodification and Social Concern: The Poetics of Modernity.* Cambridge: Cambridge University Press, 2009.

Smith, J.L. *Melodrama.* New York: Routledge, 1973.

Smither, H.E. *A History of the Oratorio*, 4 vols. Chapel Hill: University of North Carolina Press, 1977–2000.

Sondheim, S. and Wheeler, H. *Sweeney Todd: The Demon Barber of Fleet Street*. New York: Applause Theatre Book Publishers, 1991.

Sorba, C. "National Theater and the Age of Revolution in Italy." *Journal of Modern Italian Studies* 17 (2012): 400–13.

Sourvinou-Inwood, C. *Tragedy and Athenian Religion*. New York: Lexington Books, 2003.

Staves, S. *Married Women's Separate Property in England, 1660–1833*. Cambridge: Harvard University Press, 1990.

Staves, S. "Tragedy." In *The Cambridge Companion to British Theatre, 1730–1830*, edited by J. Moody and D. O'Quinn, 87–102. Cambridge: Cambridge University Press, 2007.

Steiner, G. *The Death of Tragedy*. New Haven and London: Faber and Faber, 1961.

Steiner, G. "'Tragedy,' Reconsidered." In *Rethinking Tragedy*, edited by R. Felski, 29–44. Baltimore: Johns Hopkins University Press, 2008.

Stephens, J.R. "Playwright *In Extremis*: George Dibdin Pitt Revisited." *Theatre Notebook* 53 (1999): 41–7.

Stone, L. *The Family, Sex, and Marriage in England 1500–1800*, abridged edition. New York: Harper & Row, 1979.

Strindberg, A. *Plays: 1*. Trans. M.L. Meyer. London: Bloomsbury Methuen, 2014.

Strindberg, A. *The Plays of Strindberg*. Trans. M.L. Meyer. 2 vols. New York: Vintage Books, 1976.

Strindberg, A. *Pre-Inferno Plays*. Trans. W. Johnson. New York: Norton, 1976.

Strindberg, A. *Six Plays of Strindberg*. Trans. E. Sprigge. Garden City, NY: Anchor Books, 1955.

Sublette, N. and C. *The American Slave Coast: A History of the Slave-Breeding Industry*. Chicago: Chicago Review Press, 2015.

Sypher, F.J. "Politics in the Poetry of Tennyson." *Victorian Poetry* 14 (1976): 101–12.

Szondi, P. *An Essay on the Tragic*. Trans. P. Fleming. Stanford, CA: Stanford University Press, 2002.

Theatre Royal, Haymarket. A collection of playbills from Haymarket Theatre, 1831–1833. TS British Playbills, 1754–1882, British Library, *Nineteenth Century Collections Online* (http://tinyurl.galegroup.com/tinyurl/5rAHA1).

Thorslev, P. "Incest as Romantic Symbol." *Comparative Literature Studies* 2 (1965): 41–58.

Ulmer, W. *Shelleyan Eros: The Rhetoric of Romantic Love*. Princeton: Princeton University Press, 1990.

Valladares, S. *Staging the Peninsular War: English Theatres, 1807–1815*. New York: Routledge, 2015.

Van Kooy, D. *Shelley's Radical Stages: Performance and Cultural Memory in the Post-Napoleonic Era*. New York: Routledge, 2016.

Van Kooy, D. and Cox, J.N. "Melodramatic Slaves." *Modern Drama* 55 (2012): 459–75.

Vaughan, V.M. *Othello: A Contextual History*. Cambridge: Cambridge University Press, 1994.

Vernant, J.P. and Vidal-Naquet, P. *Myth and Tragedy in Ancient Greece*. Trans. J. Lloyd. New York: Zone Books, 1988.

Wallace, D. "Bourgeois Tragedy or Sentimental Melodrama? The Significance of George Lillo's *The London Merchant*." *Eighteenth-Century Studies* 25 (1991–2): 123–43.

Wallace, J. *The Cambridge Introduction to Tragedy*. Cambridge: Cambridge University Press, 2007.

Weltman, S. Aronofsky. "Introduction: George Dibdin Pitt's 1847 *Sweeney Todd*." *Nineteenth Century Theatre and Film* 38 (2011): 1–22.

Weltman, S. Aronofsky. "Melodrama, *Purimspiel*, and Jewish Emancipation." *Victorian Literature and Culture* 46 (2018).

White, H. *Metahistory: The Historical Imagination in Nineteenth-Century Literature*. Baltimore: Johns Hopkins University Press, 1973.
Whitman, R. "Beatrice's 'Pernicious Mistake' in *The Cenci*." *PMLA* 74 (1959): 249–53.
Wilde, O. *Salome*. Trans. Lord A. Douglas. New York: Dover, 1967.
Williams, C. "Melodrama." In *The Cambridge History of Victorian Literature*, edited by K. Flint, 193–219. Cambridge: Cambridge University Press, 2012.
Williams, R. *Modern Tragedy*. Stanford, CA: Stanford University Press, 1966.
Williams, R. *The Tragic Imagination*. Oxford: Oxford University Press, 2016.
Wilson, J. "Beatrice Cenci and Shelley's Vision of Moral Responsibility." *Ariel* 9 (1978): 75–89.
Wilson, K. "Rowe's *Fair Penitent* as Global History: Or, A Diversionary Voyage to New South Wales." *Eighteenth-Century Studies* 41 (2008): 231–51.
Wollstonecraft, M. *A Vindication of the Rights of Woman*. Ed. D.S. Lynch. New York: W.W. Norton, 2009.
Woodford, C. and Schofield, B. eds. *The German Bestseller in the Late Nineteenth Century*. Rochester, NY: Camden House, 2012.
Wordsworth, W. *The Borderers*. Ed. R. Osborn. Ithaca: Cornell University Press, 1982.
Wordsworth, W. *Lyrical Ballads*. 2 vols. London: Longman, 1800.
Young, A.R. "Sarah Berhardt's Ophelia." *Borrowers and Lenders: The Journal of Shakespeare and Appropriation* 8 (2013). Available online: http://www.borrowers.uga.edu/662/show
Zola, E. "Naturalism in the Theatre." In *The Theory of the Modern Stage*, edited by E. Bentley. Harmondsworth: Penguin, 1968.

INDEX

adaptation 7, 26, 28, 32–3, 42, 54–9, 62, 66, 69, 72, 92, 113, 125, 144
Addison, Joseph
   Cato 87
Aeschylus 29, 121
   Oresteia 81, 124, 139
   The Persians 97, 124
   Prometheus Bound 124
aesthetics 4, 23, 28, 29, 31, 33, 50, 77, 80, 82, 83–6, 110, 120
affect 10, 42, 113, 126, 140, 145–6, 153
agency 49, 77–8, 108, 112–13, 114, 132–3, 154
alienation 10, 107, 121, 122–6, 129, 130–3, 136–7
Alary, Giulio 33
Aldridge, Ira 63–4
Alfieri, Vittorio 6
Alighieri, Dante 24
Anderson, Benedict 52, 105
Anderson, Mary 50
architecture of theaters 51–2, 59
Arendt, Hannah 89, 121
Aristotle 58, 75–6, 78, 132
Arnold, Matthew 99
Arthurian legend 32–5, 123
The Athenaeum 50, 69–70
audiences 3, 8–9, 26–8, 33, 47, 49, 51, 54, 56, 62–3, 65, 72–4, 91, 106, 119, 123, 126–8, 132–3, 145
Austen, Jane
   Mansfield Park 66

Badon, Edmond
   Un Duel sous Richelieu 62, 68
Baillie, Joanna 2, 32, 62, 121, 125–32, 137
   Orra 10, 123, 125–8, 130, 132, 135–7, 141, 145, 153
   Plays on the Passions 29, 126
Barbauld, Anna Letitia
   Eighteen Hundred and Eleven 126
Barish, Jonas 92
Bawr, Alexandrine de 62
Bayly, C.A. 121

Beckett, Samuel
   Waiting for Godot 103
Bell, J. 2
La Belle Assemblée 70
Benjamin, Walter 7, 10
   The Arcades Project 119
   "Paris Capital of the Nineteenth Century" 10
   "Theses on the Philosophy of History" 137
Bennett, Susan 51
Berlioz, Hector 33, 67
Bernhardt, Sarah 53, 62, 68
Blake, William 33, 96, 99
Boaden, Caroline 8, 70
   A Duel in Richelieu's Time 62, 69–70, 75
Boaden, James
   Fontainville Forest 92
Boaden, John 70
Böcklin, Alfred
   The Island of the Dead 96
body, the 83, 107, 112, 114, 130–2, 134, 144, 149, 150, 152, 153
Bonaparte, Napoleon 7, 29, 52, 66, 126, 128–9
Booth, Edwin 64
Booth, Michael 61, 64, 66, 110
Bortolotti, Gary 26
Boucicault, Dion 8, 53–4, 123, 129, 132, 137
   Corsican Brothers 54, 57
   Janet Pride 56
   London Assurance 54
   Louis XI 54–7
   The Octoroon 10, 133–5
   The Slave Market 18
Boulevard du Temple 19, 66
Boursiquot, Samuel 54
Bradley, A.C. 105
Bramin, John 70
Bratton, Jacky 53–6, 59
Brecht, Bertolt 104
Brereton, Thomas
   Esther, or Faith Triumphant 71
Brombert, Victor 25, 30–1
Brontë, Charlotte
   Villette 68

Brown, John 133
Browning, Elizabeth Barrett
    The Runaway Slave at Pilgrim's Point 31
Browning, Robert 50–1, 62
    A Blot in the 'Scutcheon 50
    Strafford 50
Büchner, Georg 104
    Woyzeck 9, 107–11, 117
Buckley, Matthew 4, 25, 106, 111
Bürger, Gottfried August 1
Burke, Edmund
    Reflections on the Revolution in France 25
Burns, Robert
    Poems, Written Chiefly in the Scottish Dialect 1
Bushnell, Rebecca 24, 28
Byron, George Gordon, Lord 121, 123, 129, 132–3, 136–7
    Cain 6, 8, 102, 103–4, 135
    Childe Harold's Pilgrimage 6
    Don Juan 6
    The Giaour 6
    Heaven and Earth 6, 8, 102–4
    Manfred 29, 95–6
    Marino Faliero 29, 104
    Sardanapalus 10, 29, 33, 104, 129–30, 132, 134, 137
    The Two Foscari 29, 130–2, 135

Cabanel, Alexandre
    Ophelia 36
Calderón de la Barca, Pedro 48
Cameron, Julia Margaret 33
    The Corpse of Elaine Arriving in the Palace of King Arthur 35
Camille 68
capital and capitalism 5, 49–52, 114, 128, 136
Carlson, Julie A. 127
Carlson, Marvin 47, 53
censorship 7, 8, 27–9, 45, 47, 52, 61–3, 67, 69, 92–3, 102, 125
Certeau, Michel de 52
Charles X (King of France) 68
Chatrian, Alexandre 107, 113
Chekhov, Anton 65
class 5, 27–8, 31, 88, 108–19, 136, 139–54
closet drama 6, 29, 105
Coleridge, Samuel Taylor 2, 24, 92–3, 121, 125–6, 132
    Death of Wallenstein 2
    Fears in Solitude 125
    Lyrical Ballads 2, 93, 125
    Osorio 2

    The Piccolomini 2
    Remorse 93, 136
Colman, George, the Younger
    Blue-Beard 92
colonialism 25, 121
comedy 2, 27, 29, 46, 61, 63, 66–8, 70, 74, 125, 133, 137
Connolly, L.W. 28
copyright 33
Corneille, Pierre 68, 140
Cox, Jeffrey N. 27, 54, 65, 75, 121, 132–3
    In the Shadows of Romance 6
Craig, Edward Gordon 57
Cruikshank, George 38–40
    Manchester Heroes 39
    Massacre at St. Peter's or "Britons Strike Home"!!! 39
Curran, Stuart 123
Cushman, Charlotte 64

Darley, Anna 54
Darwin, Charles 91
Davidoff, Leonore 140
Davis, Jim 53, 74
Davis, Tracy 110
Delacroix, Eugène
    The Death of Sardanapalus 33
    The Massacre at Chios 40
    La Mort d'Ophélie 58
Delavigne, Casimir 56
Deleuze, Gilles 107
Dickens, Charles 71
Diderot, Denis
    The Natural Son 140
Doré, Gustave 33
    The Body of Elaine on Its Way to King Arthur's Palace 34
Dostoyevsky, Fyodor 24, 29, 31
    Crime and Punishment 31
Dowden, Stephen 24
dramatic monologue 29, 31
Dryden, John 140
Duff, David 25, 26
Dumas, Alexandre 24, 27, 58
    Antony 27
    Henri III et sa cour 27
Dumas, Alexandre *fils*
    La Dame aux Camélias 68
Ducray-Duminil, Guillaume 66
Duvernoy, Alphonse 33

Eagleton, Terry 9, 23, 45, 77–8
The Echo 143

INDEX

Edwards, Lee 59
Eliot, George 6, 30
   Daniel Deronda 68
Elsner, J. 42
Emeljanow, Victor 53, 74
Emerson, Caryl 31
empire 42, 53, 65, 121, 128, 130, 133
Engels, Friedrich 145
Erckmann, Emile and Alexandre Chatrian
   Le Juif Polonais 9, 107, 113
Euripides 85, 98, 124
   Medea 139
The Examiner 129

family 93–4, 97–8, 108, 111–19, 121–37
fate 30–2, 49, 79, 81–5, 95–6, 98, 100–1, 115–16, 119, 127, 144, 149, 153
Faucit, Helen 49–50
Faure, Jean-Baptiste 58
Favret, Mary 124, 127
fear 3, 6, 23, 38, 40, 51, 60, 72–6, 88, 97, 119, 126–8, 131–3, 136, 143
Felix, Rachel 62, 68
Felski, Rita 24
Fichte, Johann Gottlieb 78–9, 81, 83
Figaro in London 71
Finney, Gail 146, 153
Fischer-Lichte, Erika 47
Flaubert, Gustave 30
   L'Éducation Sentimentale 31
   Madame Bovary 31
Foley, H.P. 42
Frederick the Great (King of Prussia) 53
freedom 77–81, 86, 93, 98, 134, 135
French Revolution 4–5, 7, 9, 23–5, 27, 31, 37, 43, 45, 59, 65, 76–8, 88–9, 91, 93, 106, 111, 125
Freud, Sigmund 7, 153

Galton, Samuel 140
Gamer, Michael 65, 74, 92
Gautier, Thomas 67
gender 111–19, 139–54
genre 6–7, 26, 28–9, 43, 45–6, 48–9, 55, 59, 62–4, 69, 72, 74–77, 80, 88, 123, 139
George IV (King of Great Britain and Ireland) 97
Gilbert, Pamela 107
Godwin, William 24, 69
Goethe, Johann Wolfgang von 1–2, 24, 67, 92–3, 96, 99–100, 104, 129, 131–2, 136–7
   Egmont 93–4

Faust 95, 133, 136
Goetz von Berlichingen 2, 66, 93
Iphigenia in Tauris 8, 10, 97–9, 102, 124–7, 129, 135
The Sorrows of Young Werther 30–1
Goldhill, Simon 4, 42, 132
gothic 26, 30, 66, 92–3, 102, 121–2, 125–8, 133, 136
Gottsched, Johann Christoph 140
Goya, Francisco de
   Disasters of War 42
   El Tres de Mayo 41
Grabbe, Christian Dietrich 8, 48
Greenberg, Robert 100
Guattari, Félix 107
The Guillotine 7, 23, 43
guilt 65, 82, 94, 113–14, 142–3, 149, 151

Hadley, Elaine 26
Haitian Revolution 25
Halévy, Ludovic 8
   Frou-Frou 68–9
Hall, Catherine 140
Hall, Edith 110
hamartia 49
Handel, George Frideric
   Esther 62
Hardy, Thomas 6, 24, 30, 104
   Tess of the D'Urbervilles 6, 104, 106, 108
Hazlitt, William 5, 7
Hegel, Georg Wilhelm Friedrich 4, 7, 9, 77, 79–85, 88–9, 108, 132
Heinrich, Anselm 49, 52
Hemans, Felicia
   Records of Woman 32
Hemmings, F.W.J. 52
Herder, Johann Gottfried von 140
heroism 3, 5, 11, 30–2, 34, 37, 45, 50, 57, 84–5, 88, 91–3, 100–1, 124, 130, 136–7
history and historicism 3, 23, 25, 27, 29–31, 33, 43, 45–7, 49, 56, 65, 69, 77, 82, 88–9, 93, 104, 127, 132, 137
Hodder, Ian 106–7
Hogle, Jerrold E. 133
Holcroft, Thomas
   A Tale of Mystery 66
Holder, Heidi 71
Hölderlin, Friedrich 7
honor 79, 133, 140, 148, 150
Horne, Richard Hengist 111
horror *see* fear
hubris 6, 49

Hugo, Victor 2, 8–9, 24, 25, 27, 62
   Cromwell 67
   Hernani 64, 67, 75, 141, 145, 153
   Les Misérables 30–1
   Marion de Lorme 64, 69, 75
   Notre-Dame de Paris 30
Hunt, James Henry Leigh 102, 129
Hutcheon, Linda 26

Ibsen, Henrik 3, 10–11, 21, 65, 93, 123, 132, 137, 145
   Brand 8, 94
   A Doll's House 10–11, 145–7, 153
   An Enemy of the People 3
   Ghosts 9–10, 106–7, 114–19, 147–9, 153
   The Master Builder 10, 135–7, 151, 153
identity
   collective 10, 48, 53, 71
   individual 81–2, 101, 131, 133
"illegitimate" theater *see* "legitimate" and "illegitimate" theater
The Illustrated London News 56
The Illustrated Sporting and Dramatic News 53
Immerman, Karl Leberecht 47
incest 93, 104, 117, 121, 135, 143, 152, 153
Inchbald, Elizabeth 24
   Lovers' Vows 66
individual, the, and individualism 3–4, 5, 9, 10, 29, 31, 49, 80, 84–5, 93, 95, 107–8, 111, 122, 125–6, 130–3, 136–7, 139 (*see also* subjectivity)
Industrial Revolution 29, 32, 49, 50, 59, 106, 128
Irving, Henry 46, 49, 53–7, 64, 113

James, Henry 6, 30
Jenkins, Henry 7
Jerrold, Douglas 46
   Black-Ey'd Susan 46, 65
   Rent Day 46, 65
The John Bull 51
Johnson, Samuel 91, 102
Joncières, Victorin de 33
Judaism 62, 70–2, 74, 82–3, 109, 113–14

Kant, Immanuel 78, 81, 83
Kean, Charles 46, 49, 54–6, 64
Kean, Edmund 63
Kean, Ellen 56
Keats, John 123
Keenlyside, Simon 57

Kelly, Katherine 116
Kelly, Michael 92
Kemble, John Philip 63
King, Jeannette 6, 30
Klee, Paul 137
Kleist, Heinrich von 2, 48, 132, 136–7
   Penthesilea 124, 130, 133
Kliger, Ilya 29, 31
Knigge, Adolph Freiherr von 140
Knowles, James Sheridan
   Virginius 9, 61, 64, 106–7, 110–14, 119
Kotzebue, August von 1, 48, 92, 125
   Das Kind der Liebe 66
Kraus, C. 42

Lafond, D.G. 58
Lane, Sarah 72–3
   Dolores 69
Larpent, John 92
law 81–3, 134–5
"legitimate" and "illegitimate" theater 27, 46, 50–2, 54, 63, 66
Legouvé, Ernest
   Adrienne Lecouvreur 68
Leonard, Miriam 7, 80, 85
Lermontov, Mikhail 24
Lessing, Gottfried Ephraim 1, 139
   Emilia Galotti 140–1, 143, 153
   Miss Sara Sampson 140
Lewes, George Henry 68, 99
Lewis, Leopold Davis
   The Bells 9, 107, 113–14, 119
Lewis, Matthew Gregory
   The Castle Spectre 92
   The Monk 92
Lillo, George
   The London Merchant; or, The History of George Barnwell 1, 27, 111, 139
Liszt, Franz 33
The Literary Gazette 70, 143
Lockroy, Édouard 68, 70
   Un Duel sous Richelieu 62
Louis XIV (King of France) 66
Louis XVI (King of France) 7
Lytton, Edward Bulwer 64–5
   England and the English 5
   Richelieu 64

MacDonald, Frances
   Ophelia 37
Machiavelli, Niccolò
   Discorsi 87

INDEX

Mackenzie, Henry 1–2, 11
    "Account of the German Theatre" 1–2
    The Lounger 1
    The Man of Feeling 1
    The Mirror 1
Mackintosh, Fiona 110
Macready, William Charles 8, 46, 48, 50–1, 53, 64, 110
madness 108, 111, 128, 132, 137, 141, 150, 153,
Malory, Thomas 32
Malkowski, Helen 57–8
Malthus, Thomas 107
Marie Antoinette (Queen of France) 7, 23, 43
Marmontel, Jean-François 139
Marston, John Westland 61
Mars, Mademoiselle (Anne Françoise Hyppolyte Boutet Salvetat) 68
Marx, Karl 7, 9, 77, 88, 106, 110
    The Eighteenth Brumaire of Louis Bonaparte 88
Matthews, Charles 54
The Matrix 33
Maturin, Charles Robert
    Bertram; or, The Castle of St Aldobrand 8, 26, 92–3
    Fredolpho 26
    Manuel 26
    Melmoth the Wanderer 26
McCarthy, Tom
    Satin Island 9, 75, 77–8
McCormick, John 52
media 11, 32–43, 59, 75, 89, 113–14, 126–7, 129, 137
Meilhac, Henri 8
    Frou-Frou 68
Meisel, Martin 37, 56
Melba, Nellie 59
melodrama 8, 10, 26–7, 30, 38, 45–50, 54–6, 59–74, 110, 121–2, 126, 128, 133, 135
Mikalson, Jon 91
Mill, John Stuart
    The Subjection of Women 145
Millais, John Everett
    Ophelia 36, 58
Milton, John 99
Mitford, Mary Russell
    Rienzi 50
Moretti, Franco 6, 108
Morgan, Lewis 145
The Morning Post 51, 56

Morton, John Maddison
    A Thumping Legacy 50–1
Moxon, Edward 33
Murray, John 102
Musser, Benjamin 23, 43
Musset, Alfred de 104, 129
    Lorenzaccio 94, 101, 132
Myers, Terry 99

Napoleon *see* Bonaparte, Napoleon
nation, the, and nationalism 10–11, 29, 52–3, 57, 87, 93, 105–19
neoclassicism 4–5, 139–40
Newey, Kate 70
The New Monthly Magazine 70, 143
Nicoll, Allardyce 61
Nietzsche, Friedrich 7, 9, 29, 77, 84–6, 94
Nilsson, Christina 58
Nodier, Charles 2
novel, the 6, 30–2, 68, 70–1, 123, 125, 140,

objects and objectification 10, 79–83, 86, 105–19, 134
opera 10, 27, 33, 49–51, 53, 57–9, 61, 70, 86, 113–15, 152
pain 4, 7, 23–4, 26–7, 30, 37–8, 40–2, 45, 49, 76, 79, 83, 96, 104, 108, 126, 132, 139, 143, 145
Paine, Thomas
    The Rights of Man 25
Patterson, Michael 48
Petterson, Orlando 133
performance 45–59, 61–2, 91, 114, 123
"Peterloo" massacre 38
Phelps, Samuel 49–50, 54–5, 64
Picasso, Pablo
    The Tragedy 42
Picciotto, James
    Sketches of Anglo-Jewish History 70
Pitt, George Dibdin 8, 61–5
    The Revolution of Paris 63
    The String of Pearls (Sweeney Todd) 72–5
Pixerécourt, René-Charles Guilbert
    Coelina, ou, l'enfant du mystère 66
Plato 92
Plotz, Jon 112
politics and the political 4–5, 9–10, 23–32, 40, 42, 51, 59, 63, 76–8, 81, 86–7, 93, 97, 105–6, 111, 121, 125–6
Polack, Elizabeth 8, 62, 70
    Esther, the Royal Jewess 62, 71, 75

Polack, Joel Samuel 71
Polack, Maria
   Fiction without Romance 70
Poole, Adrian 24
Powell, Kerry 62
Pre-Raphaelite Brotherhood 33, 58
public sphere 38, 46, 71, 132
Pushkin, Alexander
   Boris Godunov 31
   Evgenii Onegin 31
   Little Tragedies 31
Pye, Henry James 1

race 133–5, 145
Racine, Jean 47, 61, 68, 71
   Esther 62
   Phèdre 68, 139
Radcliffe, Ann
   The Mysteries of Udolpho 30
   The Romance of the Forest 92
Ramberg, Johann Heinrich
   Ophelia Falling into the Water 35
Raupach, Ernst 48
rape 31, 93, 124, 133, 142–4
religion 82–3, 91–104, 122 (*see also* Judaism)
Report of the Select Committee on Dramatic Literature 45–7
revolution 29, 31, 47, 59, 63–4, 88–9, 121, 125, 129, 132
Richardson, Samuel
   Clarissa; or, The History of a Lady 30
Richelieu, Cardinal (Armand Jean du Plessis) 67
Ritchie, Harry 110
romanticism 2–3, 5–7, 23, 25, 30, 33, 40, 47, 53, 58, 66–8, 91, 100, 115
Roach, Joseph 116
Robins, Elizabeth 62
Rousseau, Jean-Jacques 126
The Rovers; or, the Double Arrangement 92
Rowe, Nicholas
   The Fair Penitent 134–5
Ruskin, John
   The Eagle's Nest 68
Russell, Gillian 126

Sachs, Jonathan 108
sacrifice 81, 88, 97–8, 103–4, 107, 124–5, 130–1, 135, 140, 144–5,
Saglia, Diego 26–7
Sanders, Julie 51

Santley, Charles 58
Sardou, Victorien
   Patrie! 69
Sargent, John Singer 49
The Saturday Review 143
Schelling, Friedrich Wilhelm Joseph 7, 9, 76–7, 78–82, 85–6
Schiller, Friedrich von 1, 47–50, 52, 92–3, 96–7, 99, 125
   The Bride of Messina 96, 101
   Don Carlos 93, 94
   Intrigue and Love 140–1, 143, 153
   The Robbers 1, 10–11, 65, 123
   Wallenstein 93
Schlegel, August Wilhelm 27, 124
Schoch, Richard 54–5
Scott, Clement 53, 56–7
Scott, Walter 1–2, 9, 123
   The House of Aspen 1–2
   Goetz von Berlichingen 2, 66
   Waverley; or, 'Tis Sixty Years Since 6
Schopenhauer, Arthur 9, 77, 83–7, 100, 106, 108
Scribe, Eugène
   Adrienne Lecouvreur 68
Sen, Suddhaseel 57
Seneca 58
Seward, Anna 1
sexuality 66, 69, 94, 111, 114–19, 123, 133–5, 139–54
Shakespeare, William 2, 5, 46–50, 54–6, 58, 61, 63–5, 111, 132, 135
   Hamlet 37, 47–9, 57–9, 68, 92, 101, 126, 130, 143
   Henry VIII 56
   King John 56
   King Lear 61
   Macbeth 49, 55–6, 139
   The Merchant of Venice 130
   Othello 64, 130
   Richard III 56, 64, 73–4
   Romeo and Juliet 49
Shaw, George Bernard 11, 65, 93, 104, 132, 144–6, 149
   Mrs. Warren's Profession 10–11, 151
   Saint Joan 93
Shelley, Mary
   Frankenstein; or, The Modern Prometheus 6, 30–1
   The Last Man 30
Shelley, Percy Bysshe 9, 77, 89, 96–7, 99, 100, 104, 121, 132, 136–7

INDEX

The Cenci 8, 10–11, 26, 29, 93–4, 95, 122–4, 126–7, 133, 135–6, 141–5, 148, 152, 153
"A Defence of Poetry" 86–8
"England in 1819" 38
Hellas 29, 97, 124
"The Mask of Anarchy" 38
Oedipus Tyrannus; or, Swellfoot the Tyrant 97, 124
Prometheus Unbound 29, 97, 99, 124
Sheridan, Richard Brinsley
  The School for Scandal 70
Siddons, Sarah 63
Simon, Bennett 121
slavery 31–2, 40–1, 65, 133–5, 145
Smith, Charlotte 24
Smithson, Harriet 58
Socrates 85
Sondheim, Stephen
  Sweeney Todd: The Demon Barber of Fleet Street 61, 72–5
Sophocles 61, 78, 97, 107, 121
  Antigone 82, 124, 132
  Oedipus Rex 61, 79, 124, 139
Sourvinou-Inwood, Christiane 91
Spinoza, Baruch 78–9
Staël-Holstein, Anne Louise Germaine, Madame de 2
Star Wars 33
Staves, Susan 130
Steiner, George 2–3, 24–5, 45, 91
Stendhal (Henri Beyle) 27
Stowe, Harriet Beecher
  Uncle Tom's Cabin 65
Strauss, Richard 152
Strindberg, August 96, 132, 145
  A Dream Play 96
  Easter 8, 96
  The Father 10, 149–51, 153
  The Ghost Sonata 96
  Miss Julie 108–10, 151
  To Damascus 8–9, 91, 96
subjectivity 79–81, 85 (*see also* individual, the, and individualism)
Sublette, Constance 133
Sublette, Ned 133
sublime, the 27, 40, 56, 79, 84
suffering *see* pain
supernatural, the 8, 92–3, 95 (*see also* gothic)
Swedenborg, Emmanuel 96
Swinburne, Algernon Charles 96
  Atalanta in Calydon 99–100

Erechtheus 100
Szondi, Peter 78, 80, 82, 86

Talfourd, Thomas Noon 50
Taylor, Tom
  The Bottle 65
  The Ticket-of-Leave Man 65
Taylor, William, of Norwich 1
terror *see* fear
Tennyson, Alfred 32–3, 123
Terry, Ellen 49, 59, 64
theaters
  Astley's Amphitheatre (London) 64
  Berlin Opera House 53
  Bolshoi (Moscow) 17
  Boston Theater 50
  Boulevard du Temple (Paris) 19
  Britannia (London) 68, 72
  Comédie Française (Paris) 19, 21, 52, 61, 67, 75
  Covent Garden (London) 12, 18, 27, 50, 51–2, 54, 57–8, 62–5, 70, 92
  Drury Lane (London) 2, 12–13, 16, 27, 46, 48, 50–2, 63, 70, 74–5, 92–3
  Düsseldorf Theater 47–8
  Gaiety Theatre (London) 68
  Gaîté (Paris) 66
  Grand Theater (Moscow) 15
  Haymarket (London) 14, 27, 51–2, 63, 68–70
  Islington Grand Theatre (London)
  Krefeld-Moenchengladbach Theater (Krefeld, Germany) 58
  Königliches Schauspielhaus (Berlin) 53
  La Scala (Milan) 15, 57
  Liceu Theatre (Barcelona) 10, 20
  Mannheim Theater 10–11
  Metropolitan Opera (New York) 57
  National-Theater (Berlin) 53
  National Theater (Mannheim) 11
  National Theater (Oslo) 10, 21
  New Adelphi (London) 18
  Odéon (Paris) 67
  Palais Garnier (Paris) 57
  Paris Opéra 57
  Pavilion (London) 72
  Porte Saint-Martin (Paris) 13, 66
  Princess's (London) 49, 54–6, 64
  Sadler's Wells (London) 49, 64
  San Carlo (Naples) 16
  Savoy (London) 20
  Stadt-Theater (Berlin) 53

State Opera (Berlin) 17
Surrey Theatre 46, 65
Théâtre de l'Ambigu-Comique 66
Wallner Theater (Berlin) 53
Winter Garden City (New York) 133
Theatre Licensing Act (1737) 27–8, 52, 63
Theatre Regulation Act (1843) 28, 49, 51, 63
Theatres Act (1968) 63
Thomas, Ambroise 57–8
   Mignon 57
   Hamlet 57–9
Thomson, Peter 54–5
The Times 51, 56, 143
To Henry Hunt, Esq 38
tragedy
   as mode 9, 24
   in popular culture 9, 24–5, 49–50
   theories of 9, 23–4, 49–50, 58, 67, 75–89
   types of
      bourgeois 1, 27, 49, 108–19, 139–41, 149
      Early Modern 33, 64
      Greek 5–6, 29, 33, 58, 79, 81, 87, 91, 96, 99–100, 106, 121, 124, 139
      Jacobean 130
      Renaissance 106
      Roman 5, 58, 106
      Romantic 5, 91, 100, 139
      she-tragedy 134
      vernacular 77–8, 89
translation 1–2, 9, 54–5, 57, 59, 66, 69, 106, 113
Turner, J.M.W.
   The Slave Ship 40

unities 5, 67, 97

Verdi, Giuseppe 57
   Othello 61, 114
   Rigoletto 61
Verga, Giovanni 6
Vestris, Lucia Elizabeth, Madame 54

Victoria (Queen of Great Britain and Ireland) 53
violence 2, 4, 9, 10, 23, 25, 28, 38, 42, 45, 65, 73, 87, 99, 100, 108, 111–14, 119, 121, 123, 131, 141, 144, 153–4
visual arts 24, 32–43

Wade, Thomas
   The Jew of Arragon 62
Wagner, Richard 57, 86
   The Ring Cycle 115
   Tristan and Isolde 114–15
Wallace, Jennifer 3–4, 126
Walpole, Horace
   The Castle of Otranto 26
   The Mysterious Mother 26
war 6–7, 9–10, 23, 32, 37, 40, 42, 58, 65, 88, 93–4, 101, 122, 124, 126–7, 130
Waterhouse, J.W. 58
Wellesley, Arthur, Duke of Wellington 129
White, Hayden
   Metahistory 2–3
Wilde, Oscar 11, 145
   Salome 10, 152
Wilkie, David 46
   Distraining for Rent 65
   Rent Day 65
Williams, Caroline 65, 75
Williams, Raymond 3, 9, 24–5, 27, 76–8, 133
Williams, Rowen 132
Wilson, Kathleen 134, 135
Wollstonecraft, Mary
   A Vindication of the Rights of Woman 145
   The Wrongs of Woman; or, Maria 30
Wordsworth, Dorothy 2
Wordsworth, William 2, 121, 123
   The Borderers 2, 93
   Lyrical Ballads 2, 93, 125

Zola, Emile 6, 59, 65